Teacher's Annotated Edition

HOUGHTON MIFFLIN
math
CENTRAL

Reteaching

Includes Masters for:
- **Another Look Worksheets Linked to each Lesson**
- **Another Look Worksheets for Problem Solving Lessons**
- **Midchapter and Chapter Reteach Worksheets**
- **Annotations for each Worksheet**

HOUGHTON MIFFLIN

Boston · Atlanta · Dallas · Denver · Geneva, Illinois · Palo Alto · Princeton

Level 5

To the Teacher

Two types of reteaching worksheets are included in this book. Another Look worksheets are linked directly to the lessons in the Pupil's Edition of Houghton Mifflin *Math Central*. Reteach worksheets are keyed to the Chapter Reviews. Each worksheet is shown in reduced, annotated form at the point of use in the *Math Central* Teacher's Edition. These materials are designed to provide reteach opportunities to ensure that students understand the concepts of the lessons.

Contents

Contents

Name _____ Date _____

1.1 ▷ ANOTHER LOOK

Using Numbers

1776	30	*19¢*	5th	**555-7312**	12	8	
	24	100		1000	32	9:00	$3\frac{1}{2}$
90		$3.25	**212°**	29,028	*12:30*		$150

Use the numbers in the box.
Write the number that could be:

1. the price of a bicycle — **$150**

2. the number of hours in a day — **24** hours

3. the weight of a grizzly bear — **1000** pounds

4. the number of days in September — **30** days

5. the height of the world's tallest mountain — **29,028** feet

6. a telephone number — **555–7312**

7. the number of pennies in a dollar — **100** pennies

8. the length of a ruler — **12** inches

9. the number of hours a football game lasts — $3\frac{1}{2}$ hours

10. the price of a sandwich — **$3.25**

11. the time you might eat lunch — **12:30** P.M.

12. the number of ounces in a quart of milk — **32** ounces

13. the number of times your heart beats in a minute — **90**

14. the number of arms an octopus has — **8** arms

15. the temperature of boiling water — **212°** Fahrenheit

1.2 ANOTHER LOOK

Place Value

You can use a place-value chart to help you read a number and write its word name.

> The average distance of Neptune from the sun is 2,793,000,000 miles.

Billions			Millions			Thousands			Ones		
Hundreds	Tens	Ones	Hundreds	Tens	Ones	Hundreds	Tens	Ones	Hundreds	Tens	Ones
		2	7	9	3	0	0	0	0	0	0

The place-value chart shows the value of each digit in the number.

• You read this number as 2 billion, 793 million.

• You can write this number three ways:
  Short word form ⟶ 2 billion, 793 million
  Expanded form ⟶ 2,000,000,000 + 700,000,000 + 90,000,000 + 3,000,000
  Standard form ⟶ 2,793,000,000

Write the number in the place-value chart. Then write the number in expanded form.

1. 240 million, 3 thousand

Billions			Millions			Thousands			Ones		
Hundreds	Tens	Ones	Hundreds	Tens	Ones	Hundreds	Tens	Ones	Hundreds	Tens	Ones
			2	4	0	0	0	3	0	0	0

200,000,000 + 40,000,000 + 3000

2. 5 billion, 225

Billions			Millions			Thousands			Ones		
Hundreds	Tens	Ones	Hundreds	Tens	Ones	Hundreds	Tens	Ones	Hundreds	Tens	Ones
		5	0	0	0	0	0	0	2	2	5

5,000,000,000 + 200 + 20 + 5

Write the number in standard form.

3. 350 million _____ 350,000,000

4. 300,000 + 70,000 + 40 _____ 370,040

5. 70 billion, 195 million _____ 70,195,000,000

6. 367 billion, 459 thousand _____ 367,000,459,000

7. 7,000,000 + 9000 + 400 _____ 7,009,400

8. 63 billion, 592 million, 4 _____ 63,592,000,004

1.3 ◢ ANOTHER LOOK

MENTAL MATH: Sums and Differences

How can you add or subtract mentally?
• Use place-value names.
• Look for basic facts.

Add: 4000 + 3000
• Think of 4000 as **4 thousands**.
• Think of 3000 as **3 thousands**.
• Add the thousands.
  4 thousands + **3** thousands = **7** thousands

So, **4**000 + **3**000 = **7**000.

Basic fact:
4 + 3 = 7

Add: 920 + 50
• Think of 920 as **92 tens**.
• Think of 50 as **5 tens**.
• Add the tens.
  92 tens + **5** tens = **97** tens

So, **92**0 + **5**0 = **97**0.

Subtract: 6000 − 400
• Think of 6000 as **60 hundreds**.
• Think of 400 as **4 hundreds**.
• Subtract the hundreds.
  60 hundreds − **4** hundreds = **56** hundreds

So, **6**000 − 400 = **56**00.

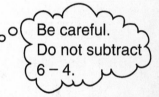

Be careful.
Do not subtract
6 − 4.

Add or subtract. Circle the letter of the correct answer.

1. 550 + 400
   a. 590
   b. 950 ⟵ circled

2. 9000 − 600
   a. 8400 ⟵ circled
   b. 3000

3. 7000 − 300
   a. 4000
   b. 6700 ⟵ circled

4. 8000 + 200
   a. 8200 ⟵ circled
   b. 10,000

Add or subtract. Use mental math.

5. 40 + 50 = __90__

6. 300 + 500 = __800__

7. 70 − 40 = __30__

8. 5000 − 2000 = __3000__

9. 900 − 600 = __300__

10. 4000 + 3000 = __7000__

11. 8000 − 500 = __7500__

12. 7000 + 300 = __7300__

13. 3000 − 900 = __2100__

14. 720 + 50 = __770__

15. 900 − 40 = __860__

16. 610 + 70 = __680__

17. 850 − 200 = __650__

18. 430 + 40 = __470__

19. 7000 + 1400 = __8400__

20. 6000 − 600 = __5400__

21. 7600 + 200 = __7800__

22. 5300 − 200 = __5100__

1.4 ANOTHER LOOK

Problem Solving Strategy: Make a Table

You start a jogging program. You will jog 2 mi a day, 5 days a week for the first 2 months. Then, every 2 months, you will add 1 mi. How far will you be running each day at the end of one year?

1. Understand

- You know that you will jog 2 miles a day the first 2 months. The next two months, you will increase that distance by 1 mi.

- You will increase the distance every 2 months for a year.

2. Plan

- Make a table to show the distance each month.

3. Try It

- Complete the table.

4. Look Back

- You will jog 2 miles each day for the first 2 months. This number will increase by 1 every 2 months to give a final amount of 7 miles each day by the end of the year.

Months	Number of Miles
Jan.–Feb.	2
Mar.–Apr.	3
May–June	4
July–Aug.	5
Sept.–Oct.	6
Nov.–Dec.	7

Solve. Use Make a Table when you can.

1. You collect tickets for the class play. Fifty people have already given you their tickets. If you collect tickets at the rate of 6 tickets per minute, how long will it take to fill 110 seats?

   10 minutes

2. The student population is growing at the Oak Ridge Middle School. This year the fifth-grade class has 19 students. Three more students will be added to the class each year for the next few years. At this rate, when will the class have more than 27 students in it? ____ **in 3 years** _____

3. A fountain releases water at the rate of 4 liters per min. Its amount is increased by 3 liters every minute. How much water will the fountain release after it has been running for 5 min? ____ **19 liters** ____

1.5 ◤ ANOTHER LOOK

Estimating Sums

You can use rounding or front-end estimation to estimate a sum.

On Mrs. Hidalgo's last trip she flew 2937 miles and then
3184 miles. About how many miles did she fly on the trip?

Rounding
Round to the greatest place.
Add the rounded numbers.

Th	H	T	O
	2	9	3 7

Look at the first 2 digits. 9 > 5,
so 2937 rounds up to 3000.

+ 3184

Look at the first 2 digits. 1 < 5,
so 3184 rounds down to 3000.

Th	H	T	O
	3	0	0 0

+ 3000
_____
6000

Rounded estimate

Mrs. Hidalgo flew about 6000 miles.

Front-end
Circle the digits in the greatest place.
Add.

②937
+ ③184

$2000 + 3000 = 5000$

Mrs. Hidalgo flew about 6000 miles.

To adjust the estimate, look in the
next place for groups of about 10.

2|9|37
+ 3|1|84

Think: 900
+ 100
_____
1000

$5000 + 1000 = 6000$

Adjusted estimate

Find the estimate by rounding and then by using front-end estimation with adjusting.
Ranges are given.

		Rounding estimate	Adjusted front-end estimate
1.	4569 + 337 + 568	5500–6000	5300–5450
2.	652 + 178 + 84	900–1000	900
3.	$32.67 + $6.42 + $57.98	$97–$100	$95–$97
4.	1205 + 477 + 6581	8000–8300	8100–8250
5.	$7.43 + $3.52 + $6.15	$17.00–$17.10	$17

1.6 ANOTHER LOOK

Estimating Sums

You can use rounding or front-end estimation to estimate a difference.

There are 6783 students in Martin Luther King, Jr., Junior High School. On one day, 435 students were absent. About how many students were in school that day?

Rounding
Round 435 to the hundreds place. Round 6783 to the same place. Subtract.

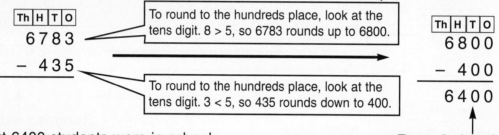

Th	H	T	O
6	7	8	3

To round to the hundreds place, look at the tens digit. 8 > 5, so 6783 rounds up to 6800.

– 435

To round to the hundreds place, look at the tens digit. 3 < 5, so 435 rounds down to 400.

Th	H	T	O
6	8	0	0

– 400

6400

Rounded estimate

About 6400 students were in school.

Front-end
Subtract the digits in the thousands place.

Th	H	T	O
6	7	8	3

– | 4 | 3 | 5

6 | 0 | 0 | 0

About 6300 students were in school.

To adjust the estimate, use the digits in the next greatest place.

Th	H	T	O
6	7	8	3

– | 4 | 3 | 5

6 | 3 | 0 | 0

Adjusted estimate

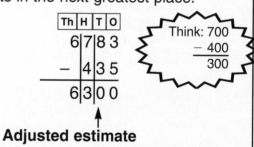

Think: 700
 – 400
 300

Find the estimate by rounding and then by using front-end estimation with adjusting.

		Rounding estimate	Adjusted front-end estimate
1.	5463 – 371	5000–5100	5100
2.	78,492 – 6304	72,000	72,000
3.	257 – 34	230	200–210
4.	5981 – 3665	2000–2300	2300–2320
5.	9584 – 238	9340–10,000	9300–9350

1.7 ◢ ANOTHER LOOK

Addition and Subtraction

When you add or subtract greater numbers, you can use squared paper to help you keep track of places.

Add: 56,748 + 35,669

Add the ones.	Add the tens.	Add the hundreds.	Add the thousands.	Add the ten thousands.

		1	
5	6,7	4	8
+ 3	5,6	6	9
			7

	1	1	
5	6,7	4	8
+ 3	5,6	6	9
		1	7

1	1	1	
5	6,7	4	8
+ 3	5,6	6	9
	4	1	7

1	1	1	1
5	6,7	4	8
+ 3	5,6	6	9
2	4	1	7

1	1	1	1
5	6,7	4	8
+ 3	5,6	6	9
9	2,4	1	7

Add. Use squared paper if it helps.

1.   4156
    + 2689
     6845

2. $63.08
    + 19.73
    $82.81

3.   16,483
    + 7,864
     24,347

4.   56,751
    + 14,582
     71,333

5. $12.69 + $43.97 = ___$56.66___

6. 15,745 + 2749 = ___18,494___

Subtract: 58,013 − 4576

Subtract the ones.	Subtract the tens.	Subtract the hundreds.	Subtract the thousands.	Subtract the ten thousands.

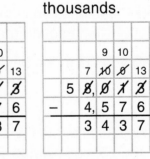

Subtract. Use squared paper if it helps.

7.   7619
    − 3745
     3874

8. $80.12
    − 55.46
    $24.66

9.   13,548
    − 7,839
     5709

10.   27,200
    − 5,346
     21,854

11. 52,743 − 9365 = ___43,378___

12. $60.00 − $14.76 = ___$45.24___

1.8 ANOTHER LOOK

Problem Solving: Using Strategies

In 1990, the attendance at a national park was 5,500,000. The attendance in 1991 increased by 25,000. In the years 1992 to 1994, the attendance increased by 5000 each year. What was the attendance at the national park in 1994?

1. Understand

- You know that in 1990 the attendance was 5,500,000. It increased by 25,000 the next year.

- Attendance increased by 5000 every year for 3 more years.

2. Plan

- Make a table to solve the problem.

3. Try It

- Complete the table.

4. Look Back

Year	Attendance
1990	5,500,000
1991	5,525,000
1992	5,530,000
1993	5,535,000
1994	5,540,000

- The table shows an increase of 25,000 in 1991. Then, the amount increases by 5000 for each year after 1991.

Use any strategy to solve.

1. Suppose you put pennies in a bank during a 10-day period. You start on day 1 with one penny. Then, the next day you double the amount. On day 3 you double the amount again. Each day you double the amount from the day before. How

   many pennies will you put in the bank on day 10? _____ **512 pennies** _____

2. There are 2 parking lots next to the school. One measures 42 meters long and 25 meters wide. The other is a square with a side of 35 meters. The owner wants to put a fence around each lot. Which lot will require more fencing? How much

   more? _____ **the square lot; 6 meters more** _____

Name _____ Date _____

MENTAL MATH: Addition

When you want to add in your head, try breaking up the numbers. Use numbers that you can add easily.

Add: 55 + 46

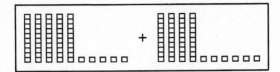

Add the tens.

50 + 40 is easy to add.
50 + 40 = 90

Add the ones.

5 + 6 is a basic fact.
5 + 6 = 11

Add 90 and 11.

That's 101.
So, 55 + 46 = 101.

Here are two other ways that you can add 55 and 46 mentally.

Break up 46 into 45 + 1.

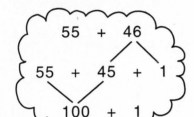

That's 101.

Break up 46 into 40 + 6.

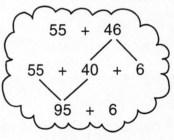

That's 101.

Write the sum. Use mental math.

1. 23 + 47 = __70__

2. 58 + 32 = __90__

3. 48 + 35 = __83__

4. $29 + $46 = __$75__

5. 28 + 55 = __83__

6. 45 + 27 = __72__

7. 27 + 24 = __51__

8. 24 + 43 = __67__

9. $66 + $35 = __$101__

10. 35 + 45 = __80__

11. 85 + 19 = __104__

12. $37 + $28 = __$65__

13. 34 + 29 = __63__

14. 58 + 13 = __71__

15. 59 + 31 = __90__

16. 35 + 53 = __88__

17. $49 + $46 = __$95__

18. 99 + 16 = __115__

The federal government claims that in 1989 there were one hundred seventy-six million, two hundred thirty-four thousand $1000-bills in circulation. The word form of this number takes up a lot of room. You can write this number in standard form to shorten it.

176,234,000

billions			millions			thousands			ones		
hundreds	tens	ones	hundreds	tens	ones	hundreds	tens	ones	hundreds	tens	ones
		1	7	6	2	3	4	0	0	0	

In this number, there are 176 millions, 234 thousands, and no hundreds, tens, or ones.

short word form:	176 million, 234 thousand
expanded form:	100,000,000 + 70,000,000 + 6,000,000 + 200,000 + 30,000 + 4,000
standard form:	176,234,000

Write the number in standard form. Make sure each answer appears in the Answer Box.

1. 500,000,000 + 30,000,000 + 2,000,000 + 700,000 + 20,000 + 6000 + 800 + 40 + 3 _____ 532,726,843

2. 502 million, 726 thousand, 843 _____ 502,726,843

3. 532 million, 700 thousand, 843 _____ 532,700,843

4. 532,000,000 + 843 _____ 532,000,843

5. 532 thousand, 843 _____ 532,843

Answer Box

532,843	502,726,843	532,000,843	532,700,843	532,726,843

▶RETEACH

2

Before you add, estimate. Use your estimate to check your exact answer for reasonableness. Add the digits one place at a time, starting from the right. Regroup.

$$\begin{array}{r} 3615 \\ +2914 \\ \hline \end{array}$$

Add the digits from the right.
Regroup where necessary.

Estimate.

$$\begin{array}{r} 4000 \\ +3000 \\ \hline 7000 \end{array}$$

$$\begin{array}{r} 3615 \\ +2914 \\ \hline 9 \end{array}$$

$$\begin{array}{r} 3615 \\ +2914 \\ \hline 29 \end{array}$$

$$\begin{array}{r} \overset{1}{3}615 \\ +2914 \\ \hline 529 \end{array}$$

$$\begin{array}{r} \overset{1}{3}615 \\ +2914 \\ \hline 6529 \end{array}$$

Since 6529 is close to 7000, the sum is reasonable.

Write the sum. Make sure each answer appears in the Answer Box.

1. $\begin{array}{r} 222{,}100 \\ +262{,}017 \\ \hline 484{,}117 \end{array}$

2. $\begin{array}{r} 570{,}833 \\ +269{,}100 \\ \hline 839{,}933 \end{array}$

3. $\begin{array}{r} 14{,}906 \\ +\ \ 7{,}094 \\ \hline 22{,}000 \end{array}$

4. $\begin{array}{r} 28\ min\ 15\ s \\ +34\ min\ 18\ s \\ \hline 62\ min\ 33\ s \end{array}$

5. $\begin{array}{r} 23\ lb\ \ 5\ oz \\ +18\ lb\ \ 6\ oz \\ \hline 41\ lb\ 11\ oz \end{array}$

6. $\begin{array}{r} 8039\ mi \\ +1162\ mi \\ \hline 9201\ mi \end{array}$

7. $345{,}799 + \$4{,}899 =$ ___$350{,}698___

8. 356 ft 6 in. + 488 ft 5 in. = ___844 ft 11 in.___

9. $5{,}289 + \$78{,}199 =$ ___$83{,}488___

Answer Box

41 lb 11 oz	$350,698	844 ft 11 in.	62 min 33 s	839,933	484,117	$83,488	22,000	9201 mi

RETEACH

3

Subtracting Whole Numbers and Units of Measure

Before you subtract, estimate. Use your estimate to check your exact answer for reasonableness. Subtract the digits one place at a time, starting from the right. To subtract a larger digit from a smaller, regroup from the place to the left.

Find the difference: 560,833 − 262,017

Estimate.

$$\begin{array}{r} 600,000 \\ -300,000 \\ \hline 300,000 \end{array}$$

Subtract the digits from the right. Regroup where necessary.

2 13	2 13	2 13	5 10 2 13	4 15 10 2 13	4 15 10 2 13
560,8̶3̶3̶	560,8̶3̶3̶	560,8̶3̶3̶	5̶6̶0̶,8̶3̶3̶	5̶6̶0̶,8̶3̶3̶	5̶6̶0̶,8̶3̶3̶
−262,017	−262,017	−262,017	−262,017	−262,017	−262,017
6	16	816	8 816	98 816	298,816

Since 298,816 is close to 300,000, the difference is reasonable.

Write the difference. Make sure each answer appears in the Answer Box.

1.
$$\begin{array}{r} 23,281 \\ -11,278 \\ \hline 12,003 \end{array}$$

2.
$$\begin{array}{r} 5354 \\ -2816 \\ \hline 2538 \end{array}$$

3.
$$\begin{array}{r} 55 \text{ lb } 11 \text{ oz} \\ -28 \text{ lb } 10 \text{ oz} \\ \hline 27 \text{ lb } 1 \text{ oz} \end{array}$$

4.
$$\begin{array}{r} 56 \text{ min } 28 \text{ s} \\ -27 \text{ min } 18 \text{ s} \\ \hline 29 \text{ min } 10 \text{ s} \end{array}$$

5. 36 ft 6 in. − 17 ft 4 in.

_____ 19 ft 2 in. _____

6. 5342 − 1899

_____ 3443 _____

7. 45 min 38 s − 19 min 4 s

_____ 26 min 34 s _____

8. 96 lb 12 oz − 38 lb 9 oz

_____ 58 lb 3 oz _____

Answer Box

19 ft 2 in.	27 lb 1 oz	12,003	3443	29 min 10 s	58 lb 3 oz	26 min 34 s	2538

1.10 ▶ ANOTHER LOOK

Understanding Tenths and Hundredths

You can write tenths as a fraction
or as a decimal.

 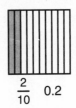

$\frac{1}{10}$ 0.1 $\frac{2}{10}$ 0.2 $\frac{5}{10}$ 0.5 $\frac{7}{10}$ 0.7 $\frac{10}{10}$ 1.0

Use Decimal Squares to complete the chart.

	Number name	Fraction	Decimal
1.	two tenths	$\frac{2}{10}$	0.2
2.	seven tenths	$\frac{7}{10}$	0.7
3.	three tenths	$\frac{3}{10}$	0.3
4.	eight tenths	$\frac{8}{10}$	0.8
5.	four tenths	$\frac{4}{10}$	0.4

You can write hundredths as
a fraction or as a decimal.

 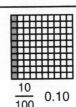 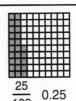 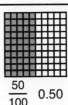

$\frac{1}{100}$ 0.01 $\frac{10}{100}$ 0.10 $\frac{25}{100}$ 0.25 $\frac{50}{100}$ 0.50

Use Decimal Squares to complete the chart.

	Number name	Fraction	Decimal
6.	eighty-five hundredths	$\frac{85}{100}$	0.85
7.	forty-five hundredths	$\frac{45}{100}$	0.45
8.	thirty hundredths	$\frac{30}{100}$	0.30
9.	ten hundredths	$\frac{10}{100}$	0.10
10.	five hundredths	$\frac{5}{100}$	0.05

1.11 ▼ ANOTHER LOOK

Understanding Thousandths

You can use a place-value chart to write thousandths.

		Ones	Tenths	Hundredths	Thousandths
$\frac{436}{1000}$	0.436	0	4	3	6
$\frac{58}{1000}$	0.058	0	0	5	8
$\frac{900}{1000}$	0.900	0	9	0	0

Complete the chart. Use a place-value chart when it helps.
The first one has been done for you.

	Number name	Fraction	Decimal
1.	two hundred sixteen thousandths	$\frac{216}{1000}$	0.216
2.	eight hundred seven thousandths	$\frac{807}{1000}$	0.807
3.	six hundred thirty thousandths	$\frac{630}{1000}$	0.630
4.	one hundred eight thousandths	$\frac{108}{1000}$	0.108
5.	nine hundred forty-four thousandths	$\frac{944}{1000}$	0.944
6.	two hundred fifty-nine thousandths	$\frac{259}{1000}$	0.259
7.	sixty-eight thousandths	$\frac{68}{1000}$	0.068
8.	twelve thousandths	$\frac{12}{1000}$	0.012
9.	four hundred three thousandths	$\frac{403}{1000}$	0.403
10.	ninety-seven thousandths	$\frac{97}{1000}$	0.097
11.	eight hundred seventy thousandths	$\frac{870}{1000}$	0.870
12.	sixty-three thousandths	$\frac{63}{1000}$	0.063

1.12 ▸ ANOTHER LOOK

Reading and Writing Decimals

You can write a decimal in standard form and in word form.

Tens	Ones	Tenths	Hundredths	Thousandths
	6	2		
4	1	6	5	
1	1	0	2	7

> Write the word *and* for the decimal point.

Standard form	Word form
6.2	six and two tenths
41.65	forty-one and sixty-five hundredths
11.027	eleven and twenty-seven thousandths

The decimals 1.7 and 1.70 have equal value.

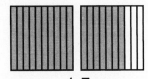

1.7
one and seven tenths

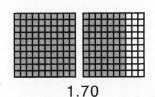

1.70
one and seventy hundredths

Write each decimal in standard form and in word form.

	Tens	Ones	Tenths	Hundredths	Thousandths
1.		2	8		
2.	1	5	3	6	
3.		9	5	0	4
4.	2	7	0	5	

Standard form	Word form
2.8	two and eight tenths
15.36	fifteen and thirty-six hundredths
9.504	nine and five hundred four thousandths
27.05	twenty-seven and five hundredths

Circle the letter of the equivalent decimal. Use Decimal Squares when you need to.

5. 3.05
  a. 3.50
  b. 3.050 ⟲

6. 6.9
  a. 6.09
  b. 6.90 ⟲

7. 12.850
  a. 12.805
  b. 12.85 ⟲

8. 58.1
  a. 58.100 ⟲
  b. 58.001

Name_____ Date _____

1.13 ANOTHER LOOK

Comparing and Ordering Decimals

You can use a place-value chart to line up the digits when you compare and order decimals.

Compare: 1.63 and 1.7

Ones	Tenths	Hundredths	Thousandths
1	⑥	3	
1	⑦		

• Compare the digits.
• Begin with the greatest place.
• Work from left to right.
  7 tenths > 6 tenths

So, 1.7 > 1.63.

Order: 3.71, 5.4, and 2.09

Ones	Tenths	Hundredths	Thousandths
③	7	1	
⑤	4		
②	0	9	

• Compare the digits.
• Begin with the greatest place.
• Work from left to right.
  5 > 3 and 3 > 2

So, 5.4 is the greatest number.

The order from greatest to least: 5.4, 3.71, and 2.09.
The order from least to greatest: 2.09, 3.71, and 5.4.

Compare. Write < or >. Use a place-value chart if you need to.

1. 0.65 ⟩ 0.51   **2.** 4.378 ⟩ 0.975   **3.** 52.6 ⟩ 9.78   **4.** 345 ⟨ 435

5. 1 ⟩ 0.50   **6.** 0.89 ⟩ 0.79   **7.** 6.08 ⟨ 6.80   **8.** 63 ⟩ 6.3

Order from greatest to least. Use a place-value chart if you need to.

9. 6.97, 6, 6.5

6.97, 6.5, 6

10. 0.478, 0, 2.7, 1.2

2.7, 1.2, 0.478, 0

11. 0.04, 0.2, 0.008

0.2, 0.04, 0.008

12. 72, 79.3, 65.9

79.3, 72, 65.9

13. 64,293,575,604; 691,553,704; 178,261,849,002

178,261,849,002; 64,293,575,604; 691,553,704

16

Name _____   Date _____

1.14 ◤ ANOTHER LOOK

Rounding Decimals

You can round decimals the same way as you round whole numbers.

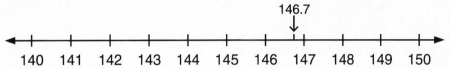

146.7

140 141 142 143 144 145 146 147 148 149 150

You can round 146.7 to the nearest whole number.

• 146.7 is between 146 and 147.
• 146.7 is closer to 147.

So, to the nearest whole number, 146.7 rounds to 147.

You can round 146.7 to the greatest place.

• 146.7 is between 100 and 200.
• 146.7 is closer to 100.

So, to the greatest place, 146.7 rounds to 100.

Round 381.68 to the nearest whole number.

1. What whole numbers is 381.68 between?   __**381 and 382**__

2. Mark 381 and 382 on the number line. Then estimate where 381.68 is and mark it on the number line.

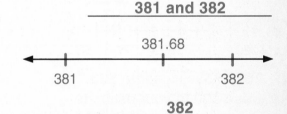

381.68

381   382

3. Which whole number does 381.68 round to?   __**382**__

Circle the digit in the greatest place. Then round the number to the greatest place.

4. 3④.8   **5.** 5⑥.25   **6.** ⑨.08   **7.** 51⑧.523   **8.** 77⑨.75

____35____   ____56____   ____9____   ____519____   ____780____

9. ②5.91   **10.** ⑧.24   **11.** $③.51   **12.** ①583   **13.** ②3.196

____30____   ____8____   ____$4____   ____2000____   ____20____

Round the number to the underlined place.

14. 2̲7.30   **15.** 51̲5   **16.** 395̲.44   **17.** 9̲8.1   **18.** 33̲3.5

____30____   ____520____   ____395____   ____100____   ____330____

1.15 ▸ ANOTHER LOOK

ESTIMATION: Adding and Subtracting Decimals

You can use rounding to estimate sums and differences.

Estimate: 3.9 + 15.2

• Round each number to the nearest whole number.

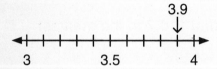

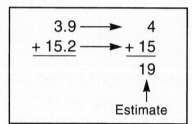

3.9 is closer to 4.
Use 4 in your estimate.

15.2 is closer to 15.
Use 15 in your estimate.

Estimate: $28.65 − $7.41

• Round each number to the greatest place.

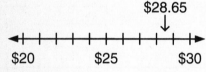

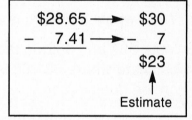

$28.65 is closer to $30.
Use $30 in your estimate.

$7.41 is closer to $7.
Use $7 in your estimate.

Round each number to the nearest whole number. Then estimate.

1. 26.93   rounds to ⟶ __27__
    + 11.37 rounds to ⟶ __+ 11__
    Add   __38__

2. 19.42   rounds to ⟶ __19__
    − 8.73   rounds to ⟶ __− 9__
    Subtract   __10__

Round each number to the greatest place. Then estimate.

3. $77.25 rounds to ⟶ __$80__
    + 21.75 rounds to ⟶ __+ 20__
    Add   __$100__

4. 965   rounds to ⟶ __1000__
    − 103   rounds to ⟶ __− 100__
    Subtract   __900__

Estimate by rounding each number to the greatest place.

5.   12.8
    + 27.3
    ___40___

6.   32.61
    − 16.78
    ___10___

7.   3.72
    + 18.43
    ___24___

8.   357.94
    − 33.71
    ___370___

9.   61.86
    + 430.64
    ___460___

Name _____ Date _____

1.16 ◢ ANOTHER LOOK

Adding Decimals

When you add decimals, you can use place-value charts to help you line up the digits.

Add: 1.48 + 2.65

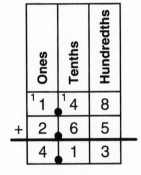

You can also use lined paper turned sideways to help you line up the digits.

Add: 23.069 + 47.583

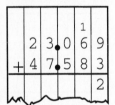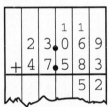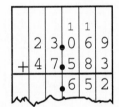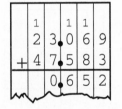

Write the sum. Use lined paper turned sideways when it helps.

1.   45.83
     + 63.29
     109.12

2.   657.5
     + 286.7
     944.2

3. $365.71
     +   49.59
     $415.30

4.   5.088
     + 15.736
     20.824

5.   43.774
     + 27.605
     71.379

6. $198.73
     +   76.55
     $275.28

7.   83.462 mi
     + 69.784 mi
     153.246 mi

8.   562.74
     + 157.78
     720.52

9. 235.76 + 154.8 = ___390.56___

10. 13.789 + 65.7 + 53.454 = ___132.943___

11. $362 + $158.76 = ___$520.76___

12. 15.53 + 0.05 + 245.8 = ___261.38___

1.17 ◢ ANOTHER LOOK

Subtracting Decimals

When you subtract decimals, you can use place-value charts to help you line up the digits.

Subtract: 2.53 – 1.28

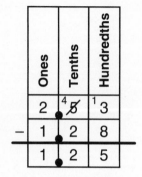

You can also use lined paper turned sideways to help you line up the digits.

Subtract: 37.2 – 5.641

Remember, 37.2 = 37.200.

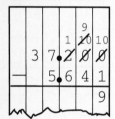  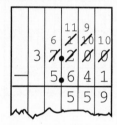 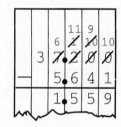 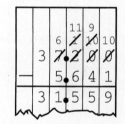

Write the difference. Use lined paper turned sideways when it helps.

1. 23.05
    – 16.77
    6.28

2. 68.00
    – 35.27
    32.73

3. 241.782
    – 67.594
    174.188

4. $39.12
    –   6.75
    $32.37

5. 3.542
    – 0.715
    2.827

6. 45.09 cm
    – 23.36 cm
    21.73 cm

7. 300.627
    – 163.479
    137.148

8. $342.25
    –   56.68
    $285.57

9. 45.6 – 26.38 = ___**19.22**___

10. $247 – $43.61 = ___**$203.39**___

11. 725.3 – 55.95 = ___**669.35**___

12. 156 – 62.74 = ___**93.26**___

Name_____ Date_____

1.18 ANOTHER LOOK

∙∙∙

MENTAL MATH: Subtraction

Subtract: $436 - 99$ ∘∘∘∘∘∘∘ (Think of 99 as 1 less than 100.)

$436 - 100 = 336$

$336 + 1 = 337$ ∘∘∘∘∘(Since you subtracted 1 too many, add 1 back.)

So, $436 - 99 = 337$.

Subtract: $\$80.00 - \$1.99$ ∘∘∘∘∘∘∘∘∘(Think of $1.99 as 1¢ less than $2.00.)

$\$80.00 - \$2.00 = \$78.00$

$\$78.00 + \$0.01 = \$78.01$ ∘∘∘∘∘(Since you subtracted 1¢ too much, add 1¢ back.)

So, $\$80.00 - \$1.99 = \$78.01$.

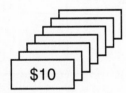

| $10 | $1 | $1 | $1 | $1 | $1 | $1 | + 1¢ |

───

Write the difference. Use mental math.

HINT: Think of 99 as 1 less than 100.

1. $236 - 99 = \underline{137}$ **2.** $700 - 99 = \underline{601}$ **3.** $785 - 99 = \underline{686}$

HINT: Think of 199 as 1 less than 200.

4. $674 - 199 = \underline{475}$ **5.** $3482 - 199 = \underline{3283}$ **6.** $5000 - 199 = \underline{4801}$

HINT: Think of $0.99 as 1¢ less than $1.00.

7. $\$3.26 - \$0.99 = \underline{\$2.27}$ **8.** $\$9.00 - \$0.99 = \underline{\$8.01}$ **9.** $\$5.75 - \$0.99 = \underline{\$4.76}$

HINT: Think of $1.99 as 1¢ less than $2.00.

10. $\$4.28 - \$1.99 = \underline{\$2.29}$ **11.** $\$5.00 - \$1.99 = \underline{\$3.01}$ **12.** $\$6.50 - \$1.99 = \underline{\$4.51}$

RETEACH

4

Reading and Writing Decimals

How can you read a decimal and write its word name? You can use a place-value chart to help you. Some decimals have a whole number part and a decimal part. To read 3.721, look at the decimal part first.

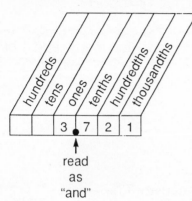

read
as
"and"

The decimal goes to the thousandths place.

The number after the decimal point is seven hundred twenty-one. So, the decimal part of the number is read as *seven hundred twenty-one thousandths.*

The decimal point is read as "and."

So, the word name for 3.721 is *three and seven hundred twenty-one thousandths.*

Write the word name for each decimal.

1. 5.12 _____ five and twelve hundredths _____

2. 34.003 _____ thirty-four and three thousandths _____

Write each decimal. Make sure each answer appears in the Answer Box.

3. two hundred and thirty-five hundredths _____ 200.35 _____

4. twenty-three and five thousandths _____ 23.005 _____

5. two and three hundred five thousandths _____ 2.305 _____

6. two hundred thirty-five thousandths _____ 0.235 _____

7. two and thirty-five thousandths _____ 2.035 _____

8. two and two hundred thirty-five thousandths _____ 2.235 _____

Answer Box

2.235	200.35	0.235	2.305	2.035	23.005

◤5◢ RETEACH   Place Value of Decimals

The value of a digit in a decimal can be found by counting how many positions to the right of the decimal point the digit is located.

Find the value of the 8, 9, and 2 in the decimal 3.892.

Places to the right of the decimal point	Place Value
one place	tenths
two places	hundredths
three places	thousandths

The digit 8 is one position to the right. Its value is **8 tenths.**
The digit 9 is two positions to the right. Its value is **9 hundredths.**
The digit 2 is three positions to the right. Its value is **2 thousandths.**

You can also use a place-value chart to find the value of any digit.

Find the value of the 7 in 12.471.

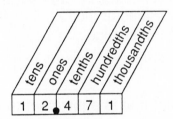

The value of the 7 is **7 hundredths.**

Circle the letter of the value of the underlined digit.

1. 3.87

   b. 7 thousandths

   (a.) 7 hundredths

2. 0.913

   (o.) 3 thousandths

   t. 3 thousand

3. 12.247

   s. 1 tenth

   (t.) 1 ten

4. 9.026

   (a.) 6 thousandths

   p. 6 tenths

5. 0.06

   (t.) 6 hundredths

   u. 6 tenths

6. 3.413

   m. 4 tens

   (w.) 4 tenths

Answer the question below by unscrambling the letters you have circled.

What is the capital of Canada?

O	t	t	a	w	a
2	3	5	4	6	1

RETEACH

6

When zeros are written at the end of a decimal, the value of the number does not change.

Are 0.1 and 0.10 equivalent decimals?

0.1 and 0.10 have the same digit in the tenths place.
0.1 has no digit in the hundredths place.
0.10 has a zero in the hundredths place.

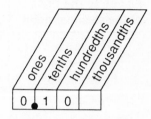 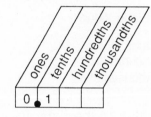

Since the only difference between 0.1 and 0.10 is the zero to the right of the 1, the two decimals are equivalent.

Are 24.7 and 24.700 equivalent decimals?

No matter how many zeros are written at the end of a decimal, its value does not change.

24.7 and 24.700 are equivalent decimals.

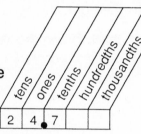 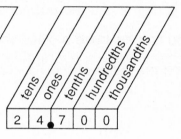

Circle the letter of each decimal that is equivalent to the given decimal.

1. 3.42

  (**H.**) 3.420

  D. 3.4

  (**i.**) 3.4200

2. 2.900

  (**i.**) 2.9

  j. 2.09

  (**a.**) 2.90

3. 0.7

  (**w.**) 0.700

  b. 0.07

  (**a.**) 0.70

4. 152.900

  (**A.**) 152.9

  (**s.**) 152.90

  c. 152.09

5. 0.4

  j. 0.004

  (**a.**) 0.40

  (**a.**) 0.400

6. 49.200

  (**l.**) 49.2

  f. 49.02

  (**k.**) 49.20

Answer the question below by unscrambling the letters.
What two states were the last to be admitted to the United States?

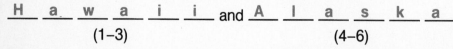

__H__ __a__ __w__ __a__ __i__ __i__ and __A__ __l__ __a__ __s__ __k__ __a__
　　　　(1–3)　　　　　　　　　　(4–6)

◢ RETEACH   Comparing and Ordering

7

You can use a place-value chart to help you order decimals.

Order from least to greatest: 0.315, 3.05, 0.309

Line up the decimal points.	Compare the digits from left to right.		Order from least to greatest.
0.315	0.315	0.315	0.309
3.05	3.05	0.309	0.315
0.309	0.309	Since 1 > 0,	3.05
	Since 3 > 0,	0.315 is	
	3.05 is the	greater than	
	greatest.	0.309.	

Order from least to greatest. Circle the letter that matches the correct order. Unscramble the circled letters to solve the riddle.

1. 2.15, 21.5, 2.05   **(q.)** 2.05, 2.15, 21.5   **k.** 2.15, 2.05, 21.5

2. 6.11, 6.10, 6.12   **j.** 6.12, 6.11, 6.10   **(s.)** 6.10, 6.11, 6.12

3. 0.03, 0.3, 0.003   **f.** 0.3, 0.003, 0.03   **(u.)** 0.003, 0.03, 0.3

4. 4.2, 0.4, 0.04   **e.** 0.4, 4.2, 0.04   **(a.)** 0.04, 0.4, 4.2

5. 0.08, 0.807, 0.47   **(s.)** 0.08, 0.47, 0.807   **i.** 0.47, 0.807, 0.08

6. 0.005, 0.051, 0.501   **(h.)** 0.005, 0.051, 0.501   **d.** 0.501, 0.051, 0.005

If you throw a pumpkin in the air, what comes down?

squash
_____

7. From which direction should you compare digits to order any number?

from left to right
_____

8 ◢ RETEACH   Rounding

You can round a number to a certain place by looking at the value of the digit to its right. Round 6851 to the greatest place.

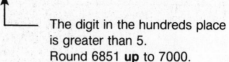

6 8 5 1

The greatest place
is the thousands.

The digit in the hundreds place
is greater than 5.
Round 6851 **up** to 7000.

Round 16.14 to the nearest whole number.

1 6.1 4

The nearest whole number ⟶

The digit in the tenths place
is less than 5.
Round 16.14 **down** to 16.

Round each number to the greatest place. Make sure each answer appears in the Answer Box.

1. $3854 ___$4000___   2. $83.98 ___$80___

3. 622 ___600___   4. $89.22 ___$90___

5. 4.48 ___4___   6. 3.88 ___4___

Round each decimal to the nearest whole number. Make sure each answer appears in the Answer Box.

7. 3.85 ___4___   8. 69.8 ___70___

9. 49.66 ___50___   10. 13.44 ___13___

11. 621.32 ___621___   12. 1.79 ___2___

13. 225.75 ___226___   14. 375.25 ___375___

Answer Box

4	4	600	$90	70	2	621	$80	$4000	13	50	4	375	226

⟋RETEACH

9

When adding decimals, be sure to line up the decimal points.

$8\,2.1\,3 + 0.4\,9\,7 + 5.6\,0\,1$

Line up the decimal points.		Add the digits.	Place the decimal point in the answer.
$\begin{array}{r} 8\,2.1\,3\,0 \\ 0.4\,9\,7 \\ +\,5.6\,0\,1 \\ \hline \end{array}$	$82.13 = 82.130$	$\begin{array}{r} 8\,2.1\,3\,0 \\ 0.4\,9\,7 \\ +\,5.6\,0\,1 \\ \hline 8\,8\ \ 2\,2\,8 \end{array}$	$\begin{array}{r} 8\,2.1\,3\,0 \\ 0.4\,9\,7 \\ +\,5.6\,0\,1 \\ \hline 8\,8.2\,2\,8 \end{array}$

Write the sum. Make sure each answer appears in the Answer Box.

1.
$$\begin{array}{r} 5\,0\,4.3\,2\,0 \\ 4\,0.6\,3\,8 \\ +\quad.0\,4\,7 \\ \hline 5\,4\,5.0\,0\,5 \end{array}$$

2.
$$\begin{array}{r} 3\,7.9\,8\,1 \\ 4\,7\,8.3\,0\,2 \\ +\,9\,0\,7.0\,0\,4 \\ \hline 1\,4\,2\,3.2\,8\,7 \end{array}$$

3.
$$\begin{array}{r} 4\,7\,9.7\,8 \\ +\,3\,2\,8.3\,0 \\ \hline 8\,0\,8.0\,8 \end{array}$$

4. $0.328 + .429 = \underline{0.757}$

5. $7.89 + 4.31 + 18.21 = \underline{30.41}$

6. $0.078 + 1.043 + 2.0 = \underline{3.121}$

7. $88.3 + 17.0 = \underline{105.3}$

8. $32.1 + 0.321 + 2.321 = \underline{34.742}$

9. $303.24 + 192.15 = \underline{495.39}$

10. $0.250 + 1.50 + 3.00 = \underline{4.75}$

11. Why is it important to line up the decimal points?

    __so that the place values will be aligned correctly__

Answer Box

4.75	34.742	3.121	808.08	30.41	0.757	495.39	105.3	1423.287	545.005

▶RETEACH

10

When subtracting decimals, be sure to line up the decimal points.

$$19.00 - 2.71$$

Line up the decimal points.	Subtract the digits.	Place the decimal point in the answer.
$\begin{array}{r} 19.00 \\ -\ 2.71 \\ \hline \end{array}$	$\begin{array}{r} 19.00 \\ -\ 2.71 \\ \hline 16\ \ 29 \end{array}$	$\begin{array}{r} 19.00 \\ -\ 2.71 \\ \hline 16.29 \end{array}$

Write the difference. Make sure each answer appears in the Answer Box.

1. $\begin{array}{r} 428.00 \\ -\ 19.76 \\ \hline 408.24 \end{array}$

2. $\begin{array}{r} 13.004 \\ -\ 8.096 \\ \hline 4.908 \end{array}$

3. $\begin{array}{r} 20.700 \\ -18.925 \\ \hline 1.775 \end{array}$

4. $\begin{array}{r} 39.05 \\ -19.95 \\ \hline 19.10 \end{array}$

5. $\begin{array}{r} 2.00 \\ -1.00 \\ \hline 1.00 \end{array}$

6. $\begin{array}{r} 47.10 \\ -27.95 \\ \hline 19.15 \end{array}$

7. $36 - 29.05 = \underline{6.95}$

8. $9 - 1.25 = \underline{7.75}$

9. $276.50 - 269.75 = \underline{6.75}$

10. $33.10 - 15.25 = \underline{17.85}$

11. How do you subtract a decimal part from a whole number?

   Add a decimal point and one or more zeros after the whole

   number. Then subtract.

Answer Box

1.00	1.775	6.95	408.24	7.75	4.908	17.85	6.75	19.10	19.15

2.1 ANOTHER LOOK

Expressions

You can write addition and subtraction expressions using letters to stand for numbers.

The letter *c* stands for the number of counters in the cup.

If you remove 2 counters, there will be *c* – 2 counters in the cup.

If you add 3 counters, there will be *c* + 3 counters in the cup.

• *c* – 2 and *c* + 3 are examples of **expressions.**

When *c* stands for 6 counters, what is *c* – 2?

> *c* – 2 is 6 – 2, or 4 counters

Write an expression to answer each question.

1. You have *b* books. You give your best friend 4 of your books. How many books do you have left?

> *b* – 4

2. You have *s* T-shirts. You get 3 more for your birthday. How many T-shirts do you have now?

> *s* + 3

3. There are *m* muffins. You bake 24 more. How many muffins are there now?

> *m* + 24

4. There are *r* raisins in a box. You eat 15 raisins. How many raisins are left?

> *r* – 15

Write the value of each expression.

5. What is *g* + 8 if *g* = 9? _____ 17

6. What is *h* – 5 if *h* = 70? _____ 65

7. What is 32 + *d* if *d* = 8? If *d* = 25? _____ 40; 57

8. What is *x* – 12 if *x* = 36? If *x* = 84? _____ 24; 72

2.2 ANOTHER LOOK

Multiplication Expressions

You can use multiplication in an expression.

There are *n* counters in each cup. The number of counters in all 3 cups is 3 × *n*, or *n* × 3.

This picture shows how the cups would look if *n* = 4. The total number is 3 × 4, or 12 counters.

Draw counters to show how the cups would look if *n* = 5.

Remember, both 3 × *n* and 3 • *n* mean *3 times n*.

Write a multiplication expression to describe each situation.

1. A dollar can be changed for 10 dimes. If *d* stands for the number of dollars Jenny has, how many dimes could she have?

   10 • *d* or *d* • 10

2. There are 3 tennis balls in a can. If *c* stands for the number of cans Hugo has, how many tennis balls does he have?

   3 • *c* or *c* • 3

3. A large pizza can be cut into 8 slices. If *p* stands for the number of pizzas sold, how many slices were sold?

   8 • *p* or *p* • 8

4. A large can of juice has 18 servings. If *c* stands for the number of cans of juice bought, how many servings are there?

   18 • *c* or *c* • 18

5. A factory packs 16 sweaters in each carton. If *c* stands for the number of cartons shipped on one day, how many sweaters were shipped?

   16 • *c* or *c* • 16

6. There are 12 eggs in a carton. If *c* stands for the number of cartons of eggs a bakery ordered, how many eggs were ordered?

   12 • *c* or *c* • 12

7. A quarter can be changed for 5 nickels. If *q* stands for the number of quarters Vincent has, how many nickels could he have?

   5 • *q* or *q* • 5

8. A dollar can be changed for 4 quarters. If *d* stands for the number of dollars Savitri has, how many quarters could she have?

   4 • *d* or *d* • 4

2.3 ◢ ANOTHER LOOK

Multiples and Least Common Multiple

To find the least common multiple of two numbers, find the
first several multiples of each number.

What is the least common multiple of 4 and 5?

    4, 8, 12, 16, **20**, 24, 28, 32, 36, **40**, 44, . . .
    5, 10, 15, **20**, 25, 30, 35, **40**, 45, 50, . . .

The top list shows the first several multiples of 4.
The bottom list shows the first several multiples of 5.
• 20 and 40 are in both lists.
• 20 and 40 are **common multiples** of 4 and 5.
• 20 comes first. So, 20 is the **least common multiple** of 4 and 5.

Use the lists below to find the least common multiple of 6 and 8.

    6, 12, 18, 24, 30, 36, 42, 48, 54, 60, . . .
    8, 16, 24, 32, 40, 48, 56, 64, 72, 80, . . .

1. Which list shows the multiples of 6? ___the top list___

2. The other list shows the multiples of what number?___8___

3. What numbers are in both lists? ___24 and 48___

4. Write two common multiples of 6 and 8. ___24, 48___

5. What is the least common multiple of 6 and 8? ___24___

**Find the least common multiple for each set of numbers.
Write the first several multiples of each number. Circle the
least common multiple.**

6. 2 and 3   multiples of 2 ___2, 4, ⑥, 8, 10, 12, 14, . . .___

    multiples of 3 ___3, ⑥, 9, 12, 15, . . .___

7. 8 and 5   multiples of 8 ___8, 16, 24, 32, ㊵, 48, 56, 64, . . .___

    multiples of 5 ___5, 10, 15, 20, 25, 30, 35, ㊵, 45, . . .___

8. 5 and 3   multiples of 5 ___5, 10, ⑮, 20, 25, 30, 35, 40, . . .___

    multiples of 3 ___3, 6, 9, 12, ⑮, 18, 21, 24, 27, . . .___

2.4 ◣ ANOTHER LOOK

Mental Math: Multiples of 10, 100, and 1000

You can use basic facts to multiply mentally by multiples of 10, 100, or 1000.

Multiply mentally: 30 × 500 ° ° ° °  **Think:**
3 × 5 **hundreds** = 15 **hundreds**

$$3 \times 500 = 1500$$

$$30 \times 500 = 15{,}000$$

Write the missing numbers.

1. 4 × 70 ⟶ 4 × 7 tens = ___28___ tens = ___280___

2. 8 × 60 ⟶ 8 × ___6___ tens = ___48___ tens = ___480___

3. 9 × 300 ⟶ 9 × 3 hundreds = ___27___ hundreds = ___2700___

4. 6 × 500 ⟶ 6 × ___5___ hundreds = ___30___ hundreds = ___3000___

5. 3 × 2000 ⟶ 3 × ___2___ thousands = ___6___ thousands = ___6000___

6. 7 × 9000 ⟶ 7 × ___9___ thousands = ___63___ thousands = ___63,000___

7. 30 × 90 ⟶ 3 × 9 tens = ___27___ tens

         3 × 90 = ___270___

         30 × 90 = ___2700___

8. 60 × 700 ⟶ 6 × 7 hundreds = ___42___ hundreds

         6 × 700 = ___4200___

         60 × 700 = ___42,000___

Write the product. Use mental math.

9. 90 × 90 = ___8100___

10. 50 × 40 = ___2000___

11. 8 × 70 = ___560___

12. 300 × 60 = ___18,000___

13. 3000 × 7 = ___21,000___

14. 900 × 4 = ___3600___

15. 50 × 50 = ___2500___

16. 90 × 400 = ___36,000___

17. 9 × 2000 = ___18,000___

18. 20 × 700 = ___14,000___

2.5 ANOTHER LOOK

Estimating Products

Remember, you can estimate a product using either rounding or front-end estimation.

At the Bay Street School, there are 12 rows of 27 seats set up for the class play. About how many people can sit and watch the play?

Use **rounding** to estimate.

12×27

$12 \longrightarrow 10$

$27 \longrightarrow 30$

$10 \times 30 = 300$ °°° (about 300 seats)

Use **front-end** estimation.

12×27

$12 \longrightarrow 10$

$27 \longrightarrow 20$

$10 \times 20 = 200$ °°° (about 200 seats)

- Both 300 and 200 are reasonable estimates.
- Rounding usually gives you the closer estimate.

Write your estimate. Use rounding or front-end estimation. Accept any reasonable estimate. Rounded estimates are given.

1. 6×93

$6 \longrightarrow \underline{6}$

$93 \longrightarrow \underline{90}$

Estimate $\longrightarrow \underline{540}$

2. 34×68

$34 \longrightarrow \underline{30}$

$68 \longrightarrow \underline{70}$

Estimate $\longrightarrow \underline{2100}$

3. 521×7

$521 \longrightarrow \underline{500}$

$7 \longrightarrow \underline{7}$

Estimate $\longrightarrow \underline{3500}$

4. 8×57

$8 \longrightarrow \underline{8}$

$57 \longrightarrow \underline{60}$

Estimate $\longrightarrow \underline{480}$

5. 75×83

$75 \longrightarrow \underline{80}$

$83 \longrightarrow \underline{80}$

Estimate $\longrightarrow \underline{6400}$

6. 4×472

$4 \longrightarrow \underline{4}$

$472 \longrightarrow \underline{500}$

Estimate $\longrightarrow \underline{2000}$

Write your estimate. Accept any reasonable estimate. Rounded estimates are given.

7. 6×34 ___180___

8. 81×42 ___3200___

9. 63×68 ___4200___

10. 74×42 ___2800___

11. 8×309 ___2400___

12. 3×875 ___2700___

13. 76×28 ___2400___

14. 240×9 ___1800___

2.6 ▸ ANOTHER LOOK

Problem Solving Decisions: Logical Reasoning

Rosa, Mark, Janell, and Tommy have new skateboards. Their skateboards are blue, green, black, and orange. Rosa's skateboard is black and Mark's skateboard is not blue. If Janell's skateboard is green, what color is Tommy's skateboard?

- The friends who have new skateboards are Rosa, Mark, Janell, and Tommy.

- The colors of the skateboards are blue, green, black, and orange.

- You know Rosa's and Janell's colors and that Mark's is not blue.

- Make a chart to show what you know.

- Write a "√" if the skateboard color is correct for the person. Make an "x" if it is not.

	Blue	Green	Black	Orange
Rosa	✗	✗	✔	✗
Mark	✗			
Janell	✗	✔	✗	✗
Tommy				

- You know that Rosa's skateboard is black and Janell's skateboard is green, so only orange and blue are left. You also know that Mark's skateboard is not blue, so it must be orange. This means that Tommy's skateboard is blue.

Decide how to sort the information. Then solve.

1. The five children in Dana's family have their dental appointments in the months of January, June, July, August, and November. Her three older sisters have their appointments in months that start with the letter J. Her brother's appointment is not during the summer. When is Dana's appointment? _____ **August**

2. The third-, fourth-, fifth-, and sixth-grade classes each have a class pet. The pets are a guinea pig, a parrot, a snake, and a crayfish. The sixth-grade pet is not a crayfish and the fourth-grade pet is a bird. If the third-grade pet is a snake, what is the fifth-grade pet? _____ **crayfish**

11 ▼ RETEACH   Writing Expressions

Geffin Airways always keeps track of the number of people on each flight. The Pawtucket to Notown flight always has a crew of 6 people. If *t* stands for the total number of people on the Pawtucket to Notown flight, which expression shows how many of the people were passengers on the flight?

a) $6 - t$ **b)** $t + 6$ **c)** $t - 6$

To solve, you must figure out which expression represents the problem.

Two pieces of information are given in the problem:
1. There are 6 crew members.
2. There are a total of *t* people on the flight.

The number of passengers on the flight is:

total number of people on the flight − the size of the crew

$$t - 6$$

The answer to the question is **c)** $t - 6$.

Circle the expression that represents each word problem.

1. The number of pages used for advertising in each issue of Pre-Teen Monthly is fixed at 16. If *p* stands for the number of pages with no advertising this month, what was the total number of pages in this month's issue?

    a. $p - 16$ **b.** $p + 16$ **c.** $16 - p$

2. Every time Julio records his bowling score he adds 23 bonus points. If *s* stands for the score Julio has written down, what would Julio's score be without the bonus points?

    a. $s + 23$ **b.** $23 - s$ **c.** $s - 23$

3. Speedy Delivery Service was supposed to deliver 132 packages for the XYZ Co, but an unknown number of packages was lost during delivery. If *d* stands for the number of packages lost during delivery, how many packages were delivered?

    a. $132 - d$ **b.** $d - 132$ **c.** $132 + d$

4. The price of admission to the movies is $7.00. At the movie, Belinda spent money on popcorn and soft drinks. If *m* is the total amount of money Belinda spent going to the movies, how much did she spend on popcorn and soft drinks?

    a. $m - 7$ **b.** $7 + m$ **c.** $7 - m$

▶RETEACH

12

Evaluating Expressions

Make sure to substitute for the variable or letter when you are finding the value of an expression.

Problem: | Find the value of the expression $8 \times p$ when $p = 7$.

Use the given value to replace the variable, or letter, in the expression.

Write an expression: $8 \times p$ $p = 7$

Replace the variable: 8×7

Multiply: $8 \times 7 = 56$

Write the value of the expression when $n = 4$. Make sure each answer appears in the Answer Box.

1. $9 \times n$	**2.** $n \times 6$	**3.** $n \times 4$	**4.** $n \times 10$
9×4	4×6	4×4	4×10
<u>36</u>	<u>24</u>	<u>16</u>	<u>40</u>

Write the value of the expression when $k = 9$. Make sure each answer appears in the Answer Box.

5. $k \times 3$	**6.** $5 \times k$	**7.** $k \times 1$	**8.** $7 \times k$
<u>9</u> $\times 3$	$5 \times$ <u>9</u>	<u>9</u> $\times 1$	$7 \times$ <u>9</u>
<u>27</u>	<u>45</u>	<u>9</u>	<u>63</u>

Write the value of each expression. Make sure each answer appears in the Answer Box.

9. $t \times 10$, when $t = 5$	**10.** $x \times 4$, when $x = 16$	**11.** $25 - s$, when $s = 12$
<u>50</u>	<u>64</u>	<u>13</u>

12. $5 \times j$, when $j = 6$	**13.** $11 \times m$, when $m = 2$	**14.** $r \times 2$, when $r = 200$
<u>30</u>	<u>22</u>	<u>400</u>

Answer Box

64	40	63	9	13	50	36	16	24	400	45	27	22	30

13 ▶ **RETEACH**   **Symbols for Multiplication**

There is more than one way to indicate multiplication.

Problem: | Write the value of the expression $8 \cdot m$, when $m = 4$.

multiply

$8 \cdot m$, when $m = 4$
$8 \cdot 4 = 32$

Remember that $8 \cdot m$ means the same thing as $8 \times m$.

Write the value of each expression. Make sure each answer appears in the Answer Box.

1. $9 \cdot p$, when $p = 12$

$9 \cdot 12 = \underline{108}$

2. $n \times 8$, when $n = 7$

$7 \times 8 = \underline{56}$

3. $b + 9$ when $b = 9$

$9 + 9 = \underline{18}$

4. $15 \cdot f$, when $f = 3$

$\underline{45}$

5. $m + 15$, when $m = 4$

$\underline{19}$

6. $q \cdot 3$, when $q = 12$

$\underline{36}$

7. $t + 7$, when $t = 21$

$\underline{28}$

8. $20 \times n$, when $n = 5$

$\underline{100}$

9. $7 \cdot z$, when $z = 10$

$\underline{70}$

10. Complete the table for the expression $t \cdot 8$. Make sure each answer appears in the Answer Box.

t	20	11	12
$t \cdot 8$	$20 \cdot 8 = \underline{160}$	$11 \cdot 8 = \underline{88}$	$12 \cdot 8 = \underline{96}$

11. What signs may be used in an expression to indicate the multiplication operation?

               A dot and a $\times$.

Answer Box

28	88	108	45	70	19	56	96	100	36	18	160

14 **RETEACH** **Multiplication Expressions**

To find the value of a multiplication expression, substitute the value of the variable and multiply.

Problem: | Find the value of $10 \cdot n$ when $n = 9$

Remember the two steps:
1. substitute the value of the variable: $10 \cdot 9$
2. multiply: $10 \times 9 = 90$

Write the value of each expression. Make sure each answer appears in the Answer Box.

1. $15 \cdot n, n = 4$

$15 \cdot 4 = \underline{60}$

2. $n \times 8, n = 16$

$16 \times 8 = \underline{128}$

3. $13 \cdot n, n = 5$

$13 \cdot 5 = \underline{65}$

4. $n \cdot 75, n = 2$

$2 \cdot 75 = \underline{150}$

5. $n \cdot 70, n = 6$

$\underline{6} \cdot 70$

$\underline{420}$

6. $18 \times n, n = 4$

$18 \times \underline{4}$

$\underline{72}$

7. $n \cdot 5, n = 20$

$\underline{20} \cdot 5$

$\underline{100}$

8. $3 \times n, n = 40$

$\underline{120}$

9. $n \cdot 12, n = 7$

$\underline{84}$

10. $6 \times n, n = 17$

$\underline{102}$

11. $n \times 22, n = 3$

$\underline{66}$

12. $9 \cdot n, n = 10$

$\underline{90}$

13. $n \times 8, n = 8$

$\underline{64}$

14. $42 \cdot n, n = 2$

$\underline{84}$

15. $n \times 35, n = 1$

$\underline{35}$

16. $n \cdot 8, n = 8$

$\underline{64}$

17. What are the two steps for finding the value of a multiplication expression?

_____ 1. Substitute the value of the variable. _____

_____ 2. Multiply. _____

Answer Box

90	65	100	420	150	128	84	72	64	120	102	60	66	84	35	64

Name _____ Date _____

15 **RETEACH** **Multiples:**
Finding the Least Common Multiple

Remember that you can find the least common multiple of 2 or more numbers by skip counting.

Problem: | Find the least common multiple of 2, 3, and 4.

2: 2, 4, 6, 8, 10, (12), 14, 16, 18, 20, 22, 24, 26, 28, 30, 32, 34, 36, 38, 40, 42

Find some multiples of each number by skip counting.

3: 3, 6, 9, (12), 15, 18, 21, 24, 27, 30, 33, 36, 39, 42

Underline the common multiples.

Circle the smallest common number. This is the least common multiple.

4: 4, 8, (12), 16, 20, 24, 28, 32, 36, 40, 44

Least common multiple = 12

Complete. Write the least common multiple. Make sure each answer appears in the Answer Box.

1. 2: 2, 4, 6, 8, 10, _12_, _14_, _16_, _18_

3: 3, 6, 9, 12, 15, 18, _21_, _24_, _27_

Common multiples: _6, 12, 18_

Least common multiple = _6_

3. 4: 4, 8, _12_, _16_, _20_, _24_

8: 8, 16, _24_, _32_, _40_, _48_, _56_

12: 12, 24, _36_, _48_, _60_

Least common multiple = _24_

5. 2: 2, 4, 6, 8, 10, 12, _14_, _16_, _18_, _20_

4: 4, 8, _12_, _16_, _20_, 24, _28_, _32_, _36_

5: 5, 10 _15_, _20_, _25_, _30_, _35_, _40_

Least common multiple = _20_

2. 3: 3, 6, _9_, _12_, _15_, _18_, _21_, _24_

9: 9, 18, 27, _36_, _45_, _54_, _63_, _72_

Common multiples: _9, 18_

Least common multiple: _9_

4. 10: 10, _20_, _30_, _40_, _50_, _60_

25: 25, _50_, _75_, _100_, _125_, _150_

Least common multiple = _50_

Answer Box

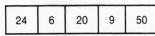

24	6	20	9	50

2.7 ANOTHER LOOK

Multiplying by 1-Digit Numbers

You can use a model to help you understand multiplication.

Multiply: 46 × 2

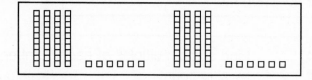

Multiply the ones.

$$\begin{array}{r} \overset{1}{46} \\ \times\ 2 \\ \hline 2 \end{array}$$

6 ones × 2 = 12 ones, *or* 1 ten 2 ones

Multiply the tens.

$$\begin{array}{r} \overset{1}{46} \\ \times\ 2 \\ \hline 92 \end{array}$$

4 tens × 2 = 8 tens
8 tens + 1 ten = 9 tens

Write the product.

1. $\begin{array}{r} 59 \\ \times\ 8 \\ \hline 472 \end{array}$
2. $\begin{array}{r} 46 \\ \times\ 3 \\ \hline 138 \end{array}$
3. $\begin{array}{r} 37 \\ \times\ 8 \\ \hline 296 \end{array}$
4. $\begin{array}{r} 75 \\ \times\ 9 \\ \hline 675 \end{array}$
5. $\begin{array}{r} 98 \\ \times\ 2 \\ \hline 196 \end{array}$

Multiply: 134 × 3

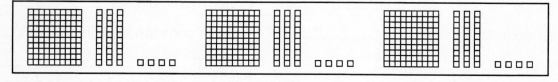

Multiply the ones.

$$\begin{array}{r} \overset{1}{1}34 \\ \times\ \ 3 \\ \hline 2 \end{array}$$

4 ones × 3 = 12 ones, *or* 1 ten 2 ones

Multiply the tens.

$$\begin{array}{r} \overset{11}{1}34 \\ \times\ \ 3 \\ \hline 02 \end{array}$$

3 tens × 3 = 9 tens
9 tens + 1 ten = 10 tens, *or* 1 hundred 0 tens

Multiply the hundreds.

$$\begin{array}{r} \overset{11}{1}34 \\ \times\ \ 3 \\ \hline 402 \end{array}$$

1 hundred × 3 = 3 hundreds
3 hundreds + 1 hundred = 4 hundreds

Write the product.

6. $\begin{array}{r} 519 \\ \times\ \ 4 \\ \hline 2076 \end{array}$
7. $\begin{array}{r} 386 \\ \times\ \ 6 \\ \hline 2316 \end{array}$
8. $\begin{array}{r} 305 \\ \times\ \ 7 \\ \hline 2135 \end{array}$
9. $\begin{array}{r} 228 \\ \times\ \ 5 \\ \hline 1140 \end{array}$
10. $\begin{array}{r} 147 \\ \times\ \ 8 \\ \hline 1176 \end{array}$

2.8 ⬛ ANOTHER LOOK

Multiplying by 2-Digit Numbers

You can think of multiplying large numbers as several simpler problems. Squared paper can help you line up the digits.

Multiply: 258 × 34 °°°(Think: 34 = 30 + 4)

First, multiply
258 × 4.

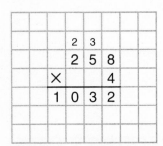

Next, multiply
258 × 30.

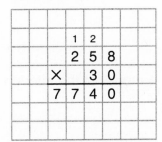

Then, add the
two products.

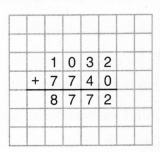

Write the product. Use squared paper if it helps.

1. 193 × 20 = **3860**	**2.** 47 × 35 = **1645**	**3.** 275 × 18 = **4950**	**4.** 105 × 93 = **9765**
5. 59 × 77 = **4543**	**6.** $8.29 × 51 = **$422.79**	**7.** 268 × 82 = **21,976**	**8.** 367 × 60 = **22,020**
9. 273 × 78 = **21,294**	**10.** 65 × 50 = **3250**	**11.** $4.09 × 48 = **$196.32**	**12.** 792 × 29 = **22,968**

13. 12 mL × 46 = ___**552 mL**___

14. 25 × $3.42 = ___**$85.50**___

15. 305 × 98 = ___**29,890**___

16. 263 × 26 = ___**6838**___

2.9 ◣ ANOTHER LOOK

....

Problem Solving Strategy: Act It Out

You are installing a new tile kitchen floor. The room is 12 ft long by 8 ft wide. You put a border of blue tiles around the edge. Each tile is 1 square ft. How many tiles will you need to complete the border?

1. Understand

- The room measures 12 ft × 8 ft.

- The border will extend around all 4 sides of the room.

- The tiles are 1 square ft.

2. Plan

- Use cubes or color tiles to make a model of the kitchen floor.

- Count the number of border tiles.

3. Try It

- Build a rectangle to represent the kitchen floor.

- Count the tiles that make up the border.

4. Look Back

- Remember not to count the corner tiles twice.

- The total number of tiles needed is 36.

Solve. Use Act It Out when you can.

1. The community gardening club decided to plant yellow tulip bulbs. The bulbs are to be planted one foot apart. There are to be 20 bulbs down each row and 10 bulbs across each row. How many bulbs will be needed in all?

   _____ **200 bulbs** _____

2. The club wants to have a border of red tulips around the garden. It decides to replace the outer bulbs with red ones.

   How many red bulbs are needed? _____ **56 red bulbs** _____

3. If the club plants the red border and plants yellow tulips in the

   interior, how many yellow tulips are needed? _____ **144 yellow bulbs** _____

Name _____   Date _____

2.10 ◢ ANOTHER LOOK

Multiplying by 3-Digit Numbers

You can think of multiplying large numbers as several simpler problems. Squared paper can help you keep the digits in the correct places.

Multiply: 291 × 326 °°°○ Think: 326 = 300 + 20 + 6

First, multiply 291 × 6.	Multiply 291 × 20.	Multiply 291 × 300.	Then, add the three products.

Write the product. Use squared paper if it helps.

1. 346 × 110 38,060	**2.** 283 × 246 69,618	**3.** $5.49 × 503 $2761.47	**4.** 181 × 437 79,097
5. 270 × 716 193,320	**6.** 526 × 456 239,856	**7.** 750 × 320 240,000	**8.** 193 × 208 40,144
9. 498 × 957 476,586	**10.** 707 × 707 499,849	**11.** $6.66 × 869 $5787.54	**12.** $2.50 × 305 $762.50

13. 365 × 308 = __112,420__   **14.** 920 × $1.46 = __$1343.20__

15. 115 × 422 = __48,530__   **16.** 728 × 256 = __186,368__

2.11 ANOTHER LOOK

Problem Solving: **Using Strategies**

The Voyager spacecraft left Earth in 1977. It arrived at the planet Neptune 12 years later. About how many days was the Voyager in space?

1. Understand

- You know there are 365 days in a year.

- It took the Voyager 12 years to reach Neptune.

2. Plan

- You can multiply to find out about how many days the Voyager was in space.

3. Try It

- Multiply 365 × 12 to find the number of days.

4. Look Back

- The Voyager reached Neptune after being in space for about 4380 days.

Use any strategy to solve.

1. There are 44 classrooms in the new high school. Each classroom has between 1 and 5 boards.

   a. If all the classrooms are being used, what is the greatest possible number of boards that are in use? _____ 220 _____

   b. If 12 rooms are not being used, what is the greatest possible number of boards in use? _____ 160 _____

2. A dripping faucet can waste up to 75 gal of water in one week.

   About how much water is this in one year? _____ 3900 gal a year _____

3. Suppose you have juice to pour into cups for a school fair. You need to pour 288 cups. You can pour 32 cups from one gallon.

   How many gallons do you need? _____ 9 gal _____

2.12 ANOTHER LOOK

Mental Math: **Multiplication**

You can use mental math to multiply 2-digit and 3-digit numbers that are not multiples of 10, 100, or 1000.

Multiply: 4 × 199 ∞∘{ Think: 199 is close to 200. }

You can multiply 4 × 199 mentally by first multiplying 4 × 200.   4 × 200 = 800

Since 199 is 1 less than 200, subtract 1 from each 200.

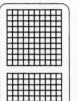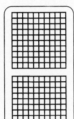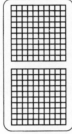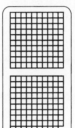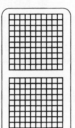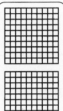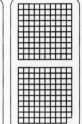

So, to multiply 4 × 199 mentally, think: 4 × 200 = 800
                                           4 × 1 = 4
                                           800 − 4 = 796

Write the product. Use mental math.

1. 5 × 19 = ___95___

2. 7 × 29 = ___203___

3. 6 × 99 = ___594___

4. 4 × 49 = ___196___

5. 8 × 99 = ___792___

6. 7 × 199 = ___1393___

7. 6 × 29 = ___174___

8. 3 × $0.19 = ___$0.57___

9. 3 × $0.49 = ___$1.47___

10. 5 × 49 = ___245___

11. 9 × 199 = ___1791___

12. 5 × 99 = ___495___

13. 6 × 19 = ___114___

14. 2 × 49 = ___98___

15. 3 × $1.99 = ___$5.97___

16. 8 × 199 = ___1592___

17. 4 × $0.99 = ___$3.96___

18. 7 × 19 = ___133___

▶ RETEACH

16

Multiplying by 1-Digit Numbers: Failing to Regroup

You can write the product of each place value on a separate line to help you multiply 3-digit numbers.

Problem: | 3×271 |

```
  271        Multiply each place value. Then add the partial products to
×   3        find the final product.
    3 = 3 × 1    ⟶ Multiply the ones. Write the product on the first line.
  210 = 3 × 70   ⟶ Multiply the tens. Write the product on the second line.
  600 = 3 × 200  ⟶ Multiply the hundreds. Write the product on the third line.
  813           ⟶ Add partial products.
```

Write the product. Make sure each answer appears in the Answer Box.

1.
```
    521
  ×   8
─────────
      8 = 8 × 1
    160 = 8 × 20
   4000 = 8 × 500
   4168
```

2.
```
    286
  ×   2
─────────
     12 = 2 × 6
    160 = 2 × 80
    400 = 2 × 200
    572
```

3.
```
    478
  ×   3
─────────
     24
    210
   1200
   1434
```

4.
```
    348
  ×   4
─────────
     32
    160
   1200
   1392
```

5.
```
    931
  ×   6
─────────
      6
    180
   5400
   5586
```

6.
```
    802
  ×   9
─────────
     18
    000
   7200
   7218
```

7. $738 \times 2 =$ __1476__

8. $890 \times 7 =$ __6230__

9. $648 \times 5 =$ __3240__

10. What steps can you do to help you multiply 3–digit numbers?

   __Multiply each place value. Write each partial product on a__

   __separate line. Add partial products.__

Answer Box

1476	1434	4168	5586	6230	1392	572	3240	7218

RETEACH

17

Multiplying by 1-Digit Numbers: Multiply Before Adding

Be sure to multiply first. Then add a regrouped number to the product.

Problem: | 4×532 |

```
   +1
   532
 ⊗   4
  2128
```

Multiply.
$4 \times 5 = 20$
Add.
$20 + 1 = 21$

Remember to multiply first; then add the regrouped number. Write the regrouped number in the next place as a reminder to add it after multiplying.

Write the product. Make sure each answer appears in the Answer Box.

1.
```
   +2
   629
 ⊗   3
  1887
```

2.
```
   +1
   748
 ⊗   2
  1496
```

3.
```
   +2
   851
 ⊗   5
  4255
```

4.
```
   543
 ×   6
  3258
```

5.
```
   409
 ×   5
  2045
```

6.
```
 $3.90
 ×    9
 $35.10
```

7.
```
   276
 ×   4
  1104
```

8.
```
 $9.90
 ×    3
 $29.70
```

9.
```
   374
 ×   2
   748
```

10.
```
   617
 ×   6
  3702
```

11.
```
 $3.69
 ×    7
 $25.83
```

12.
```
   545
 ×   3
  1635
```

13. When do you add regrouped numbers?

    _____ after multiplying _____

Answer Box

2045	1887	748	1635	3702	1496	$25.83	$35.10	4255	1104	3258	$29.70

18

RETEACH

Multiplying by 2-Digit Numbers

Remember to start multiplying at the right and work your way to the left.

Problem: | 26×413 |

```
      1
  4 1 ③
×   2 6  ←
  2 4 7 8
  8 2 6 0
1 0 , 7 3 8
```

When adding, subtracting, or multiplying, remember to start at the right and work to the left, opposite to the way you read.

Your first step is 6×3.

Write the product. Make sure each answer appears in the Answer Box.

1.
```
  8 2 ⑧
×   1 6  ←
  13,248
```

2.
```
  3 2 ④
×   1 5  ←
   4860
```

3.
```
  5 9 ⓪
×   2 7  ←
  15,930
```

4.
```
  7 3 4
×    3 3
  24,222
```

5.
```
  4 3 0
×    1 9
   8170
```

6.
```
  6 0 4
×    3 8
  22,952
```

7.
```
  1 8 7
×    6 8
  12,716
```

8.
```
  2 8 0
×    5 6
  15,680
```

9.
```
  9 0 4
×    2 7
  24,408
```

10.
```
  9 2 5
×    4 6
  42,550
```

11.
```
  1 2 0 1
×      7 7
  92,477
```

12.
```
  3 1 2 4
×      2 5
  78,100
```

Answer Box

22,952	42,550	78,100	24,408	13,248	92,477	12,716	24,222	15,680	15,930	4860	8170

RETEACH

19

When multiplying money by a whole number, always place the decimal point two places from the right in the answer. You must also remember to include the dollar sign in the answer.

Multiply. Write the product.

$3.25 × 15 = _____

Multiply as you normally would.

```
      2
  $ 3 . 2 5
  ×     1 5
  ─────────
          5
```

```
    1 2
  $ 3 . 2 5
  ×     1 5
  ─────────
        2 5
```

```
    1 2
  $ 3 . 2 5
  ×     1 5
  ─────────
    1 6 2 5
```

```
    1 2
  $ 3 . 2 5
  ×     1 5
  ─────────
    1 6 2 5
    3 2 5 0
  ─────────
    4 8 . 7 5
```

Write the dollar sign in the answer.
  $3.25 × 15 = $48.75

Notice that the decimal point is 2 places from the right.

Multiply. Write the product. Make sure each answer appears in the Answer Box.

1. $2.30 × 8 = __$18.40__

2. $7.52 × 10 = __$75.20__

3. $4.45 × 5 = __$22.25__

4. $9.08 × 12 = __$108.96__

5. $1.50 × 27 = __$40.50__

6. $14.83 × 4 = __$59.32__

7. The admission to the Museum of Folk Art is $2.75. How much would it cost for 25 people to visit the museum?

   _____$68.75_____

8. Each postcard in the museum gift shop costs $0.45. Nica decides to buy 6 postcards. How much does Nica spend on postcards?

   _____$2.70_____

9. The museum gift shop has a set of wooden bowls. There are 11 bowls in the set. If each bowl costs $5.90, how much would the whole set cost?

   _____$64.90_____

10. Nica liked the little wooden animals so much that she bought all 32 of them. If each animal cost $1.49, how much did this cost Nica?

    _____$47.68_____

Answer Box

$2.70	$22.25	$59.32	$18.40	$68.75	$75.20	$47.68	$108.96	$40.50	$64.90

Name _____ Date _____

Remember to include zeros in the partial products of multiplication problems.

Problem: 313×529

$$
\begin{array}{r}
\overset{2}{5}\,2\,9 \\
\times 3\,1\,3 \\
\hline
1\,5\,8\,7 \\
5\,2\,9\,0 \\
1\,5\,8\,7\,0\,0 \\
\hline
1\,6\,5\,5\,7\,7
\end{array}
\qquad
\begin{array}{l}
3 \times 5\,2\,9 \\
1\,0 \times 5\,2\,9 \\
3\,0\,0 \times 5\,2\,9
\end{array}
$$

Pay attention to the place value of the factor. Remember to include as many zeros in the partial products as there are in the factor. By doing this you can be sure that the place values are lined up.

Write the product. Make sure each answer appears in the Answer Box.

1.
$$
\begin{array}{r}
3\,8\,1 \\
\times 4\,8\,3 \\
\hline
1\,1\,4\,3 \\
3\,0\,4\,8\,0 \\
1\,5\,2\,4\,0\,0 \\
\hline
184{,}023
\end{array}
$$

2.
$$
\begin{array}{r}
6\,3\,4 \\
\times 9\,8\,5 \\
\hline
3\,1\,7\,0 \\
5\,0\,7\,2\,0 \\
5\,7\,0\,6\,0\,0 \\
\hline
624{,}490
\end{array}
$$

3.
$$
\begin{array}{r}
5\,3\,5 \\
\times 8\,0\,1 \\
\hline
5\,3\,5 \\
0\,0\,0 \\
4\,2\,8\,0\,0\,0 \\
\hline
428{,}535
\end{array}
$$

4.
$$
\begin{array}{r}
9\,2\,1 \\
\times\ \ 3\,8 \\
\hline
34{,}998
\end{array}
$$

5.
$$
\begin{array}{r}
5\,2\,9 \\
\times 1\,1\,7 \\
\hline
61{,}893
\end{array}
$$

6.
$$
\begin{array}{r}
\$3.85 \\
\times\ \ 2\,9\,8 \\
\hline
\$1147.30
\end{array}
$$

7. $\$4.39 \times 628 = \underline{\$2756.92}$

8. $709 \times 319 = \underline{226{,}171}$

9. $72 \times 643 = \underline{46{,}296}$

10. $267 \times 324 = \underline{86{,}508}$

11. $920 \times 184 = \underline{169{,}280}$

12. $834 \times 529 = \underline{441{,}186}$

13. How can you line up the place values in partial products? <u>by including as many zeros in</u>
<u>the partial products as there are in the factor</u>

Answer Box

46,296	$2756.92	34,998	169,280	184,023	61,893	428,535	226,171	$1147.30	624,490
441,186	86,508								

21 ⟩RETEACH Multiplying by 2- and 3-Digit Numbers: Regrouping Numbers

···

When multiplying, be careful to keep track of regrouped numbers.

Problem: | 149 × 872 |

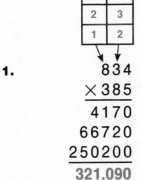

```
    2
    6̶ ̶4̶
   8 7 2
 × 1 4 9
   7 8 4 8
  34 8 8 0
  87 2 0 0
 129,928
```

Remember to cross out the first set of regrouped numbers. Write the second set of regrouped numbers in a different row. This way you won't add the incorrect regrouped number.

Write the product. As you multiply, write the regrouped numbers in the correct boxes. Cross out regrouped numbers as you add them. Make sure each answer appears in the Answer Box.

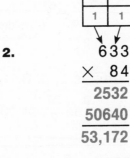

1.
1	1
2	3
1	2

```
       834
     × 385
      4170
     66720
    250200
    321,090
```

2.
2	2
1	1

```
       633
     ×  84
      2532
     50640
     53,172
```

3.
4	1
3	1
6	2

```
       583
     × 648
      4664
     23320
    349800
    377,784
```

4. 458 × 79 = ____36,182____

5. 729 × 83 = ____60,507____

6. $2.36 × 936 = ____$2208.96____

7. How can you be sure that you add in the correct regrouped numbers when multiplying 2- and 3-digit numbers?

   Cross out each regrouped number as it is added and

   write the next set in a different row.

Answer Box

60,507	53,172	321,090	$2,208.96	36,182	377,784

3.1 ▸ ANOTHER LOOK

Division Expressions

There are many different ways to represent division.

Jack has 6 goldfish. He wants to share them equally with Akiko. How many goldfish does Jack give Akiko?

Draw a picture.	Use division symbols.	Write a fraction.

$6 \div 2 = 3$ or $2\overline{)6}^{\,3}$

$\frac{6}{2} = 3$

Suppose you do not know how many goldfish Jack has. You can write a division expression, using a letter to stand for the number of goldfish.

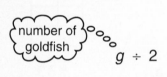

number of goldfish → $g \div 2$ or $\frac{g}{2}$ ← number of goldfish

• If the number of goldfish (g) is 6, then $\frac{g}{2}$ is $\frac{6}{2}$, or 3.

• If the number of goldfish (g) is 20, then $\frac{g}{2}$ is $\frac{20}{2}$, or 10.

Write the value of each expression when $y = 5$.
Then write the value of each expression when $y = 10$.

1. $\frac{30}{y} =$ _____ 6, 3

2. $20 \div y =$ _____ 4, 2

3. $y + 6 =$ _____ 11, 16

4. $y \div 5 =$ _____ 1, 2

5. $7 \cdot y =$ _____ 35, 70

6. $\frac{100}{y} =$ _____ 20, 10

Write an expression to describe each situation.

7. Mario wants to know how many dollars he can get for his collection of quarters. If q stands for the number of quarters, what expression tells the number of dollars?

   $\frac{q}{4}$ or $q \div 4$

8. A basket of muffins is shared equally by 6 friends. If m stands for the number of muffins, what expression tells how many muffins each friend gets?

   $\frac{m}{6}$ or $m \div 6$

3.2 ANOTHER LOOK

Estimating Quotients with Compatible Numbers

You can use **compatible numbers** to help you estimate quotients.
Compatible numbers are numbers that are easy to work with mentally.
To find compatible numbers, look for basic facts.

Estimate: $4\overline{)191}$ What number close to 191 is easy to divide by 4?

- 190 is close to 191. → $4\overline{)190}$ is not easy to divide mentally.
- 180 is close to 191. → $4\overline{)180}$ is not easy to divide mentally.

- 200 is close to 191. → $4\overline{)200}$ 4 and 200 are compatible numbers. $20 \div 4$ is basic fact.

$191 \div 4$ is about 50.

You can make another estimate.

- 4 and 160 are also compatible numbers. → $4\overline{)160}$ (40)

Both 40 and 50 are reasonable estimates.

Circle the letter of the compatible numbers.

1. $6\overline{)497}$ **a.** $6\overline{)400}$ **(b.)** $6\overline{)480}$ **c.** $6\overline{)495}$

2. $3834 \div 5$ **a.** $3800 \div 5$ **b.** $3300 \div 5$ **(c.)** $4000 \div 5$

3. $8\overline{)62,555}$ **a.** $8\overline{)60,000}$ **b.** $8\overline{)62,000}$ **(c.)** $8\overline{)64,000}$

Write the compatible numbers you would use to estimate the quotient. Then write the estimate. Answers may vary.

4. $4\overline{)3593}$

   $4\overline{)3200}$ (800)   or $4\overline{)3600}$ (900)

5. $7\overline{)694}$

   $7\overline{)630}$ (90)   or $7\overline{)700}$ (100)

6. $225 \div 9$

   $180 \div 9 = 20$ or $270 \div 9 = 30$

7. $5\overline{)715}$

   $5\overline{)500}$ (100)   or $5\overline{)1000}$ (200)

8. $6\overline{)4554}$

   $6\overline{)4200}$ (700)   or $6\overline{)4800}$ (800)

9. $1712 \div 8$

   $1600 \div 8 = 200$ or $2400 \div 8 = 300$

3.3 ANOTHER LOOK

Dividing by a 1-Digit Divisor

Estimating can help you find the number of places in the quotient.

Divide: 3)118 ∘∘∘(What number close to 118 is easy to divide by 3? **120 ÷ 3**)

```
  40  ← The estimate has two digits.
3)120    So, the quotient will have two digits.
```

Write the tens digit. Multiply and subtract.	Write the ones digit. Multiply and subtract.	Write the remainder, if there is one.

```
     3                    3 9                     3 9  R 1
3)1  1  8           3)1  1  8              3)1  1  8
  - 9  ←3 × 3 tens    - 9                     - 9
    2  8                2  8                    2  8
                     - 2  7 ←3 × 9 ones       - 2  7
                          1                        1
```

The quotient is 39 with a remainder of 1.

Complete the division. Write the missing numbers.

```
            9  R 7
1. 8)7  9
  -[7][2] ←8 × 9 ones
     [7]
```

```
            6  4  R 2
2. 3)1  9  4
   - 1  8  ←3 × 6 tens
     [1][4]
   -[1][2] ←3 × 4 ones
        [2]
```

```
            8  5  R 3
3. 5)4  2  8
  -[4][0] ←5 × 8 tens
     [2][8]
   -[2][5] ←5 × 5 ones
        [3]
```

```
            8  R 6
4. 9)7  8
```

```
            9  9  R 5
5. 6)5  9  9
```

```
            3  6
6. 7)2  5  2
```

3.4 ▸ ANOTHER LOOK

Zeros in the Quotient

Divide: $4\overline{)1635}$ ∘∘∘ (First estimate.)

400 ← The estimate has three digits.
$4\overline{)1600}$ The quotient will have three digits.

Write the hundreds digit. Multiply and subtract.	There are no tens. Write zero in the tens place of the quotient.	Write the ones digit. Multiply and subtract. Write the remainder.

Write the hundreds digit.
Multiply and subtract.

```
        4
  4)1 6 3 5
  - 1 6        ← 4 × 4
  _____      hundreds
      3 5
```

There are no tens.
Write zero in the tens
place of the quotient.

```
      4 0
  4)1 6 3 5
  - 1 6
  _____
      3 5
```

Write the ones digit.
Multiply and subtract.
Write the remainder.

```
      4 0 8  R 3
  4)1 6 3 5
  - 1 6
  _____
      3 5
    - 3 2   ← 4 × 8
    _____     ones
        3
            ↑
        Remainder
```

The quotient is 408 with a remainder of 3.

> When the quotient has no tens, write a zero in the tens place.
> When the quotient has no ones, write a zero in the ones place.

Complete the division. Write the missing numbers.

1.
```
      8 0  R 2
  4)3 2 2
  - 3 2    ← 4 × 8  tens
  _____
      2
```

2.
```
      3 0 3
  3)9 0 9
  - 9      ← 3 × 3  hundreds
  ____
    0 9
  - 9      ← 3 × 3  ones
  ____
      0
```

3.
```
      8 0  R 3
  9)7 2 3
```

4.
```
      5 5 0  R 1
  3)1 6 5 1
```

5.
```
      7 0 2
  5)3 5 1 0
```

3.5 ANOTHER LOOK

Choose a Computation Method

For a party, you purchased paper plates, napkins, plastic forks, and plastic cups. The total cost of these items was $12.60. You are sharing the cost with your best friend. How much will each of you have to pay?

- You know that the total cost is $12.60. Two people will be sharing the cost.

- You can divide the numbers in the problem easily using mental math.

- Since each of you will be paying one half, divide $12.60 by 2 to get $6.30.

- In this problem, it is quicker to use mental math than to use a calculator.

Decide whether to use a calculator or mental math. Then solve.

1. The team needs 600 points to win the track meet. It already has 150, 270, and 135 points. It hopes to get 72 points in the last event. Will this be enough to win the meet?
   methods may vary; calculator; yes, it is 27 points more

2. The team traveled 45 minutes by bus each way for the meet. How long did they travel in all?
   methods may vary; mental math; 90 min

3. Suppose you need to pack 360 books in 9 boxes. How many books will you put in each box?
   methods may vary; mental math; 40 books

4. A customer made these purchases: 3 books for $6.99 each, 1 calendar for $5.99, a bookmark for $1.50, and a magazine for $2.99. What is the total cost of the purchases?
   methods may vary; calculator; $31.45

5. Suppose you want to put 120 new photos in your photo album, but you have run out of blank pages. If refill pages hold 6 photos on each side, how many new pages should you buy? _____ *10 pages*

22 ▷ **RETEACH** .... **Division Expressions**

You already know two ways to write a division sentence.
You know that $3\overline{)12} = 12 \div 3$. There is also a third way to write

12 divided by 3; you can write it as a fraction: $\frac{12}{3}$.

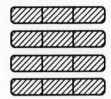

Look at these fraction bars.

Each bar is divided into thirds, and each bar shows three thirds,

or 1. So, the 4 bars together show $\frac{12}{3}$, or 4. You can check that

$\frac{12}{3} = 4$ by writing $\frac{12}{3}$ in simplest form.

$$\frac{12}{3} = \frac{4}{1} = 4$$

Any division sentence can be written as a fraction. Write the
dividend as the numerator and the divisor as the denominator. The
simplest form of the fraction (or the whole number it is equivalent
to) is the quotient.

$$12 \div 3 = \frac{12}{3} = \frac{4}{1} = 4$$

**Write each division sentence as a fraction. Then write the
fraction in simplest form and give the whole-number quotient.**

1. $21 \div 3 = \frac{21}{3} = \frac{7}{1} = $ ___7___

2. $18 \div 6 = \frac{18}{6} = \frac{3}{1} = $ ___3___

3. $30 \div 5 = \frac{30}{5} = \frac{6}{1} = $ ___6___

4. $27 \div 3 = \frac{27}{3} = \frac{9}{1} = $ ___9___

Write the equivalent whole number.

1. $\frac{14}{2} = $ ___7___

2. $\frac{36}{6} = $ ___6___

3. $\frac{21}{7} = $ ___3___

4. $\frac{16}{4} = $ ___4___

Name _____ Date _____

When you divide, remember to write the remainder as part of your answer.

Problem: 355 ÷ 4

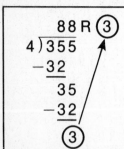

```
      88 R ③
  4)355
    -32
     35
    -32
      ③
```

Always record the remainder in the answer.

Write the answer. Make sure each answer appears in the Answer Box.

```
       81 R  1                    561 R  3                 100 R  4
1. 3)244                  2. 8)4491              3. 7)704
  -24                       -40                    -7
    4                        491                    ④
   -3                       -48
    ①                        11
                            -8
                             ③
```

```
     334 R6                    52 R1                   2370 R2
4. 7)2344                 5. 2)105               6. 4)9482
```

7. 9)40,362 = ___4484 R6___   8. 6)399 = ___66 R3___   9. 6)5500 = ___916 R4___

10. 5)634 = ___126 R4___   11. 3)2482 = ___827 R1___   12. 6)11,402 = ___1900 R2___

13. What does the remainder stand for? What do you know about its value?

   Answers may vary. It reflects the part that is left when the divisor does not divide the

   dividend exactly. It must be smaller than the divisor.

Answer Box

| 561 R3 | 52 R1 | 1900 R2 | 100 R4 | 916 R4 | 126 R4 | 2370 R2 | 66 R3 | 81 R1 | 334 R6 | 4484 R6 | 827 R1 |

▗RETEACH

Completing the Division

24

Remember to record each step on a separate line when you do long division.

Problem: $3\overline{)329}$

Remember to follow these steps before you begin dividing:
- Decide how many digits are in the whole number quotient.
- Decide what the first digit is.

Write the hundreds digit. Multiply. Subtract.	There are not enough tens. Write a zero in the tens place in the quotient.	Write the ones digit. Multiply. Subtract. Is there a remainder?
$\begin{array}{r} 1\,\_\,\_ \\ 3\overline{)329} \\ -3 \quad\leftarrow 3\times 1 \\ \hline 29 \end{array}$	$\begin{array}{r} 10\,\_ \\ 3\overline{)329} \\ -3 \\ \hline 29 \end{array}$ 2 tens and 9 ones—not enough tens.	$\begin{array}{r} 109\,\text{R2} \\ 3\overline{)329} \\ -3 \\ \hline 29 \\ -27 \leftarrow 3\times 9 \\ \hline 2 \end{array}$

Write the answer. Make sure each answer appears in the Answer Box.

1. $\begin{array}{r} 154 \\ 3\overline{)462} \\ -3 \\ \hline 162 \\ -15 \\ \hline 12 \\ -12 \\ \hline 0 \end{array}$

2. $\begin{array}{r} 49\,\text{R2} \\ 4\overline{)198} \\ -16 \\ \hline 38 \\ -36 \\ \hline 2 \end{array}$

3. $\begin{array}{r} 604\,\text{R5} \\ 8\overline{)4837} \\ -48 \\ \hline 37 \\ -32 \\ \hline 5 \end{array}$

4. $\begin{array}{r} 301 \\ 4\overline{)1204} \end{array}$

5. $\begin{array}{r} 80\,\text{R8} \\ 9\overline{)728} \end{array}$

6. $\begin{array}{r} 300\,\text{R5} \\ 8\overline{)2405} \end{array}$

7. $\begin{array}{r} 75\,\text{R2} \\ 7\overline{)527} \end{array}$

Answer Box

80 R8	49 R2	154	75 R2	300 R5	301	604 R5

Name _____ Date _____

25 ▷ **RETEACH**   **Zeros in the Quotient**
··

Estimating before you divide will help you to avoid making errors.

Problem: | 6024 ÷ 3 |

Before dividing, estimate the quotient by using compatible numbers.

1. 6024 is close to 6000.
2. 6000 ÷ 3 = 2000.
3. Now you know that your answer will have 4 digits and be close to 2000.

```
      2 0 0 8    Compare the quotient with your estimate. Is it close?
   3 )6 0 2 4
    − 6        ◄── 3 × 2
       2 4
     − 2 4     ◄── 3 × 8
         0
```

Notice that you first multiply by 2000 and then by 8. The quotient is 2008.

Estimate. Then find the quotient. Make sure each answer appears in the Answer Box.

1. 10,500 ÷ 5

   a. 10,500 is close to ____**10,000**____

   b. 10,000 ÷ 5 = ____**2000**____

   c. 10,500 ÷ 5 = ____**2100**____

2. 3015 ÷ 3

   a. 3015 is close to ____**3000**____

   b. 3000 ÷ 3 = ____**1000**____

   c. 3015 ÷ 3 = ____**1005**____

3. 9021 ÷ 3 = ___**3007**___

4. 100,208 ÷ 4 = ___**25,052**___

5. 90,081 ÷ 9 = ___**10,009**___

6. 75,010 ÷ 5 = ___**15,002**___

7. 32,024 ÷ 8 = ___**4003**___

8. 1806 ÷ 6 = ___**301**___

9. What can you do to help you check your answer when you divide?

   Estimate the quotient. Compare your estimate to the answer.

Answer Box

| 301 | 4003 | 15,002 | 10,009 | 25,052 | 3007 | 1005 | 2100 |

60

3.6 ◢ ANOTHER LOOK

··

Problem Solving Strategy: Guess and Check

In the Snack Shop, the cost of an order of toast and a small juice is $1.80. The toast costs twice as much as the juice. Find the cost of each item.

1. Understand

- The total cost of the toast and juice is $1.80.

- The cost of the toast is 2 times the cost of the juice.

2. Plan

- Use Guess and Check to help solve the problem. Organize the guesses in a table.

Guesses for Cost of Juice	Cost of Toast	Total
$.30	2 × $.30 = $.60	$.90
$.50	2 × $.50 = $1.00	$1.50
$.60	2 × $.60 = $1.20	$1.80

3. Try It

- Make a first guess. Try $.30 for the cost of the juice.

- Make your next guess higher because $1.80 > $.90.

4. Look Back

- Each time you make a guess, decide how close you are to the target number of $1.80. Then, your next guess can be closer.

- You know the juice cost $.60 and the toast cost $1.20 because together they cost $1.80.

Solve. Use Guess and Check when you can.

1. You went to the grocery store to buy milk and cereal. The cereal cost $2.89 per box and the milk cost $1.19 per container. You spent $10.54. How many of each item did you buy? _____**2 boxes of cereal, 4 containers of milk**_____

2. Your classmate bought red and blue markers for her school project. Red markers cost $.59 and blue markers cost $.69. She paid $6.30 for 10 markers. How many of each did she buy? _____**6 red markers, 4 blue markers**_____

3. You have 11 coins that total $.79 in your drawer. Only one of the coins is a quarter. What are the other coins?
4 dimes, 2 nickels, 4 pennies
_____

3.7 ANOTHER LOOK

Mental Math: **Dividing by Multiples of Ten**

You can use what you know about place value to help you divide
multiples of 10 mentally.

Divide: 80 ÷ 20   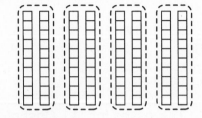   **8** tens ÷ **2** tens = **4**

80 ÷ 20 = 4

Divide: 210 ÷ 7

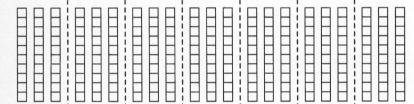   **21** tens ÷ **7** = **3** tens

210 ÷ 7 = 30

Divide: 600 ÷ 30   Divide: 3500 ÷ 50

60 tens ÷ **3** tens = **20**   **350** tens ÷ **5** tens = **70**

600 ÷ 30 = 20   3500 ÷ 50 = 70

Circle the letter of the correct quotient. Use mental math.

1. 270 ÷ 30   (**a.**) 9   **b.** 90   **c.** 900

2. 3600 ÷ 6   **a.** 6   **b.** 60   (**c.**) 600

3. 50)‾1500‾   **a.** 3   (**b.**) 30   **c.** 300

Write the quotient. Use mental math.

4. 30)‾60‾ = **2**   **5.** 20)‾800‾ = **40**   **6.** 50)‾1500‾ = **30**   **7.** 40)‾2400‾ = **60**

8. 9)‾450‾ = **50**   **9.** 7)‾4900‾ = **700**   **10.** 30)‾2400‾ = **80**   **11.** 30)‾90,000‾ = **3000**

12. 350 ÷ 70 = __**5**__   **13.** 5600 ÷ 8 = __**700**__   **14.** 2000 ÷ 50 = __**40**__

15. 270 ÷ 9 = __**30**__   **16.** 20,000 ÷ 20 = __**1000**__   **17.** 16,000 ÷ 40 = __**400**__

Name _____ Date _____

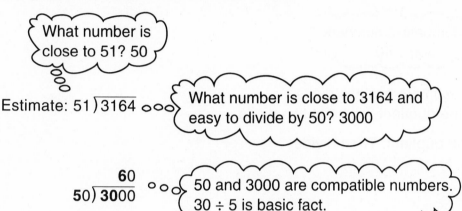

3.8 ANOTHER LOOK

Estimation: Quotients with 2-Digit Divisors

You can use compatible numbers to help you estimate quotients.
Sometimes it helps to change both the divisor and the dividend to
compatible numbers. Look for basic facts.

What number is close to 51? 50

Estimate: $51\overline{)3164}$

What number is close to 3164 and easy to divide by 50? 3000

$\dfrac{60}{50\overline{)3000}}$

50 and 3000 are compatible numbers. 30 ÷ 5 is basic fact.

3164 ÷ 51 is about 60.

Circle the letter of the compatible numbers.

1. $60\overline{)563}$ **a.** $60\overline{)500}$ **(b.)** $60\overline{)540}$ **c.** $60\overline{)570}$

2. 779 ÷ 23   **(a.)** 800 ÷ 20   **b.** 700 ÷ 20   **c.** 800 ÷ 30

3. $70\overline{)2203}$ **a.** $70\overline{)2000}$ **b.** $70\overline{)2200}$ **(c.)** $70\overline{)2100}$

4. 3983 ÷ 47   **a.** 4000 ÷ 47   **(b.)** 4000 ÷ 50   **c.** 3900 ÷ 50

5. $28\overline{)6512}$ **(a.)** $30\overline{)6000}$ **b.** $30\overline{)6500}$ **c.** $30\overline{)7000}$

6. 9466 ÷ 92   **a.** 9500 ÷ 90   **(b.)** 9000 ÷ 90   **c.** 9000 ÷ 92

**Write the compatible numbers you would use to estimate
the quotient. Then write the estimate.** Answers may vary.

7. $34\overline{)884}$

$\dfrac{20}{30\overline{)600}}$ or $\dfrac{30}{30\overline{)900}}$

8. $55\overline{)1800}$

$\dfrac{30}{60\overline{)1800}}$

9. 7282 ÷ 30

6000 ÷ 30 = 200
or 9000 ÷ 30 = 300

10. $41\overline{)1823}$

$\dfrac{40}{40\overline{)1600}}$ or $\dfrac{50}{40\overline{)2000}}$

11. $20\overline{)7219}$

$\dfrac{300}{20\overline{)6000}}$ or $\dfrac{400}{20\overline{)8000}}$

12. 2278 ÷ 29

2100 ÷ 30 = 70
or 2400 ÷ 30 = 80

3.9 ◤ ANOTHER LOOK

··

Dividing by 2-Digit Divisors

To divide by 2-digit divisors, follow the same steps you use to divide by 1-digit divisors.

Divide: $39\overline{)741}$

• First estimate.

Use compatible numbers.
$800 \div 40$

$\phantom{40\overline{)}}20$ ← The estimate has two digits.
$40\overline{)800}$ So, the quotient will have two digits.

• Write the tens digit in the quotient. Then divide.

$$
\begin{array}{r}
\boxed{1}\ \boxed{9}\quad R\ \boxed{2} \\
39\overline{)7\ \ 4\ \ 3} \\
-\ 3\ \ 9 \quad\leftarrow 39 \times \mathbf{1}\ \text{ten} \\
\hline
3\ \ 5\ \ 3 \\
-\ 3\ \ 5\ \ 1 \leftarrow 39 \times \mathbf{9}\ \text{ones} \\
\hline
2 \leftarrow \text{Remainder}
\end{array}
$$

The quotient is 19 with a remainder of 2.

Complete the division. Write the missing numbers.

1.
$$
\begin{array}{r}
\boxed{8}\quad R\ \boxed{1}\ \boxed{3} \\
45\overline{)3\ \ 7\ \ 3} \\
-\boxed{3}\ \boxed{6}\ \boxed{0} \leftarrow 45 \times 8 \\
\hline
\boxed{1}\ \boxed{3}
\end{array}
$$

2.
$$
\begin{array}{r}
\boxed{4}\ \boxed{6} \\
29\overline{)1\ \ 3\ \ 3\ \ 4} \\
-\ 1\ \ 1\ \ 6 \quad\leftarrow 29 \times \boxed{4}\ \text{tens} \\
\hline
\boxed{1}\ \boxed{7}\ \boxed{4} \\
-\boxed{1}\ \boxed{7}\ \boxed{4} \leftarrow 29 \times \boxed{6} \\
\hline
\boxed{0}
\end{array}
$$

Write the answer.

3. $\overset{24}{16\overline{)384}}$

4. $\overset{13\ R1}{56\overline{)729}}$

5. $\overset{9\ R4}{75\overline{)679}}$

6. $\overset{83}{7\overline{)581}}$

7. $670 \div 83 = \underline{\ 8\ R6\ }$

8. $832 \div 32 = \underline{\ \ 26\ \ }$

9. $2213 \div 67 = \underline{\ 33\ R2\ }$

Name _____ Date _____

3.10 ◢ ANOTHER LOOK

Dividing Greater Numbers

A roll of red ribbon is 4719 inches long. There are
36 inches in 1 yard. How many one-yard ribbons
can be cut from the roll?

You can divide 4719 by 36 to find the equivalent measure.

Divide: 36)4719

• First estimate.

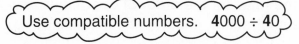
Use compatible numbers.   4000 ÷ 40

     100 ◄— The estimate has three digits.
40)4000   So, the quotient will have three digits.

• Write the hundreds digit in the quotient. Then divide.

```
      1  3  1   R 3
36) 4  7  1  9
  - 3  6          ◄— 36 × 1  hundred
    1  1  1  9
  - 1  0  8       ◄— 36 × 3  tens
       3  9
     - 3  6  ◄— 36 × 1  one
          3 ◄— Remainder
```

So, 131 one-yard ribbons can be cut from the roll.

Write the answer.

1. 12)3924 **327**

2. 64)9857 **154 R1**

3. 90)6578 **73 R8**

4. 18)1692 **94**

5. 24)5664 **236**

6. 52)4439 **85 R19**

7. 73)9205 **126 R7**

8. 16)6896 **431**

9. 2206 ÷ 7 = __315 R1__ 10. 5280 ÷ 80 = __66__ 11. 2669 ÷ 37 = __72 R5__

3.11 ▸ ANOTHER LOOK

Order of Operations

Find the answer: $3 + 5 \times (4 - 2)$

 16?   13?

Gordon and Savilla got different answers. Who is right?

- Gordon did not follow the rules for the order of operations. He added first, then he subtracted, and then he multiplied.

- Savilla followed the order of operations. She did the operation in parentheses first, then she multiplied, and then she added. Her answer, 13, is correct.

Order of Operations

$3 + 5 \times (4 - 2)$ ◂— $3 + 5 \times 2$	*First*, do any operations in parentheses.
$3 + 5 \times 2$ ◂— $3 + 10$	*Next*, multiply or divide, working from left to right.
$3 + 10 = 13$ ◂—	*Then*, add or subtract, working from left to right.

Complete each step. Then write the answer. The first one has been started for you.

1. $8 - 6 \div 2$

$8 - \underline{3} = \underline{5}$

2. $(2 + 4) \times 3$

$\underline{6} \times 3 = \underline{18}$

3. $4 \times 2 + (2 + 5)$

$4 \times 2 + \underline{7}$

$\underline{8} + \underline{7} = \underline{15}$

Write the answer. Circle the operation you did first.

4. $5 + (6 \div 2) = \underline{8}$

5. $(36 - 3) + 6 = \underline{39}$

6. $(16 - 4) \div 6 = \underline{2}$

7. $(40 \div 4) \times 3 = \underline{30}$

8. $23 \times (5 \div 5) = \underline{23}$

9. $(5 + 20) \times 4 = \underline{100}$

10. $8 - 2 + (3 \times 1) = \underline{9}$

11. $7 \times (9 - 7) + 7 = \underline{21}$

12. $(22 - 2) \div 5 = \underline{4}$

13. $(18 \div 3) \times 4 = \underline{24}$

14. $(15 - 12) \times 11 = \underline{33}$

15. $2 \times 2 + (6 \div 3) = \underline{6}$

Name _____ Date _____

3.12 ANOTHER LOOK

Divisibility

One number is **divisible** by another if the remainder of the division is zero.

12 is divisible by 4.

24 is divisible by 6.

18 is divisible by 9.

4 groups of 3, no remainder   4 groups of 6, no remainder   2 groups of 9, no remainder

Circle the divisible numbers. Use counters to check.

1. Divisible by 4: (24) (48) 31 19 (44) 27

2. Divisible by 6: 16 (30) (36) 45 32 (18)

3. Divisible by 9: (27) 17 23 (9) 47 (36)

Divisibility rules can help you decide if one number is divisible by another number. This is helpful when you divide large numbers.

• A number is **divisible by 4** if the number formed by the tens and ones digits is divisible by 4.

Example: 3<u>24</u>   ⟨ 24 is divisible by 4. ⟩

• A number is **divisible by 6** if it is divisible by both 2 and 3.

Example: 210   ⟨ 210 ÷ 2 = 105 and 210 ÷ 3 = 70 ⟩

• A number is **divisible by 9** when the sum of the digits is divisible by 9.

Example: 4554   ⟨ 4 + 5 + 5 + 4 = 18, which is divisible by 9. ⟩

Circle the divisible numbers. Use a calculator to check.

4. Divisible by 4: (632) 738 (208) (9040) 3415 (12,416)

5. Divisible by 6: (486) 165 (306) (8136) 7341 15,200

6. Divisible by 9: 109 (576) 253 (1170) 4504 (80,001)

67

Name _____ Date _____

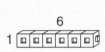 **ANOTHER LOOK**

Greatest Common Factor

Numbers that are multiplied to form a product are called **factors.**
You can use centimeter cubes to model the factors of a number.

These four solids show the factors of 6.

$1 \times 6 = 6$ $2 \times 3 = 6$ $3 \times 2 = 6$ $6 \times 1 = 6$

The factors of 6 are 1, 2, 3, and 6.

You will need 20 centimeter cubes.

1. Use 10 cubes to show the factors of 10. Write a
   multiplication expression for each.

   $1 \times 10 = 10$ $2 \times 5 = 10$ $5 \times 2 = 10$ $10 \times 1 = 10$

2. What are the factors of 10? _____ **1, 2, 5, and 10** _____

3. Use 16 cubes to show the factors of 16. Write a
   multiplication expression for each.

   $1 \times 16 = 16$ $2 \times 8 = 16$ $4 \times 4 = 16$ $8 \times 2 = 16$ $16 \times 1 = 16$

4. What are the factors of 16? __ **1, 2, 4, 8, and 16** __

5. Use cubes to find the factors of 12 and 18.

   a. What are the factors of 12? _____ ①, ②, ③, 4, ⑥, and 12

   b. What are the factors of 18? _____ ①, ②, ③, ⑥, 9, and 18

6. Circle the factors that are the same for 12 and 18. These are
   called their **common factors.**

7. Draw a box around the greatest number that is a factor of 12
   and 18. This is called their **greatest common factor.**

8. Find the factors of 15 and 20. Use cubes if you need to.

   a. What are the common factors of 15 and 20? _____ **1 and 5** _____

   b. What is the greatest common factor of 15 and 20? _____ **5** _____

3.14 ANOTHER LOOK

Prime and Composite Numbers

Some numbers have exactly two factors, 1 and the number itself. They are **prime numbers.**

Using 5 centimeter cubes, you can make only two solid arrays.

$$1 \times 5 = 5 \qquad 5 \times 1 = 5$$

• 1 and 5 are the only factors of 5.
• The number 5 is a prime number.

Other numbers have more than two factors. They are **composite numbers.**

Using 4 cubes, you can make three different solid arrays.

$$1 \times 4 = 4 \qquad 2 \times 2 = 4 \qquad 4 \times 1 = 4$$

• 1, 2, and 4 are factors of 4.
• The number 4 is a composite number.

Use 10 centimeter cubes to help you complete the chart.

	Number of Cubes	How Many Solids?	What Are the Factors?	Is It Prime or Composite?
1.	2	2	1, 2	prime
2.	3	2	1, 3	prime
3.	4	3	1, 2, 4	composite
4.	5	2	1, 5	prime
5.	6	4	1, 2, 3, 6	composite
6.	7	2	1, 7	prime
7.	8	4	1, 2, 4, 8	composite
8.	9	3	1, 3, 9	composite
9.	10	4	1, 2, 5, 10	composite

3.15 ◤ ANOTHER LOOK

Prime Factorization

Every composite number can be shown as the product of prime factors. This is called **prime factorization.** You can use a calculator to help you find the prime factorization of a number.

Find the prime factorization of 36.

• Enter 36.

• To start, try dividing by 2. ⬜ 18 Factors: 2 and 18

• Try dividing by 2 again. ⬜ 9 Factors: 2 and 9

> To keep track, make a list of the factors.

• Is 9 divisible by 2? No. ⬜ 3 Factors: 3 and 3
  Divide by 3.

• Stop when the number on your calculator display is prime. Look back at your list of factors.

• Use only the prime numbers in your list to write the prime factorization of 36. Then rewrite using exponents.
  $$2 \times 2 \times 3 \times 3 \longrightarrow 2^2 \times 3^2$$

To check the prime factorization, multiply the prime factors.
  $$2^2 \times 3^2 = 4 \times 9 = 36$$

Use a calculator to find the prime factorization of each number. Make a list of the factors. Then write the prime factorization. Check by multiplying.

1. 20 (First divide by 2.)   **2.** 15 (First divide by 3.)   **3.** 16 (First divide by 2.)

_____$2^2 \times 5$_____   _____3×5_____   _____2^4_____

4. 30   **5.** 36   **6.** 28

_____$2 \times 3 \times 5$_____   _____$2^2 \times 3^2$_____   _____$2^2 \times 7$_____

3.16 ANOTHER LOOK

··

Problem Solving: Using Strategies

Each American discards about 4 lb of trash each day. On a city block, there are about 30 homes. Each home has about 4 family members. About how many pounds of trash are discarded each week on one city block?

1. Understand

- You know that 1 person discards about 4 lb of trash each day. On one city block, four people live in each of the 30 homes.

- You need to find how much trash is discarded in 7 days.

2. Plan

- Use a chart to organize the information.

- Use multiplication to find the amount for each family and the amount for the city block.

3. Try It

- Make the chart and multiply.

4. Look Back

- The chart shows that about 3360 lb of trash is discarded in 1 week on a city block.

Number of People in 1 Home	About 4
Amount of Trash for 1 Home for 1 Day	4×4 lb = 16 lb
Amount of Trash for 30 Homes for 1 Day	30×16 lb = 480 lb
Amount of Trash for 30 Homes for 7 Days	7×480 lb = 3360 lb

Use any strategy to solve.

1. Trash is collected on Tuesday each week. If the first Tuesday of September is the 3rd, what is the date of the last collection for the month?

Sept. 24

2. Your relatives moved into a new home. Their new garden is 22 ft wide and 42 ft long. It is twice as wide and three times as long as their old garden. What was the length and width of their old garden?

11 ft wide and 14 ft long

Name _____ Date _____

Remainders in division answers can be used in different ways. How
you use remainders depends on the question you are answering.

Nino is helping pack eggs at his
grandparents' farm.
A carton holds 12 eggs.
He has 19 eggs to pack.

How many cartons will Nino fill?
You are talking about a whole carton, so do not use the remainder.
Nino will fill 1 carton.

$$\begin{array}{r} 1 \text{ R7} \\ 12\overline{)19} \\ -12 \\ \hline 7 \end{array}$$

How many cartons does Nino need?
Nino needs a second carton to hold the 7 remaining eggs. Now all
of the eggs are in 2 cartons.

How many eggs will be in the partially filled carton?
In this case, the remainder alone will answer the question.
There will be 7 eggs in the second carton.

You can also use the remainder as a fraction.
What fraction of the second carton will be filled?
To report the remainder as a fraction, use the remainder as the
numerator and the divisor as the denominator.
$\frac{7}{12}$ of the second carton will be filled.

**Write the answer. Make sure each answer appears in the
Answer Box.**

1. Nino gives his friend Pieter $50 to buy
   chicken feed. A bag of feed costs $8.
   How many bags of feed can Pieter buy?

   6 bags

2. Pieter bought 40 pounds of feed. There
   are 30 chickens. Exactly how many
   pounds of feed are there for each
   chicken?

   $1\frac{1}{3}$ **pounds**

3. Nino is freezing corn. He has 50 ears of
   corn. Each freezer bag holds 4 ears. How
   many bags does he need?

   13 bags

4. Nino and Pieter plowed 14 acres in 5
   hours. Exactly how many acres did they
   plow each hour?

   $2\frac{4}{5}$ **acres**

Answer Box

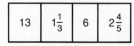

| 13 | $1\frac{1}{3}$ | 6 | $2\frac{4}{5}$ |

27 **RETEACH**   **Division: 2-Digit Divisors**

Use basic multiplication facts to help you divide.

Problem: | 320 ÷ 16 |

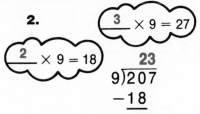

16)32̲0 →

32 ÷ 16 = 2
2 × 16 = 32

②
16)320 →

2⓪ → Be sure to write a zero in
16)320   the ones place. 16 × 20 = 320
−32
   0

Remember to use basic multiplication facts
when you divide.

**Complete the multiplication facts. Then write the quotient. Make
sure each answer appears in the Answer Box.**

1.
0 × 6 = 0

6 × 6 = 36   60
           60)3600
           −36
              0

2.
3 × 9 = 27

2 × 9 = 18   23
           9)207
           −18
             27
           −27
             0

3.
9 × 7 = 63

7 × 7 = 49   79
           7)553
           −49
             63
           −63
             0

**Write the quotient. Make sure each answer appears in the
Answer Box.**

4. 50)25,100   quotient: 502

5. 2)634   quotient: 317

6. 60)84,300   quotient: 1405

7. 4392 ÷ 3 = ___1464___

8. 20,840 ÷ 40 = ___521___

9. 64,160 ÷ 80 = ___802___

10. What will help you divide?

   __One possible answer: Using basic multiplication facts.__

Answer Box

79	1464	502	60	1405	317	521	802	23

28 ⟩ RETEACH   Factors and Greatest Common Factor

···

The greatest common factor of two or more numbers is the greatest number that is a factor of each number.

Problem: | Find the greatest common factor of 12, 16, and 24.

To find the greatest common factor:

1. List all the factors of each number.   12 : 1, 2, 3, ④, 6, 12
2. <u>Underline</u> all the factors that are the same.   16 : <u>1</u>, <u>2</u>, ④, 8, 16
3. ⟨Circle⟩ the common factor that is greatest.   24 : <u>1</u>, <u>2</u>, 3, ④, 6, 8, 12, 24

Write the greatest common factor. Make sure each answer appears in the Answer Box.

1. 3: 1, 3
6: 1, 2, 3, 6
9: 1, 3, 9
___3___

2. 8: 1, 2, 4, 8
10: 1, 2, 5, 10
12: 1, 2, 3, 4, 6, 12
___2___

3. 7: 1, 7
14: 1, 2, 7, 14
28: 1, 2, 4, 7, 14, 28
___7___

4. 6, 11, 15 ___1___

5. 4, 8, 12 ___4___

6. 10, 15, 20 ___5___

7. 12, 24, 48 ___12___

8. 8, 16, 24 ___8___

9. 18, 27, 36 ___9___

10. What steps can you do that will help you find the greatest common factor of a set of numbers?

<u>List all the factors for each number. Underline the common</u>

<u>factors. Circle the underlined factor that is the greatest.</u>

Answer Box

4	8	1	3	9	12	7	5	2

Prime Numbers and Prime Factorization

29 ▸ **RETEACH**

When you find the prime factorization of a number, remember to factor the number completely to prime numbers.

Problem: | Write the prime factorization of 24.

Remember: A prime number is a number greater than 1 that has exactly two factors, itself and 1.

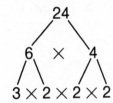

Start with any two factors.
$6 \times 4 = 24$
Neither 6 nor 4 is a prime number. Continue factoring until all the factors are prime.

The last line is the prime factorization of 24. So, the prime factorization of 24 is $3 \times 2 \times 2 \times 2$.

Circle the letter of the correct prime factorization of each number. Then use the circled letters to answer the riddle.

1. 54   **a.** 9×6 ⓔ $2 \times 3 \times 3 \times 3$ **f.** $3 \times 3 \times 6$

2. 32   **t.** $2 \times 2 \times 8$ **o.** $2 \times 4 \times 4$ ⓡ $2 \times 2 \times 2 \times 2 \times 2$

3. 90   ⓢ $2 \times 3 \times 3 \times 5$ **p.** $2 \times 5 \times 9$ **m.** $10 \times 3 \times 3$

4. 78   **d.** 39×2 ⓔ $3 \times 13 \times 2$ **e.** $2 \times 2 \times 3 \times 6$

5. 48   ⓝ $2 \times 2 \times 2 \times 2 \times 3$ **b.** $8 \times 3 \times 2$ **a.** 8×6

6. 126   **i.** $2 \times 3 \times 21$ ⓣ $2 \times 3 \times 3 \times 7$ **s.** $2 \times 7 \times 9$

7. 135   **r.** $3 \times 3 \times 15$ ⓔ $3 \times 3 \times 3 \times 5$ **l.** $3 \times 5 \times 9$

8. 30   ⓐ $2 \times 3 \times 5$ **o.** 5×6 **p.** 2×15

What is 2 feet long, has 32 eyes, and 2 tongues?

<u>a</u> <u>n</u> <u>e</u> <u>l</u> <u>e</u> <u>p</u> <u>h</u> <u>a</u> <u>n</u> <u>t</u> <u>'s</u>
   5   7   1   8   6

<u>s</u> <u>n</u> <u>e</u> <u>a</u> <u>k</u> <u>e</u> <u>r</u> <u>s</u>
3   4   2

Name _____ Date _____

4.1 ANOTHER LOOK

Stem-and-Leaf Plot

Twenty students sold plants to raise money. Here are the numbers of plants each sold.

| 1, 18, 26, 7, 4, 9, 17, 13, 7, 23, 7, 15, 8, 29, 7, 10, 5, 14, 22, 0 |

You can use place value to arrange these data on a stem-and-leaf plot.

The digits in the greatest place will be the "stems." The greatest place is tens, so write the tens digits in the left column. Use 0 tens to show numbers less than 10.

Stems	
0	
1	
2	

Write the ones digits in the right column. These will be the "leaves." Use the data to complete the graph.

Stems	Leaves
0	1, 7, 4, 9, 7, 7, 8, 7, 5, 0
1	8, 7, 3, 5, 0, 4
2	6, 3, 2, 9

The graph will be more useful if you rewrite the leaves in order from least to greatest in each row.

0	0, 1, 4, 5, 7, 7, 7, 7, 8, 9
1	0, 3, 4, 5, 7, 8
2	2, 3, 6, 9

Use the stem-and-leaf plot to answer.

1. How many students sold fewer than 10 plants? _____ 10 _____

2. How many students sold no plants? _____ 1 _____

3. What was the greatest number of plants sold by any student? _____ 29 _____

4.2 ▶ ANOTHER LOOK

Mean and Range

The **range** is the difference between the greatest number and the least number in a set. **Mean** is another name for "average." You can show the range and mean using centimeter cubes.

Start with 24 cubes. Arrange them in these 4 stacks.

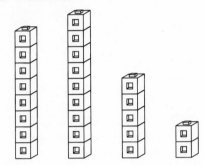

There are 9 cubes in the tallest stack and 2 cubes in the shortest stack.

The range is 7 cubes.

Move the cubes until each stack has the same number.

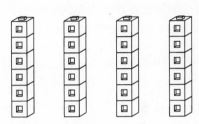

The mean is 6 cubes.

Here is another way to find the mean.

• Find the sum of the numbers: 8 + 9 + 5 + 2 = 24

• Then divide by the number of addends: 24 ÷ 4 = 6

Use centimeter cubes. Write the range for each set. Then write the mean.

1. 7, 11, 3

   range 8; mean 7

2. 5, 12, 6, 9

   range 7; mean 8

3. 8, 15, 7, 10, 5

   range 10; mean 9

Circle the least and greatest number in each set. Then write the range and the mean. You may use a calculator.

4. (15) cm, 34 cm, (56) cm

   range 41 cm; mean 35 cm

5. 13 mi, (41) mi, (9) mi, 25 mi

   range 32 mi; mean 22 mi

6. $21, $35, ($6,) $10, ($55)

   range $49.00; mean $25.40

7. 3 h, (9) h, (2) h, 7 h, 5 h, 4 h

   range 7 h; mean 5 h

4.3 ◤ ANOTHER LOOK

....

Median

The **median** is the middle number when you arrange a set of numbers in order from least to greatest. You can show the median with centimeter cubes.

Find the median of 8, 6, 3, 1, and 7.

• First, make a stack of cubes to represent each number.

• Then, arrange the stacks in order from shortest to tallest.

The median is 6.

The mean is 5.

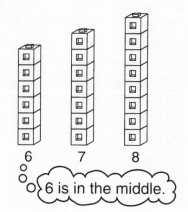

1   3   6   7   8

 6 is in the middle.

8 + 6 + 3 + 1 + 7 = 25
25 ÷ 5 = 5

Order the numbers from least to greatest. Then write the median.

1.

15 in.   27 in.   19 in.

_____**15 in., 19 in., 27 in.**_____

median _____**19 in.**_____

2.

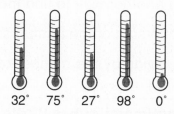

32° 75° 27° 98° 0°

_____**0°, 27°, 32°, 75°, 98°**_____

median _____**32°**_____

3. 5 lb, 9 lb, 2 lb, 7 lb, 3 lb

_____**2 lb, 3 lb, 5 lb, 7 lb, 9 lb**_____

median _____**5 lb**_____

4. 21¢, 80¢, 59¢, 68¢, 76¢, 33¢, 9¢

_____**9¢, 21¢, 33¢, 59¢, 68¢, 76¢, 80¢**_____

median _____**59¢**_____

5. 49 m, 45 m, 48 m, 43 m, 47 m

_____**43 m, 45 m, 47 m, 48 m, 49 m**_____

median _____**47 m**_____

6. $112, $85, $222, $128, $403

_____**$85, $112, $128, $222, $403**_____

median _____**$128**_____

4.4 ANOTHER LOOK

···

Problem Solving Decisions: Is the Answer Reasonable?

Students in a fifth-grade class decide to compare the weights of six
large dogs. The lightest weight is 70 pounds and the range of the
weights is 20. They predict that the weight of the sixth dog is 102
pounds. Is their prediction reasonable?

• The least number is 70.

• The range between the least number and greatest number is 20.

• Add 20 to 70 to find the greatest number in the set of numbers:
20 + 70 = 90. The greatest number is 90, so the numbers in the
set range from 70 to 90.

• Then, the prediction of 102 is not reasonable, because it is not
within the set of numbers from 70 to 90.

Decide if the answer is reasonable. Then solve.

1. Your friend read 6 books during the school vacation. The
   longest book she read had 312 pages. She says that she read
   about 2500 pages. Is her statement reasonable?

   No, because the number cannot be greater than 1872.

2. Three friends each buy a pair of shoelaces. One pair is striped,
   one is gold, and one is purple. Kristi does not buy the gold
   pair. Brian buys the purple pair and concludes that Midori
   bought the gold pair. Is his conclusion reasonable?

   Yes, because Kristi must have bought the striped pair, since she did not buy the

   gold or purple pair. Brian bought the purple, so the only color left for Midori to buy

   is gold.

3. Four numbers have a sum of 550. Three of the numbers are
   150, 125, and 225. Is it reasonable to say that the range of
   numbers is 100? Explain.

   No, the range is 175. The fourth number is 50, so the range is from 50 to 225.

◣ RETEACH

30

Mean

During a heat wave in Miami, Florida, the daily high temperatures were 102°, 95°, 99°, 97°, 105°, 103°, 98°, 105°, and 96°F. What was the mean daily high temperature?

The mean is the average of a group of numbers. You can find the mean by adding the numbers and dividing the sum by the number of items in the group.

Add the numbers.	$102 + 95 + 99 + 97 + 105 + 103 + 98 + 105$ $+ 96 = 900$
Count the items.	102°, 95°, 99°, 97°, 105°, 103°, 98°, 105°, 96° 1 2 3 4 5 6 7 8 9

Sum of the items ÷ number of items = mean $900 ÷ 9 = 100$
The mean daily high temperature during the heat wave was 100°F.

Find the mean of each set of numbers. Make sure each answer appears in the Answer Box.

1. 75, 72, 81, 94, 73
$75 + 72 + 81 + 94 + 73 = 395$
5 items
395 = sum of the items

mean = $395 ÷ 5 =$ __79__

2. 19, 5, 36, 26, 12, 23, 26
$19 + 5 + 36 + 26 + 12 + 23 + 26$
__7__ items
__147__ sum of the items

mean = __147__ ÷ __7__ = __21__

3. 87, 11, 67, 55

mean = __55__

4. 103, 2, 129, 118, 133, 97

mean = __97__

5. 8, 7, 30, 65, 25

mean = __27__

6. 200, 107, 546, 196, 631

mean = __336__

Answer Box

21	55	97	79	27	336

RETEACH

31

During the second week in January, daily snowfall in Boulder, Colorado was: 2 in., 1 in., 10 in., 12 in., 14 in., 12 in., and 5 in. What was the range for the week?

The range can tell you how far apart your numbers or data are. Find the range by subtracting the least number in the set from the greatest.

2 in., 1 in., 10 in., 12 in., 14 in., 12 in., and 5 in.	
greatest number	14
least number	1
greatest − least = range	14 − 1 = 13

The range of snowfall during the week was 13 in.

Write the range for each set of data. Make sure each answer appears in the Answer Box.

1. 169, 99, 129, 89, 179, 159
greatest number = 179
least number = 89
range = 179 − 89 = __90__

2. 48, 51, 55, 69, 57
greatest number = __69__
least number = __48__
range = __21__

3. 62 m, 15 m, 88 m, 96 m, 10 m
range = __86 m__

4. 25, 46, 52, 19, 21, 45
range = __33__

5. 30, 40, 21, 27, 98, 35
range = __77__

6. 8 ft, 9 ft, 2 ft, 11 ft, 3 ft
range = __9 ft__

7. 1, 2, 3, 4, 5, 6
range = __5__

8. 75, 25, 99, 40, 90
range = __74__

Answer Box

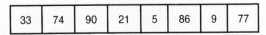

| 33 | 74 | 90 | 21 | 5 | 86 | 9 | 77 |

32 RETEACH   **Median**

The median is the middle number in the list when the numbers are put in order from least to greatest.

Here are Jenny's scores on the first five math tests: 96, 98, 95, 99, 97

Arrange numbers from least to greatest.	95, 96, 97, 98, 99
Find the middle number in the list.	the 3rd number, or 97

The median score is 97.

Find the median of each set of numbers. Make sure each answer appears in the Answer Box.

1. 23, 45, 78, 16, 21
arranged from least to greatest
16, 21, 23, 45, 78

median = __23__

2. 5, 18, 34, 56, 22, 72, 26
arranged from least to greatest
5, 18, 22, 26, 34, 56, 72

median = __26__

3. 78, 65, 1, 112, 77

median = __77__

4. 245, 199, 168, 201, 124

median = __199__

5. 6, 12, 25, 79, 33, 44, 52

median = __33__

6. 45, 62, 42, 34, 50, 51, 51, 48, 13

median = __48__

7. 45, 3, 79, 86, 45

median = __45__

8. 24, 25, 7, 16, 65, 90, 30

median = __25__

Answer Box

45	77	25	48	23	199	26	33

4.5 ▸ ANOTHER LOOK

Estimation: Reading Graphs

Make a bar graph about the following information. Use estimation to make the bars.

> This year the town librarian ordered 625 novels, 350 biographies, 475 history books, and 125 sports books.

You will need 4 strips of paper of equal length, 1 sheet of paper, and crayons.

1. Fold each strip of paper into 8 equal parts. These are the bars for your graph.

2. Count by 100's to 700. Write the numbers on the fold lines as shown at the right.

3. Label each bar. Write *Novels, Biographies, History*, or *Sports*.

4. Color the bar labeled *Novels* to show 625 novels.

```
700 -----
600 -----
500 -----
400 -----
300 -----
200 -----
100 -----
0
```

- 650 is halfway between 600 and 700. Place a mark at 650.

- 625 is halfway between 600 and 650. Place a mark at 625.

- Color the bar from 0 up to 625.

5. The librarian ordered 350 biographies. 350 is halfway between 300 and 400. Estimate and color the bar labeled *Biographies* to show 350.

6. Estimate and color the bars to show the number of history books and sports books the librarian ordered.

7. Tape or paste the 4 bars side-by-side along a line on a blank sheet of paper. Label the graph *Books Ordered*.

4.6 ▶ ANOTHER LOOK

Line Graphs

You can use a line graph to show change over time.

Mr. Brown's fifth-grade class had a recycling drive. This graph shows the number of aluminum cans students collected in one week.

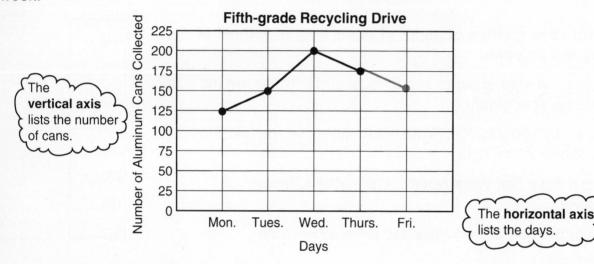

The **vertical axis** lists the number of cans.

The **horizontal axis** lists the days.

Use the graph to answer each question.

1. How many aluminum cans did the students collect on Monday?

   125 cans

2. Did the number of cans collected go up or go down between Monday and Tuesday?

   _up_

3. How many more cans were collected on Wednesday than Thursday?

   25 cans

4. On Friday, the students collected 150 aluminum cans. Draw a dot on the graph to show that. Then draw a line to connect the dots for Thursday and Friday.

5. Did the number of cans collected increase or decrease between Thursday and Friday?

   decrease

6. On which day of the week were the greatest number of cans collected?

   Wednesday

7. Between which two days did the number of cans collected increase the most?

   between Tuesday and Wednesday

4.7 ▶ ANOTHER LOOK

Interpreting Graphs

A **double-line graph** can help you compare two sets of data. This graph shows the growth of two bean sprout plants during one week.

- The dashed line shows the growth of plant A. The solid line shows the growth of plant B.

- You can see that plant A was taller than plant B at the end of one week.

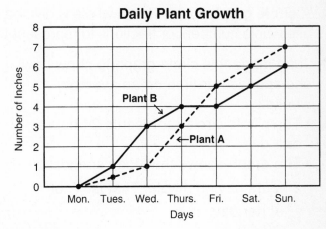

Daily Plant Growth

Use the double-line graph to answer each question.

1. Which plant was taller on Tuesday?   *plant B*

2. Which plant grew more between Wednesday and Friday?   *plant A*

3. How much did plant A grow in one week?   *7 inches*

A **double-bar graph** can also help you compare two sets of data. This graph compares the amount of snow and rain during four months in Wintertown.

- The key shows which bar stands for snow and which bar stands for rain.

- The double-bar graph makes it easy to see that there was more snow than rain in December.

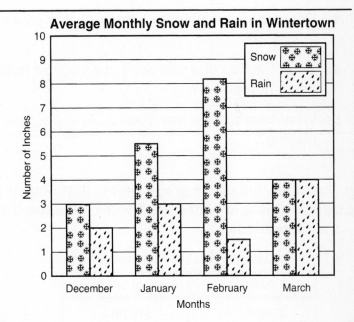

Average Monthly Snow and Rain in Wintertown

Use the graph to answer each question.

4. Which month had the least amount of snow?   *December*

5. Which month had the same amounts of rain and snow?   *March*

6. In which month did the amounts of snow and rain differ the most?   *February*

85

4.8 ▶ ANOTHER LOOK

Circle Graphs

A **circle graph** shows how a whole is divided into parts. You can use whole numbers or fractions to represent the parts.

Joan made this circle graph to show how she spends her time on an average weekday.
- The whole circle represents 24 hours, or 1 day.
- The graph shows that Joan spends 2 hours having meals. That is $\frac{2}{24}$, or $\frac{1}{12}$ of her day.

Joan's Day

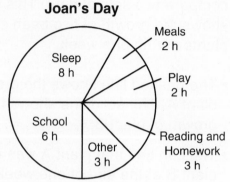

Use Joan's circle graph to answer each question.

1. How many hours does Joan sleep in a 24-hour day?

   _____ 8 hours _____

2. How many hours does Joan spend at school? What fraction of 24 hours is that?

   6 hours; $\frac{6}{24}$, or $\frac{1}{4}$

3. Does Joan spend more time each day playing or in school?

   _____ in school _____

4. What fraction of a day does Joan spend reading and doing homework?

   $\frac{3}{24}$, or $\frac{1}{8}$

5. What fraction of a day does Joan spend having meals and playing?

   $\frac{4}{24}$, or $\frac{1}{6}$

Complete the circle graph below that shows how Kelvin spends his allowance each week. Use the information from the table below.

6. **Kelvin's Weekly Allowance**

Activity	Amount of Money
Lunch	$10 or $\frac{1}{2}$
Magazines	$5 or $\frac{1}{4}$
Hobbies	$5 or $\frac{1}{4}$

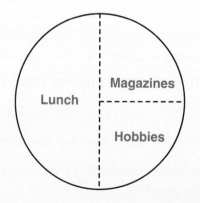

4.9 ANOTHER LOOK

Problem Solving Strategy: **Look for a Pattern**

A bus is traveling through the United States. On the first day, it travels 100 mi; on the second day, 150 mi; on the third day, 199 mi; on the fourth day, 247 mi; and on the fifth day, 294. If this pattern continues, how many miles will the bus travel on the sixth day?

1. Understand

- You know the miles the bus travels each day for 4 days.

- There is a pattern in the distances traveled from day to day.

2. Plan

- Look for a pattern.

- Find the difference in the number of miles traveled from day to day.

3. Try It

- Subtract to find each difference.
  Between the first and second day: $150 - 100 = 50$
  Between the second and third day: $199 - 150 = 49$
  Between the third and fourth day: $247 - 199 = 48$
  Between the fourth and fifth day: $294 - 247 = 47$

- Notice the pattern: each difference is 1 less than the difference before it. So, the next difference should be 46.

4. Look Back

- On the sixth day, the bus will travel 294 mi + 46 mi, or 340 mi.

Solve. Use Look for a Pattern when you can.

1. You have a collection of kitchen magnets. The first has a length of 2 in. The second has a length of 3 in., the third has a length of 5 in., and the fourth has a length of 9 in. If this pattern continues, what will be the length of the

fifth magnet? _____ **17 inches** _____

2. The neighborhood library charges $.15 for each book that is returned a day late. If 100 books are turned in one day late each month, how many months will it take for the library to

collect $75.00 in fees for books that are one day late? _____ **5 months** _____

4.10 ANOTHER LOOK

Problem Solving: **Using Strategies**

You are collecting seeds for a project. In the first hour, you collect 3 seeds. The second hour, you collect 10 seeds. The third hour, you collect 17 seeds, and in the fourth hour, 24 seeds. If you continue this pattern, how many will you collect in the seventh hour?

1. Understand

- You know that you collected 3, 10, 17, and 24 seeds in the first four hours.

- You need to find how many seeds you will collect in the fifth, sixth, and then, seventh hour.

2. Plan

- Use a table to organize the information.

- Look for a pattern to predict the number of seeds.

3. Try It

- Make a table.

Hour	1	2	3	4	5	6	7
Number of Seeds	3	10	17	24			

- Find the number added each time.

  $3 + 7 = 10$ $10 + 7 = 17$ $17 + 7 = 24$

- So, the pattern is: add 7 each time.

4. Look Back

- You will collect 31 seeds in the fifth hour, 38 seeds in the sixth, and 45 seeds in the seventh hour.

Use any strategy to solve.

1. You have $12.60. You buy 12 juice drinks that cost $.69 each and return each bottle for a $.05 refund. Then, you buy a notebook for $.75. How much money do you have left? _____ $4.17

2. You plant one seed in each section of a 36-section tray. Only the 7th, 15th, 22nd, and 28th seeds sprout. If this pattern continues, will the 36th seed sprout? Explain.

    No; the next seed to sprout will be the 33rd, then the 37th.

33 ▼RETEACH

....

Line Graphs

The graph below is a line graph. Notice that the line is not straight. A line graph shows changes that happen over time. The line at the bottom of the graph is called the horizontal axis. The line at the side of the graph is called the vertical axis. How much money was raised at the fair in 1986?

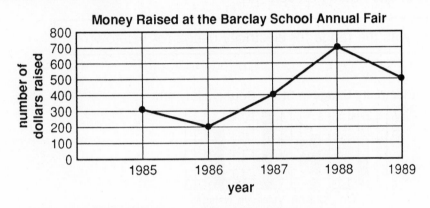

Money Raised at the Barclay School Annual Fair

To see how much money was raised in 1986, find that year on the horizontal axis. Notice that there is a point on the graph above 1986. Now look across to the vertical axis. You can see that the point is at the 200 level on the vertical axis.
So, about $200 was raised in 1986.

Use the graph to answer the questions. Make sure each answer appears in the Answer Box.

1. What was the most money raised in a single year? ___$700___

2. In which year was the most money raised? ___1988___

3. In which year was the least money raised? ___1986___

4. How much money was raised in 1985? ___$300___

5. Between which 2 years did the greatest decrease in money raised occur? ___1988 and 1989___

6. How much money was raised in 1987? ___$400___

Answer Box

1988–1989	$400	$700	1988	$300	1986

Name _____ Date _____

∙∙∙

A double-bar graph lets you picture a range for a set of data. It helps you compare the greatest and least numbers of the set of data so you can calculate the range between these numbers.

The double-bar graph below shows the high and low electricity usage in four towns in one county on July 4th.

Problem: | What was the range for electricity usage for Valetown?

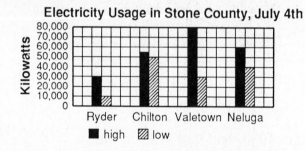

Electricity Usage in Stone County, July 4th

Look at the two bars above Valetown. The bar that shows the high is closest to 80,000 on the scale. The bar that shows the low is closest to 30,000. Subtract the low from the high to find the range: 80,000 − 30,000 = 50,000.

The range for electricity usage in Valetown was 50,000 kilowatts. The graph shows that Valetown had the greatest range of electricity usage. The difference between the high and low is greater for Valetown than for the other towns.

Use the graph to answer these questions.

1. About what was the highest electricity usage for Chilton?

   _____55,000 kilowatts_____

2. About what was the range for Chilton? _____5000 kilowatts_____

3. Which town had the smallest range of electricity usage? __Chilton__

4. By about how much greater was the range of Ryder than the

   range of Chilton? _____15,000 kilowatts_____

5. Were the ranges of Ryder and Neluga greater or less than the

   range of Valetown? _____less_____

35 ▼ RETEACH

Circle Graphs

Circle graphs show the relationship between a whole and its parts.
Each section of the circle represents a part of the whole.

Sections in New Times Journal

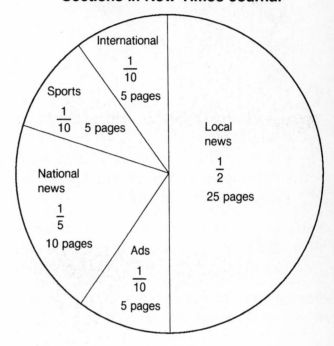

The circle graph shows the size of the
various sections of the New Times Journal.
Each part of the graph tells what fraction of
the paper that section represents. It also tells
the number of pages.

Use the graph to answer these questions.

1. How much of the newspaper is sports
news?

$\frac{1}{10}$ **or 5 pages**

2. What fraction of the newspaper is used
for ads?

$\frac{1}{10}$

3. How much of the New Times Journal is
used for national news?

$\frac{1}{5}$ **or 10 pages**

4. How many pages are in the New Times
Journal in all?

50 pages

5. Are the number of pages in the sports,
ads, and international news sections
together more or less than the number of
pages in the national section?

more

6. If the national news and the international
news are put together in one section, how
many pages would be in that section?

15 pages

5.1 ANOTHER LOOK

Measurement Sense

You can ask many questions about a milk carton.
- How heavy is it?
- How cold is the milk inside the carton?
- How much milk does the carton hold?
- How tall is the carton?

You can answer these questions by making some measurements.
First, you need to choose an appropriate unit of measure and a tool
for measuring.

For example, to measure the height of the carton, you might
measure in inches and use a ruler.

Complete the chart. Answers may vary.

		What unit will you use?	What instrument will you use?
1.	How long is the pencil?	inch or centimeter	ruler
2.	How much does the carton hold?	cup	measuring cup
3.	How cold is the ice cube?	degrees Fahrenheit or degrees Celsius	thermometer
4.	How heavy is the pencil?	ounce or gram	scale
5.	How much string is in the ball?	yard or meter	ruler or yardstick
6.	How tall is the puppy?	inch or centimeter	ruler
7.	How much does the puppy weigh?	pound	scale

Name _____   Date _____

5.2 ◣ ANOTHER LOOK

Measuring to the $\frac{1}{8}$ Inch

You can use a ruler to measure objects to the nearest inch, $\frac{1}{2}$ inch, $\frac{1}{4}$ inch, or $\frac{1}{8}$ inch.

This pencil is between 3 and 4 inches long.

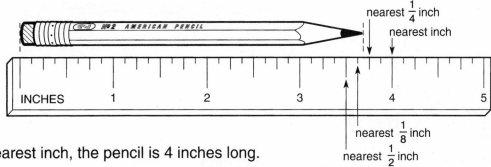

- To the nearest inch, the pencil is 4 inches long.

- To the nearest $\frac{1}{2}$ inch, the pencil is $3\frac{1}{2}$ inches long.

- To the nearest $\frac{1}{4}$ inch, the pencil is $3\frac{3}{4}$ inches long.

- To the nearest $\frac{1}{8}$ inch, the pencil is $3\frac{5}{8}$ inches long.

Use a ruler to measure each object to the nearest inch and $\frac{1}{2}$ inch.

1.
    a. nearest inch   1 in.

    b. nearest $\frac{1}{2}$ inch $1\frac{1}{2}$ in.

2.
    a. nearest inch   3 in.

    b. nearest $\frac{1}{2}$ inch $2\frac{1}{2}$ in.

Use a ruler to measure each object to the nearest $\frac{1}{4}$ inch and $\frac{1}{8}$ inch.

3.
    a. nearest $\frac{1}{4}$ inch $1\frac{3}{4}$ in.

    b. nearest $\frac{1}{8}$ inch $1\frac{7}{8}$ in.

4.
    a. nearest $\frac{1}{4}$ inch $2\frac{1}{4}$ in.

    b. nearest $\frac{1}{8}$ inch $2\frac{1}{8}$ in.

Name_____ Date_____

5.3 ▶ ANOTHER LOOK

··

Estimation: Length

You can use a measure you know to estimate another measure.

The pen is 6 inches long.   The desk is about 4 pen lengths wide.

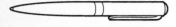

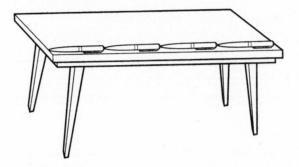

• 4 × 6 inches = 24 inches

• The desk is about 24 inches wide.

_____

Measure the length of your pen to the nearest inch.

1. length of your pen ____Answers may vary.____

Complete the chart. Use the length of your pen to help you estimate. Then use a ruler to measure.

	Object	About how many pen lengths?	Your estimate in inches	Actual length
2.	Height of your chair	Answers may vary.		
3.	Length of your shoe			
4.	Width of your desk			
5.	Your own height			
6.	Width of classroom door			
7.	Width of your mathbook			

5.4 ANOTHER LOOK

Problem Solving Strategy: **Work Backward**

City Music put all of its holiday music on sale for half price. One week later, they decided to mark it down one half again. The final sale price is now $3.99 for each CD. What was the original price of the holiday CDs?

1. Understand

- The store cut the price in half 2 times.

- The final price is $3.99.

2. Plan

- Work backward from the final price to find each amount.

3. Try It

- The final price is half of the first sale price. So, the first sale price must be 2 × $3.99, or $7.98. You can check that this is correct: $7.98 divided in half is $7.98 ÷ 2, or $3.99.

- The first sale price is half of the original price. So, the original price must be 2 × $7.98, or $15.96. You can check this: $15.96 divided in half is $15.96 ÷ 2, or $7.98.

4. Look Back

- The original price was $15.96.

Solve. Use Work Backward when you can.

1. You and your friend both brought carrot sticks to the school picnic. Your friend put his carrot sticks in a bowl. Then, you added your carrot sticks, and it doubled the total. Fifteen carrot sticks were eaten and 9 were left. How many carrot sticks did you bring?

12 carrot sticks

2. The school librarian has money to buy new books. She purchases 12 math books at $12.95 each, 10 science books at $9.25 each, and 6 history books at $8.50 each. She still has $43.10 left. How much money did she originally have?

$342.00

Name _____ Date _____

5.5 ANOTHER LOOK

Using Customary Measures

The chart below shows relationships between different units of measure. Notice that the smaller units are to the left of the equals sign.

Capacity	Length	Weight
8 fl oz = 1 c 2 c = 1 pt 2 pt = 1 qt 4 qt = 1 gal	12 in. = 1 ft 36 in. = 1 yd 3 ft = 1 yd 5280 ft = 1 mi	16 oz = 1 lb 2000 lb = 1 T

Equivalent measures are the same values expressed in different ways. Use the information in the chart to write equivalent measures.

Divide to change to larger units.

Solve: 6 c = _____ pt
Pints are larger than cups, so you need to divide. Read the chart to find the divisor: 2 c = 1 pt
6 ÷ 2 = 3 So, 6 c = 3 pt

Multiply to change to smaller units.

Solve: 3 ft = _____ in.
Inches are smaller than feet, so you need to multiply. Read the chart to find the multiplier: 12 in. = 1 ft
3 × 12 = 36 So, 3 ft = 36 in.

Use the chart above to find the equivalent measure.

1. 20 ft = __240__ in.

2. 10 gal = __40__ qt

3. 48 oz = __3__ lb

4. 18 yd = __54__ ft

5. 6000 lb = __3__ T

6. 16 c = __8__ pt

7. 5 ft = __60__ in.

8. 2 T = __4000__ lb

9. 18 qt = __9__ pt

10. 128 oz = __8__ lb

11. 8 pt = __16__ c

12. 2 mi = __10,560__ ft

13. 28 pt = __14__ qt

14. 22 yd = __66__ ft

15. 28 qt = __7__ gal

16. 4 lb = __64__ oz

17. 3 c = __48__ fl oz

18. 72 in. = __6__ ft

19. 64 fl oz = __8__ c

20. 6 c = __3__ pt

21. 108 in. = __3__ yd

36 ▸**RETEACH**

Choosing an Appropriate Measurement Tool

When you measure anything, it is important to choose the correct measurement tool. Here is how you can decide which ones to use:

If you need to measure:	The tool(s) you can use are:
length, width, or height	centimeter ruler, inch ruler, yardstick, or meter stick
capacity	measuring cup or measuring spoon
weight or mass	scale, balance
temperature	thermometer
time	clock

Choose the correct measurement tool. Write the letter of the correct tool in the space above the number of the problem. The letters will spell the answer to the question.

1. the weight of a horse
   - K. measuring spoon
   - M. ruler
   - (O.) scale

2. cinnamon for a batch of muffins
   - (L.) measuring spoon
   - B. ruler
   - E. scale

3. the length of a box
   - C. scale
   - (G.) ruler
   - T. thermometer

4. flour for a cake
   - A. clock
   - (E.) measuring cup
   - F. scale

5. the temperature of a fish tank
   - I. scale
   - (A.) thermometer
   - R. ruler

6. the time it takes to run a mile
   - E. scale
   - P. ruler
   - (L.) clock

What is the name of the scientist who studied the stars and invented the first thermometer in 1593?

G A L I L E O
3 5 6   2 4 1

▶RETEACH

37

Problem:	What unit should you use to find the weight of an airmail letter?

- You have to find the weight of the letter.

- Since the letter does not weigh much, you would use an ounce or a gram as the unit of measure.

To measure:	Some of the units you can use are:
length, width, or height	inch, foot, yard, mile, millimeter, centimeter, or kilometer
capacity	teaspoon, tablespoon, cup, pint, quart, gallon, milliliter, or liter
weight or mass	ounce, pound, gram, or kilogram
temperature	degree Fahrenheit or degree Celsius
time	second, minute, or hour

Choose the correct unit of measure. Circle the letter of the correct unit. The letters will spell the answer to the riddle at the bottom of the page.

1. the weight of a horse
   - **P.** meter
   - **(Y.)** kilogram
   - **O.** liter

2. cinnamon for a batch of muffins
   - **L.** pint
   - **(S.)** teaspoon
   - **C.** degree

3. the length of a box
   - **(D.)** centimeter
   - **O.** cup
   - **T.** ounce

4. flour for a cake
   - **B.** liter
   - **(A.)** cup
   - **F.** hour

5. the temperature of a fish tank
   - **I.** pound
   - **A.** foot
   - **(T.)** degree

6. the time it takes to run a mile
   - **E.** yard
   - **(W.)** minute
   - **L.** gram

What has six feet and cannot move?

$\underset{5}{\text{T}}\ \underset{6}{\text{W}}\ \text{O}\quad \underset{1}{\text{Y}}\ \underset{4}{\text{A}}\ \text{R}\ \underset{3}{\text{D}}\ \underset{2}{\text{S}}$

38 ▶ **RETEACH**

Measuring to the Nearest ¼ Inch or ⅛ Inch

Be sure to use the correct scale when measuring with a ruler.

Problem: What is the length of the key to the nearest $\frac{1}{4}$ inch? Nearest $\frac{1}{8}$ inch?

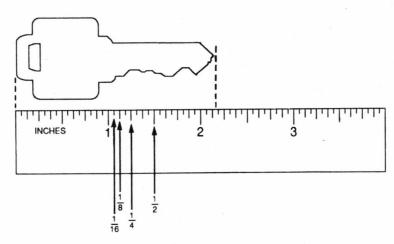

To measure the key to the nearest $\frac{1}{4}$ inch and $\frac{1}{8}$ inch, it is important to remember:

Each tiny mark is $\frac{1}{16}$ of an inch, so each group of 2 tiny marks is $\frac{2}{16}$ or $\frac{1}{8}$ of an inch. Each group of 4 tiny marks is $\frac{4}{16}$, or $\frac{1}{4}$ of an inch.

The key is $2\frac{1}{4}$ inches to the nearest $\frac{1}{4}$ inch and $2\frac{1}{8}$ inches to the nearest $\frac{1}{8}$ inch.

Write the length of the object.

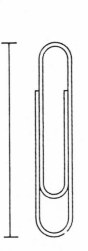

1. What is the length of the bottle cap to the nearest $\frac{1}{4}$ inch?

   $\frac{3}{4}$ in.

2. What is the length of the paper clip to the nearest $\frac{1}{8}$ inch?

   2 in.

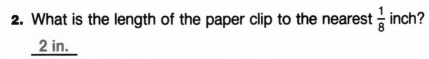

3. What is the length of the newt to the nearest $\frac{1}{4}$ inch? $3\frac{3}{4}$ in.

5.6 ANOTHER LOOK

Measuring Polygons

A **polygon** is a closed figure that is formed by line segments. In a **regular polygon**, all sides are the same length and all angles have the same measure. In an **irregular polygon**, the sides are not the same length and/or the angles do not have the same measure.

The figure below is made from 4 toothpicks.

- All sides have the same length.
- All angles have the same measure.
- The figure is a regular polygon.

You can use the same 4 toothpicks to make this figure.

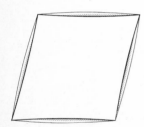

- All sides have the same length.
- Not all angles have the same measure.
- The figure is an irregular polygon.

Is each polygon regular or irregular? Write *regular* or *irregular*.
Trace or measure the polygon if it helps.

1.

irregular

2.

regular

3.

regular

4.

regular

5.

irregular

6.

regular

5.7 ANOTHER LOOK

Diagonals in Polygons

A **diagonal** is a line segment that joins two vertices of a polygon. It is not a side of a polygon.

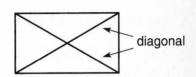
diagonal

Draw the diagonals in each figure. Complete the chart.
Look for a counting pattern to help you.

	Polygon	Number of sides	Number of diagonals	How many more diagonals than in the figure above?
1.	Triangle	3	0	—
2.	Quadrilateral	4	2	2
3.	Pentagon	5	5	3
4.	Hexagon	6	9	4
5.	Heptagon	7	14	5
6.	Octagon	8	20	6

Name _____ Date _____

5.8 ▶ ANOTHER LOOK

Perimeter

The distance around the outside of a figure is the figure's **perimeter**.

The figure at the right is drawn on squared paper. Each square is 1 centimeter long and 1 centimeter wide.

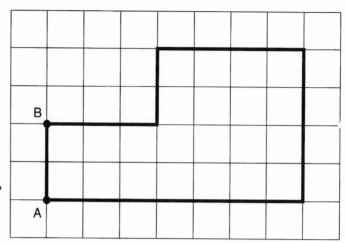

If an ant were to crawl from A to B, it would travel 2 centimeters.

To go around the figure back to A, the ant would travel these distances:

2 cm + 3 cm + 2 cm + 4 cm + 4 cm + 7 cm, or 22 cm in all.

So, the perimeter of the figure is 22 cm.

Write the perimeter of each polygon.

1.

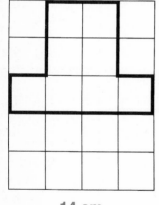

_____ 14 cm _____

2.

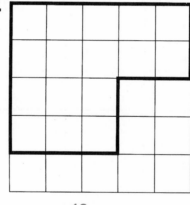

_____ 18 cm _____

3.

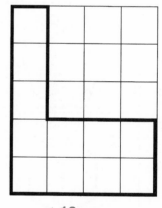

_____ 18 cm _____

4.

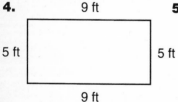

9 ft

5 ft   5 ft

9 ft

_____ 28 ft _____

5.

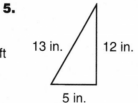

13 in.   12 in.

5 in.

_____ 30 in. _____

6.

8 cm   8 cm

8 cm   8 cm

_____ 32 cm _____

7.

6 m
5 m   2 m
3 m   6 m
3 m

_____ 25 m _____

5.9 ANOTHER LOOK

Perimeter and Polygons

Your knowledge of regular polygons can help you find perimeters quickly.

The figure below is a regular polygon.

- It has 4 sides of equal length.
- Each side is 3 centimeters.

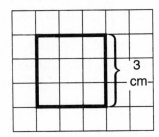

To find the perimeter,

- you can add:
  3 cm + 3 cm + 3 cm + 3 cm = 12 cm
- you can multiply: 4 × 3 cm = 12 cm

The figure below is not regular, but opposite sides are equal in length.

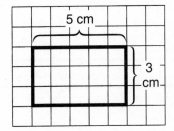

To find the perimeter, you can multiply each length by 2 and add the products.

- Perimeter = (2 × 5 cm) + (2 × 3 cm)
  = 10 cm + 6 cm
  = 16 cm

Find the perimeter of each figure.

1.

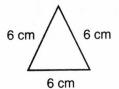

6 cm   6 cm

6 cm

_____ 18 cm _____

2.

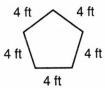

4 ft   4 ft

4 ft   4 ft

4 ft

_____ 20 ft _____

3.

9 in.

9 in.   9 in.

9 in.

_____ 36 in. _____

4.

5 m

5 m   5 m

5 m   5 m

5 m

_____ 30 m _____

5.

6 cm

4 cm   4 cm

6 cm

_____ 20 cm _____

6.

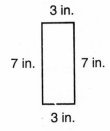

3 in.

7 in.   7 in.

3 in.

_____ 20 in. _____

7.

8 ft

3 ft   3 ft

8 ft

_____ 22 ft _____

8.

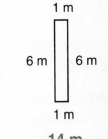

1 m

6 m   6 m

1 m

_____ 14 m _____

Name _____   Date _____

5.10 ANOTHER LOOK

Circumference

1.

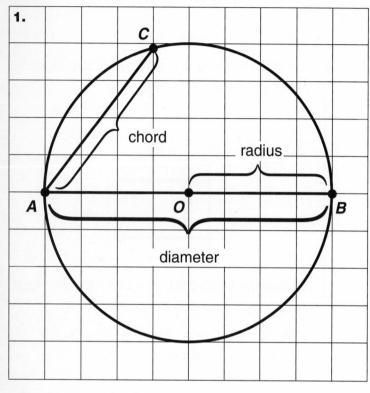

- A **chord** is a line segment connecting any two points on a circle. Find chord *AC*. Find the other chord in the diagram.

- **Radius** *OB* is 4 cm. Write: *r* = 4 cm. Use a centimeter ruler to measure the length of another radius.

- Use a centimeter ruler to measure **diameter** *AB*. The diameter of the circle is twice the length of the radius, or 8 cm. Write: *d* = 8 cm.

- Lay a piece of string around the **circumference** of the circle. Measure the string with a centimeter ruler. The circumference is a little more than 3 times the length of the diameter.

Use your compass to draw 2 circles on a sheet of paper. Draw one circle with radius = 1 cm and one circle with radius = 2 cm. For each circle, write the length of the diameter. Then estimate the circumference. Use string to check your estimate.

2. radius = 1 cm
    diameter _____2 cm_____

    circumference ___6cm–7cm___

3. radius = 2 cm
    diameter _____4 cm_____

    circumference ___12cm–13 cm___

4. In each circle, the circumference is a little more than ___3___ times the length of the diameter.

In any circle, the circumference is exactly *pi* (π) times the length of the diameter. This is written: *C* = π × *d*. The value of pi is approximately 3.14.

Write the diameter. Then multiply to find the approximate circumference.

5. radius = 1 cm ___2 cm; 6.28 cm___

6. radius = 2 cm ___4 cm; 12.56 cm___

7. radius = 4 cm ___8 cm; 25.12 cm___

Name_____ Date_____

Elapsed Time

You can use counting on to find elapsed time.

| Problem A | Darien left New York City on a plane at 10:30 A.M. He arrived in Miami at 1:15 P.M. What was the elapsed time of the flight? |

• Count on from 10:30 A.M. to 12 noon.
  From 10:30 A.M. to 12 noon = 1 hour and 30 minutes
  From 12 noon to 1:15 P.M. = 1 hour 15 minutes

• To find the total travel time, add:
$$\begin{array}{r} 1\ h\ 30\ min \\ +\ 1\ h\ 15\ min \\ \hline 2\ h\ 45\ min \end{array}$$

| Problem B | How much time will pass from 1:08 P.M. to 7:53 P.M.? |

• Count on as far as possible without changing the minutes.
  From 1:08 P.M. to 7:08 P.M. = 6 hours

• Subtract to find the elapsed time from 7:08 P.M. to 7:53 P.M.
$$\begin{array}{r} 53\ min \\ -\ \ 8\ min \\ \hline 45\ min \end{array}$$

• Then add to find the total time: 6 h + 45 min = 6 h 45 min

Write how much time will pass.

1. from 6:04 A.M. to 9:37 A.M.

_____3 h 33 min_____

2. from 2:12 P.M. to 8:31 P.M.

_____6 h 19 min_____

3. from 7:25 P.M. to 1:16 A.M.

_____5 h 51 min_____

4. from 4:09 A.M. to 2:45 P.M.

_____10 h 36 min_____

Write the answer.

5.
$$\begin{array}{r} 15\ h\ \ 9\ min \\ +\ \ 7\ h\ \ 8\ min \\ \hline 22\ h\ 17\ min \end{array}$$

6.
$$\begin{array}{r} 23\ h\ 35\ min \\ -\ 15\ h\ 17\ min \\ \hline 8\ h\ 18\ min \end{array}$$

7.
$$\begin{array}{r} 30\ min\ 28\ s \\ +\ 17\ min\ 31\ s \\ \hline 47\ min\ 59\ s \end{array}$$

8.
$$\begin{array}{r} 46\ min\ 38\ s \\ -\ 16\ min\ 25\ s \\ \hline 30\ min\ 13\ s \end{array}$$

◤5.12◢ ANOTHER LOOK

Problem Solving Decisions: Is the Answer Reasonable?

You visit a group of caverns with your class. The first part of the tour is an elevator ride. A sign inside the elevator reads: "Maximum Load: 850 lb." Your friend says that each person weighs about 80 lb., so the elevator can hold $10\frac{1}{2}$ people. Is that reasonable?

• 80 lb. is a reasonable estimate for the weight of a fifth-grader.

• $10\frac{1}{2} \times 80$ is between $10 \times 80 = 800$ and $11 \times 80 = 880$, so your friend's calculation is reasonable.

• Half a person cannot ride in an elevator. The answer doesn't make sense.

Tell whether the answer is reasonable. Then solve.

1. The elevator ride takes 60 seconds. When the elevator stops at the bottom, the guide says that you are 6 miles below ground. Is this reasonable?

    <u>No: to travel 6 miles in 60 s you would have to average 6 x 60 = 360 miles an hour,</u>

    <u>the speed of a commercial jetliner.</u>

2. The guide tells your class, "The tour will last three hours. You will be back at your school before lunch." Is this reasonable?

    <u>When you will return to school also depends on what time the tour starts</u>

    <u>and how long the trip back is. If the tour starts before 9:00 it would be over</u>

    <u>before 12:00, so the guide's estimate might be reasonable.</u>

3. You and two of your friends try to join hands around a huge stalactite, but your arms altogether are about 1 ft short. Your friend says, "The diameter is about 6 yd." Is this reasonable?

    <u>Your armspan is about 2 yd or less. If your friend had said the circumference</u>

    <u>was about 6 yd., that would have been reasonable; but the diameter is about</u>

    <u>$\frac{1}{3}$ of the circumference, so it is closer to 2 yd.</u>

4. After the tour, Samuel wants to buy some items from the gift shop. He wants a patch for $3.15, a coloring book for $1.50, and a box of crayons for $2.98. He asks to borrow a $10 bill from you. If he does not have any money of his own with him, is this a reasonable amount?

    <u>Yes: the 3 items together cost about $8, so $5 would not be enough and $20</u>

    <u>would be too much.</u>

5.13 ANOTHER LOOK

Time Zones

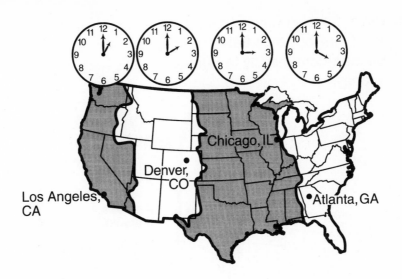

Earth is divided into 24 time zones. The United States has 4 time zones, not counting Alaska and Hawaii.

To find the time in different time zones, add as you move to the right on the map, subtract as you move to the left.

Los Angeles	Denver	Chicago	Atlanta
+1 h	+1 h	+1 h	
5:00 P.M. →	6:00 P.M. →	7:00 P.M. →	8:00 P.M.
9:30 A.M. ←	10:30 A.M. ←	11:30 A.M. ←	12:30 P.M.
−1 h	−1 h	−1 h	

Use the map. Write the time in Chicago when it is:

1. 4:00 A.M. in Denver.

_____5:00 A.M._____

2. 7:30 P.M. in Los Angeles.

_____9:30 P.M._____

3. 3:00 A.M. in Atlanta.

_____2:00 A.M._____

Write the time in Los Angeles when it is:

4. 5:45 P.M. in Atlanta.

_____2:45 P.M._____

5. 6:20 P.M. in Denver.

_____5:20 P.M._____

6. 8:45 A.M. in Chicago.

_____6:45 A.M._____

Write the time in Denver when it is:

7. 3:30 A.M. in Atlanta.

_____1:30 A.M._____

8. 8:50 A.M. in Los Angeles.

_____9:50 A.M._____

9. 4:45 P.M. in Chicago

_____3:45 P.M._____

Name_____ Date_____

5.14 ANOTHER LOOK

Using a Calendar

Four friends plan to travel in Europe during July and August. If they buy their train passes in the United States before they fly to Europe, they will save money.

July

Sun	Mon	Tues	Wed	Thur	Fri	Sat
	1	2	3	4	5	6
7	8	9	10	11	12	13
14	15	16	17	18	19	20
21	22	23	24	25	26	27
28	29	30	31			

August

Sun	Mon	Tues	Wed	Thur	Fri	Sat
				1	2	3
4	5	6	7	8	9	10
11	12	13	14	15	16	17
18	19	20	21	22	23	24
25	26	27	28	29	30	31

Discount European Train Passes

3 Weeks	$179
4 Weeks	$209
5 Weeks	$229
8 Weeks	$319

Must be purchased at least 2 weeks before departure from U.S.A. Refunds available up to 1 week before departure.

Solve each problem.

1. Ronnie plans to fly to Europe on July 16. What is the latest date on which she can buy a train pass in the United States? HINT: Try counting backward. _July 2_

2. Si is flying to Europe on July 26. She plans to be back in the United States for her birthday on August 22. What is the most she will pay for a train pass? HINT: How many weeks are there from July 26 to August 22? _$209_

3. Tatania buys her train pass on July 1. She plans to begin her trip in Europe on July 26. If she cancels her trip, what is the latest date she can get a refund for the train pass? _July 19_

4. Mazie purchases a train pass on July 8. She plans to fly to Europe as soon as she can. She must fly back to the United States by August 25. Which train pass will be the best buy for Mazie? HINT: Remember, the train pass must be purchased at least two weeks before departure. _5-week pass_

5.15 ANToR LOOK

5.15 ANOTHER LOOK

Temperature

Two different scales are commonly used to record temperatures. The Fahrenheit scale has a greater range of numbers than the Celsius scale.

Circle the letter of the more reasonable temperature:

1. hot soup

    a. 120°C

    (b.) 75°C

2. cold milk

    (a.) 40°F

    b. 20°F

3. ice cube

    (a.) 30°F

    b. 50°F

4. snowy day

    a. 25°C

    (b.) − 5°C

5. hot chocolate

    (a.) 180°F

    b. 45°F

6. ice cream

    (a.) 30°F

    b. 65°F

Circle the letter of the Fahrenheit temperature that most closely resembles the Celsius temperature:

7. 35°C

    (a.) 95°F   **b.** 40°F

8. 4°C

    a. 80°F   **(b.)** 40°F

9. ⁻15°C

    (a.) 5°F   **b.** 35°F

10. 100°C

    (a.) 212°F   **b.** 32°F

11. 0°C

    a. 0°F   **(b.)** 32°F

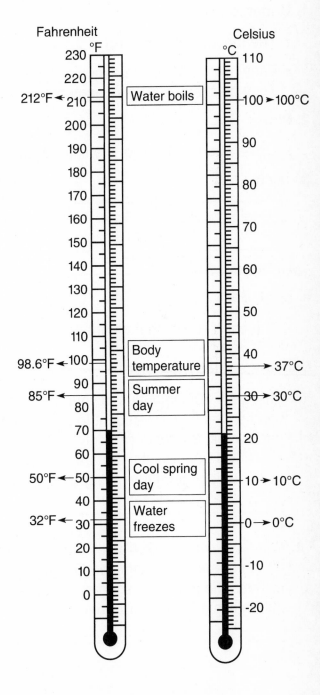

5.16 ANOTHER LOOK

Problem Solving: Using Strategies

A group of friends take a canoe trip down the Delaware River. They begin at 7 A.M. They row for 2 h, then take a 15-min break. They row for 2 h more, then take a 30-min lunch break. After lunch, they row for 2 h, and take another 15-min break. They row 2 h more to complete the trip. At what time do they finish the trip?

1. Understand

- The friends begin the trip at 7 A.M.

- They row for four 2-h periods and take two 15-min breaks. They also take a 30-min lunch break.

2. Plan

- Use a chart that shows the time for rowing, breaks, and lunch.

3. Try It

Begin Rowing	Row for 2 h	Break for 15 min	Row for 2 h	Break for 30 min	Row for 2 h	Break for 15 min	Row for 2 h
7:00 A.M.	9:00 A.M.	9:15 A.M.	11:15 A.M.	11:45 A.M.	1:45 P.M.	2:00 P.M.	4:00 P.M.

4. Look Back

- The chart shows that the friends complete the trip at 4:00 P.M.

Use any strategy to solve.

1. There are 20 computers in your school's computer lab. Your teacher wants each student to use a computer for 30 minutes each week. Students can only use a computer between 9:00 A.M. and 11:30 A.M. If there are 32 students in your class, can each student get a turn using a computer? Explain.

   No. There are $25\frac{1}{2}$-hour periods, so 7 more half-hour periods are needed.

2. You have two picture frames that you want to decorate with ribbon around the perimeter. One frame is $5\frac{1}{2}$ inches by $3\frac{1}{2}$ inches. The other is a square frame with a side of $4\frac{1}{2}$ inches. If ribbon costs $.40 a yard, which frame will cost more to cover?

   Neither, because their perimeters are the same.

39 **RETEACH**

Diagonals in Polygons

In the hexagon below, segment AC is a diagonal. Segment AB is not. Remember: A diagonal is a line segment that joins two vertices of a polygon but is not a side of the polygon.

Problem:

What is the greatest number of diagonals that can be drawn from one vertex of a hexagon?

What is the greatest number of diagonals that can be drawn in the hexagon?

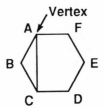

Use this rule to find the greatest number of diagonals that can be drawn from one vertex of any polygon:

number of sides of the polygon − 3 = number of diagonals per vertex

You can use the rule to figure out the first problem.

   6   −   3   =   3

number of   number of
sides of   diagonals
the polygon   per vertex

Use this rule to find the total number of diagonals that can be drawn in a polygon:

number of vertices of the polygon × number of diagonals per vertex ÷ 2 = total number of diagonals

You can use the rule to figure out the second problem.

   6   × 3 = 18;   18 ÷ 2 = 9

number of   number of   total
vertices of diagonals number of
the polygon per vertex diagonals

Find the number of diagonals that can be drawn from one vertex in the following polygons. Then find the total number of diagonals that can be drawn for each polygon.

1.

number of diagonals from one vertex ___7___

total number of diagonals ___35___

2.

number of diagonals from one vertex ___5___

total number of diagonals ___20___

3.

number of diagonals from one vertex ___6___

total number of diagonals ___27___

4.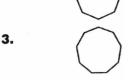

number of diagonals from one vertex ___2___

total number of diagonals ___5___

40 **RETEACH**   **Perimeters of Polygons**
···

To find the perimeter of a polygon, add the lengths of all the sides.

Problem: | Find the perimeter of this polygon:

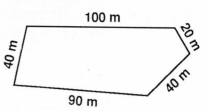
100 m
20 m
40 m
40 m
90 m

Remember that **perimeter** is the distance around a figure.

Find the distance by adding the lengths of all the sides of the polygon. Make sure you have as many addends as there are sides.

Write the lengths of the sides of the polygon.
20 m + 90 m + 40 m + 40 m + 100 m
Check: 5 sides, 5 addends

290 m is the perimeter.

Find the perimeter. Make sure each answer appears in the Answer Box

42 ft
25ft

rectangle

10 m

square

213 cm

regular pentagon

1.
_____ 134 ft _____

2.
_____ 40 m _____

3.
_____ 1065 cm _____

10 m   10 m
10 m

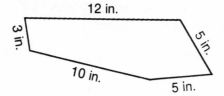
12 in.
3 in.
5 in.
10 in.
5 in.

3 ft
4 ft

4.
_____ 30 m _____

5.
_____ 35 in. _____

6.
_____ 14 ft _____

Answer Box

| 40 m | 14 ft | 30 m | 134 ft | 35 in. | 1065 cm |

◢ **RETEACH** **Elapsed Time**

41

Remember that when you are finding how much time has passed, you are measuring the number of hours and minutes.

Problem: | Elisha started studying for the math test at 3:30 P.M. He stopped studying at 7:40 P.M. How much time did he spend studying?

First count the number of full hours that passed.

3:30 ⟶ 4:30 ⟶ 5:30 ⟶ 6:30 ⟶ 7:30
    1   2   3   4   4 hours

Then count the number of minutes that passed.
    7:30 ⟶ 7:40   10 minutes

Put them together. Elisha studied 4 hours 10 minutes.

Find how much time has passed. Make sure each answer appears in the Answer Box.

1.

elapsed time:

__2__ h __5__ min

2.

elapsed time:

__3__ h __55__ min

3.

elapsed time:

__10__ h __10__ min

4. 9:15 A.M. to 1:40 A.M.

        __4 h 25 min__

5. 12:13 P.M. to 12:05 A.M.

        __11 h 52 min__

6. 8:01 P.M. to 8:00 A.M.

        __11 h 59 min__

7. 11:50 A.M. to 12:49 P.M.

        __59 min__

8. What steps do you do to find out how much time has passed?

        __Count the hours; then count the minutes.__

Answer Box

59 min	11 h 59 min	11 h 52 min	4 h 25 min	10 h 10 min	3 h 55 min	2 h 5 min

RETEACH

42

Problem: | 3 h 23 min + 6 h 18 min |

You can add and subtract numbers of hours, minutes, and seconds
the same way you add and subtract other numbers and units.

```
  3 h 23 min
+ 6 h 18 min
  9 h 41 min
```
**Add the minutes,
then add the hours.**

```
  8 min 48 s
- 5 min 22 s
  3 min 26 s
```
**Subtract the seconds,
then subtract the minutes.**

Circle the letter of the correct answer.

1.
```
  15 h 25 min
+  4 h 16 min
```
    a. 11 h 9 min   **b.** 19 h 41 min   **c.** 20 h 41 min

2.
```
  16 min 13 s
+ 12 min 20 s
```
    a. 28 min 33 s   **b.** 38 min 33 s   **c.** 4 min 7 s

3.
```
  12 h 35 min
-  8 h 18 min
```
    a. 20 h 17 min   **b.** 4 h 17 min   **c.** 4 h 27 min

4.
```
  9 h 20 min
- 6 h 14 min
```
    a. 15 h 34 min   **b.** 3 h 16 min   **c.** 3 h 6 min

Write the answer.

5.
```
  3 h 15 min
+ 7 h  5 min
 10 h 20 min
```

6.
```
  11 h 32 min
-  4 h 25 min
   7 h  7 min
```

7.
```
  18 h 40 min
- 12 h 22 min
   6 h 18 min
```

Name_____ Date_____

6.1 ANOTHER LOOK

Multiplication of Decimals

Models can help you think about how to multiply decimals by whole numbers.

Each tenths square is divided into 10 equal parts, or tenths.
One whole tenths square = 10 tenths.

3 × 5 tenths   equals   15 tenths

So, 3 × 0.5 = 1.5.

Complete.

1. 1.2 = 1 and __2__ tenths

2. 3.5 = 3 and __5__ tenths

3. 2.9 = __2__ and __9__ tenths

4. 1.3 = __1__ and __3__ tenths

Complete each multiplication sentence. Use squared paper to make a model.

5. 4 × 3 tenths = __12__ tenths, or 1 and __2__ tenths

6. 2 × 8 tenths = __16__ tenths, or __1__ and __6__ tenths

7. 7 × 0.4 = __28__ tenths, or 2 and __8__ tenths

8. 6 × 0.7 = __42__ tenths, or 4 and __2__ tenths

Write each product. Color the model to show the number of tenths in the product.

9.

2 × 7 tenths = __14__ tenths

2 × 0.7 = __1.4__

10.

4 × 5 tenths = __20__ tenths

4 × 0.5 = __2.0__

11. 6 × 0.3 = __1.8__

12. 8 × 0.4 = __3.2__

6.2 ANOTHER LOOK

Mental Math: Multiplying by 10, 100, and 1000

Look for patterns in mathematics to help you use mental math to solve problems.

Look at the patterns.

Multiply by 10	**Multiply by 100**	**Multiply by 1000**
$3.0 \times 10 = 30$	$3.0 \times 100 = 300$	$3.0 \times 1000 = 3000$
$0.3 \times 10 = 3$	$0.3 \times 100 = 30$	$0.3 \times 1000 = 300$
$0.03 \times 10 = 0.3$	$0.03 \times 100 = 3$	$0.03 \times 1000 = 30$

Answer each question.

1. What pattern do you notice when you multiply by 10?

     The decimal point in the product moves 1 space to the right.

2. What pattern do you notice when you multiply by 100?

     The decimal point in the product moves 2 spaces to the right.

3. What pattern do you notice when you multiply by 1000?

     The decimal point in the product moves 3 spaces to the right.

Use a calculator to find each product. Look for patterns.

4. $4.5 \times 10 =$ __45__

   $4.5 \times 100 =$ __450__

   $4.5 \times 1000 =$ __4500__

5. $36.07 \times 10 =$ __360.7__

   $36.07 \times 100 =$ __3607__

   $36.07 \times 1000 =$ __36,070__

6. $5.865 \times 10 =$ __58.65__

   $5.865 \times 100 =$ __586.5__

   $5.865 \times 1000 =$ __5865__

Use the patterns to write each product. Then use a calculator to check.

7. $0.2 \times 10 =$ __2__

8. $0.004 \times 1000 =$ __4__

9. $7.45 \times 10 =$ __74.5__

10. $22.63 \times 100 =$ __2263__

11. $106.7 \times 100 =$ __10,670__

12. $3.461 \times 10 =$ __34.61__

6.3 ANOTHER LOOK

Estimation: Products

At a school book sale, books cost $1.29. You have $8.59. Can you buy 4 books?

Estimate how many books you can buy. What dollar amounts does $1.29 fall between?

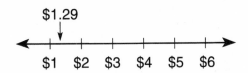

$1.29

$1 $2 $3 $4 $5 $6

Low Estimate
Since $1.29 is greater than $1.00,
4 × $1.29 will be more than
4 × $1.00, or $4.00.

High Estimate
Since $1.29 is less than $2.00,
4 × $1.29 will be less than
4 × $2.00, or $8.00.

You have more than $8.00, so you will be able to buy 4 books.

Use high and low estimates to complete.

1. 3 × $2.60

$2.60

$1 $2 $3 $4 $5
Mark $2.60 on the number line.
$2.60 is between $2 and $3.

3 × $2 = __$6__   3 × $3 = __$9__

3 × $2.60 is between $6 and $9.

2. 4 × $4.70

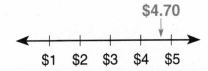

$4.70

$1 $2 $3 $4 $5
Mark $4.70 on the number line.
$4.70 is between $4 and $5.

4 × $4 = __$16__   4 × $5 = __$20__

4 × $4.70 is between $16 and $20.

**Write the whole-dollar amounts that each price falls between.
Then complete the estimate.**

3. $3.56 is between __$3__ and __$4__.

4 × __$3__ = $12   4 × __$4__ = $16

4 × $3.56 is between __$12__ and __$16__.

4. $9.22 is between __$9__ and __$10__.

2 × __$9__ = $18   2 × __$10__ = $20

2 × $9.22 is between __$18__ and __$20__.

5. $11.75 is between __$11__ and __$12__.

5 × __$11__ = $55   5 × __$12__ = $60

5 × $11.75 is between __$55__ and __$60__.

6. $0.89 is between __$0__ and __$1__.

3 × __$0__ = $0   3 × __$1__ = $3

$0.89 × 3 is between __$0__ and __$3__.

6.4 ANOTHER LOOK

Decimals and Whole Numbers

Using a model can help you understand multiplying a decimal by a whole number.

Multiply: 3×2.4

    Estimate. $3 \times 2 = 6$ $3 \times 3 = 9$ The product is between 6 and 9.

You can use a model to find the product.

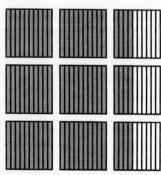

          3×24 tenths = 72 tenths
          $3 \times 2.4 = 7.2$

You also can multiply as you would with whole numbers.

$$\begin{array}{r} 2.4 \\ \times\ 3 \\ \hline 7.2 \end{array}$$

24 tenths $\times$ 3 = 72 tenths

Write the decimal point.

Predict which answer is most reasonable. Circle a, b, or c. Then write the missing numbers.

1. $6.4 \times 7 =$ **a.** 448   **b.** 4.48   (**c.**)44.8   because $6 \times 7 =$ __42__ and $7 \times 7 =$ __49__.

2. $3 \times 2.7 =$ **a.** 81   (**b.**)8.1   **c.** 0.81   because $3 \times 2 =$ __6__ and $3 \times 3 =$ __9__.

3. $5.9 \times 4 =$ **a.** 236   (**b.**)23.6   **c.** 2.36   because $5 \times 4 =$ __20__ and $6 \times 4 =$ __24__.

Write the product. Use a model if it helps.

4. $2 \times 0.6 =$ __1.2__   **5.** $1.2 \times 8 =$ __9.6__   **6.** $4 \times 5.3 =$ __21.2__

7. $0.8 \times 3 =$ __2.4__   **8.** $7 \times 1.3 =$ __9.1__   **9.** $5 \times 2.5 =$ __12.5__

10. $\begin{array}{r} 2.6 \\ \times\ 3 \\ \hline 7.8 \end{array}$ **11.** $\begin{array}{r} 9.1 \\ \times\ 2 \\ \hline 18.2 \end{array}$ **12.** $\begin{array}{r} 7.4 \\ \times\ 4 \\ \hline 29.6 \end{array}$ **13.** $\begin{array}{r} 25.5 \\ \times\ 5 \\ \hline 127.5 \end{array}$

Name _____ Date _____

6.5 ▶ ANOTHER LOOK

Zeros in the Product

Sometimes when you multiply a decimal, you need to write zeros in the product in order to place the decimal point.

Tenths are written **1** place to the right of the decimal point.

Hundredths are written **2** places to the right of the decimal point.

Thousandths are written **3** places to the right of the decimal point.

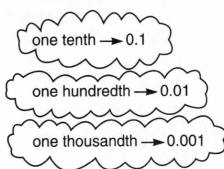

one tenth → 0.1

one hundredth → 0.01

one thousandth → 0.001

Multiply: 3×0.009

$$
\begin{array}{r}
9 \text{ thousandths} \\
\times \qquad 3 \\
\hline
27 \text{ thousandths}
\end{array}
$$

27 thousandths = 0.027

You need to write a zero in the product to place the decimal point.

$$
\begin{array}{r}
0.009 \\
\times \qquad 3 \\
\hline
0.027
\end{array}
$$

Write the product.

1.
$$
\begin{array}{r}
0.008 \\
\times \quad 7 \\
\hline
0.056
\end{array}
$$

2.
$$
\begin{array}{r}
0.04 \\
\times \quad 2 \\
\hline
0.08
\end{array}
$$

3.
$$
\begin{array}{r}
0.034 \\
\times \quad 2 \\
\hline
0.068
\end{array}
$$

4.
$$
\begin{array}{r}
0.025 \\
\times \quad 3 \\
\hline
0.075
\end{array}
$$

5.
$$
\begin{array}{r}
0.003 \\
\times \quad 5 \\
\hline
0.015
\end{array}
$$

6.
$$
\begin{array}{r}
\$0.09 \\
\times \quad 8 \\
\hline
\$0.72
\end{array}
$$

7.
$$
\begin{array}{r}
1.09 \\
\times \quad 7 \\
\hline
7.63
\end{array}
$$

8.
$$
\begin{array}{r}
0.006 \\
\times \quad 9 \\
\hline
0.054
\end{array}
$$

9.
$$
\begin{array}{r}
0.014 \\
\times \quad 6 \\
\hline
0.084
\end{array}
$$

10.
$$
\begin{array}{r}
0.07 \\
\times \quad 4 \\
\hline
0.28
\end{array}
$$

11.
$$
\begin{array}{r}
1.03 \\
\times \quad 7 \\
\hline
7.21
\end{array}
$$

12.
$$
\begin{array}{r}
5.04 \\
\times \quad 5 \\
\hline
25.20
\end{array}
$$

Name _____ Date _____

6.6 ▸ ANOTHER LOOK

··

Problem Solving Strategy: **Make a List**

At a carnival, there is one tank with 4 purple balls and one tank
with 4 yellow balls. The balls in each tank are numbered 1 through
4. You pick a ball from each tank and add the scores. If the sum is
5, you win. How many different ways can you make 5 and win?

1. Understand

- There are 4 possible numbers for the purple ball and 4
  possible numbers for the yellow ball.

- So, there are 16 combinations possible when you pick 1
  purple and 1 yellow ball.

- You need to find how many combinations have a sum of 5.

2. Plan

- Make a tree diagram to show all the possible combinations.

- Use the diagram to find the winning combinations.

3. Try It

- Complete the diagram to show all the possible combinations.

Purple   1   2   3   4

Yellow   1 2 3 4

- Add to find each sum. Then circle the winning sums.

Purple   1   2   3   4

Yellow   1 2 3 4   1 2 3 4   1 2 3 4   1 2 3 4

Sums   2 3 4 ⑤   3 4 ⑤ 6   4 ⑤ 6 7   ⑤ 6 7 8

4. Look Back

- List each combination that makes a winning sum.

- There are 4 winning combinations: P1 and Y4, P2 and Y3, P3
  and Y2, and P4 and Y1.

Solve. Use Make a List when you can.

1. Four classmates are friends. If each friend telephones each of

   the other three, how many telephone calls are made? _____ **12 telephone calls**

2. You want to buy a hat of one color and a shirt of another color.
   There are white and black hats for sale. The shirts for sale are
   red, green, blue, and yellow. How many different combinations

   of 1 hat and 1 shirt can you buy? _____ 8

120

Name _____ Date _____

6.7 ANOTHER LOOK

Choose a Computation Method

A star chart in an encyclopedia measures 8 in. by 10 in. In one square inch of the chart, you can see 10 stars. About how many stars are in the entire chart?

1. Understand

- You want to find how many stars are in the star chart.

2. Plan

- You decide you are going to find an estimate because the number of stars in each square may vary.

- You will need to find the area of the star chart.

- You will then multiply the area of the chart by the number of stars in one square inch.

3. Try It

- Multiply the length by the width to find the area.
  8 in. × 10 in. = 80 sq in.

- Multiply the area of the star chart by the number of stars in one square inch.
  80 square inches by 10 stars = 800 stars

4. Look Back

- There are about 800 stars in the entire star chart.

Decide whether an estimate or an exact answer is needed. Then solve.

1. The largest passport processing center in the U.S. is in Portsmouth, New Hampshire. It can process about 30,000 passports each week. If this pattern continues, can the center process 700,000 passports in 6 months? Explain your answer.
   Yes. The center can process about 780,000 passports in 6 mo (about 26 wk)

2. The Boston Public Library has more than 6,529,000 volumes of books and audio material. The Jacksonville Public Library has more than 2,561,000 volumes. How many more volumes does Boston have than Jacksonville? _____ Boston has about 4 million more volumes.

43 ▲ RETEACH   Placing the Decimal Point

You can figure out where to place the decimal point in the product by counting decimal places in the factors.

Problem: | 5.64 × 3 |

5.64 ← 2 places   Start from the right and count left.
×   5 ← 0 places   If there is no decimal point, count zero
———   places.
2820

28.20 ← 2 places   Add the places. Count that many places
                      from the right of the product to place
                      the decimal point.

28.2∅   When there is a zero in the last decimal
                      place, you can cross it out.

Write the product. Make sure each answer appears in the Answer Box.

1. 4.53 2 places   **2.** 3.7 1 place   **3.** 8.62 2 places
×   3 0 places   ×   4 0 places   ×   7 0 places
————   ———   ————
13.59 2 places   14.8 1 place   60.34 2 places

4. 0.45   **5.** 0.072   **6.** 5.5   **7.** 9.3   **8.** 3.44
×   2   ×   4   ×   5   ×   7   ×   7
———   ————   ———   ———   ————
0.9   0.288   27.5   65.1   24.08

9. 63.1   **10.** 2.4   **11.** 4.8   **12.** 0.09   **13.** 0.111
×   3   ×   6   ×   2   ×   9   ×   3
———   ———   ———   ———   ————
189.3   14.4   9.6   0.81   0.333

14. How can you decide where to place the decimal point in the

product? _____ Add the places in the two factors and _____

count over that many places from the right in the product.

Answer Box

13.59	0.9	9.6	0.288	24.08	0.333	27.5	14.8	189.3	60.34	65.1	14.4	0.81

44 ▼ RETEACH

Regrouping with Decimals

If your partial product has more than one digit, you must regroup.

Problem: 2×4.8

Write down the regrouped number to remind yourself to add it.

```
 +1
  4.8    2 × 8 = 16
×   2    Write 6 in the product.
    6    Regroup ①.
```

```
 +1
  4.8
×   2
  9.6    2 × 4 + 1 = 9
```

Write the product. Make sure each answer appears in the Answer Box.

1.
```
 +1
  5.3    3 × 4 = 12
×   4    Write 2 in the product.
 21.2    Regroup ____1____
```

2.
```
 +5
  7.7    7 × 8 = 56
×   8    Write 6 in the product.
 61.6    Regroup ____5____
```

3.
```
  1.9
×   8
 15.2
```

4.
```
  4.5
×   6
   27
```

5.
```
  8.6
×   3
 25.8
```

6.
```
  4.71
×    2
  9.42
```

7.
```
  0.15
×    5
  0.75
```

8.
```
  0.39
×    7
  2.73
```

9.
```
  2.33
×    4
  9.32
```

10.
```
  11.4
×    9
 102.6
```

11.
```
  0.48
×    6
  2.88
```

12.
```
  0.57
×    3
  1.71
```

13.
```
  5.8
×   2
 11.6
```

14.
```
  6.2
×   5
 31.0
```

15.
```
  2.19
×    3
  6.57
```

16.
```
  3.7
×   8
 29.6
```

17.
```
  88.9
×    7
 622.3
```

18. How can you tell if a partial product needs to be regrouped?

If it has more than one digit, it will need to be regrouped.

Answer Box

2.88	11.6	21.2	29.6	9.42	25.8	61.6	2.73	0.75	27.0	102.6	622.3	15.2	1.71	31.0
9.32	6.57													

RETEACH
45

Placing Zeros in Decimal Products

Place zeros carefully in multiplication products.

Problem: | 0.007×8

Multiply as you would with whole numbers. Make sure you have enough zeros in your product. If there is a zero in the last decimal place of your product, you can cross it out.

$$
\begin{array}{r}
0.007 \\
\times \quad 8 \\
\hline
0.056
\end{array}
\qquad
\begin{array}{r}
0.035 \\
\times \quad 4 \\
\hline
0.14\cancel{0}
\end{array}
$$

Write the product. Make sure each answer appears in the Answer Box.

1.
$$
\begin{array}{r}
0.006 \\
\times \quad 7 \\
\hline
0.042
\end{array}
$$

2.
$$
\begin{array}{r}
0.05 \\
\times \quad 2 \\
\hline
0.10
\end{array}
$$

3.
$$
\begin{array}{r}
2.004 \\
\times \quad 3 \\
\hline
6.012
\end{array}
$$

4. $0.008 \times 7 =$ ___0.056___

5. $0.5 \times 8 =$ ___4___

6. $0.004 \times 6 =$ ___0.024___

7. $1.007 \times 4 =$ ___4.028___

8. $0.02 \times 4 =$ ___0.08___

9. $0.0002 \times 5 =$ ___0.001___

10. $9 \times 2.004 =$ ___18.036___

11. $5 \times 0.006 =$ ___0.03___

12. $4.007 \times 3 =$ ___12.021___

Answer Box

0.08	0.001	4.028	4	0.042	6.012	0.03	12.021	18.036	0.1	0.056	0.024

6.8 ► ANOTHER LOOK

Placing the Decimal Point

Look for patterns to discover the rules for placing decimal points.

Use a calculator to find each product.

1. $4 \times 3 =$ __12__

$4 \times 0.3 =$ __1.2__

$4 \times 0.03 =$ __0.12__

2. $5 \times 7 =$ __35__

$0.5 \times 7 =$ __3.5__

$0.05 \times 7 =$ __0.35__

3. $14 \times 16 =$ __224__

$1.4 \times 16 =$ __22.4__

$1.4 \times 1.6 =$ __2.24__

4. $9 \times 8 =$ __72__

$9 \times 0.8 =$ __7.2__

$0.9 \times 0.8 =$ __0.72__

5. When there is 1 factor with 1 decimal place, how many decimal places are in the product? _____1_____

6. When there is 1 factor with 2 decimal places, how many decimal places are in the product? _____2_____

7. When there is 1 factor with 1 decimal place and another factor with 1 decimal place, how many decimal places are in the product? _____2_____

How many decimal places will there be in the product?

8. 4×8.06 __2__ decimal place(s)

9. 0.4×80.6 __2__ decimal place(s)

10. 4×80.6 __1__ decimal place(s)

11. 0.4×8.06 __3__ decimal place(s)

Write the decimal point in the product. Use a calculator to check.

12. $3.7 \times 6 = 2\ 2.2$

13. $4.2 \times 0.7 = 2.9\ 4$

14. $8 \times 0.03 = 0.2\ 4$

15. $5 \times 0.09 = 0.4\ 5$

16. $3 \times 0.6 = 1.8$

17. $0.3 \times 0.28 = 0.0\ 8\ 4$

6.9 ▸ ANOTHER LOOK

Multiplying Decimals

You can use the following rule to place a decimal point in a product.

> The number of decimal places in a product equals the total number of decimal places in the factors.

```
  6.3  ◄— 1 decimal place          4.9  ◄—1 decimal place
×  4  ◄— 0 decimal places       × 0.7  ◄—1 decimal place
─────                           ──────
 25.2 ◄— 1 decimal place         3.43 ◄—2 decimal places
```

Write the missing numbers. Then rewrite the product with its decimal point.

1. 0.9   _1_ decimal place(s)
     × 3   _0_ decimal place(s)
     ─────
      2 7   _1_ decimal place(s)
     _2.7_

2. 12.73   _2_ decimal place(s)
     ×   1.3 _1_ decimal place(s)
     ──────
     1 6 5 4 9 _3_ decimal place(s)
       _16.549_

3.   19.5 _1_ decimal place(s)
     ×   1.5 _1_ decimal place(s)
     ──────
      2 9 2 5 _2_ decimal place(s)
       _29.25_

4.   207 _0_ decimal place(s)
     ×   4.25 _2_ decimal place(s)
     ──────
      8 7 9 7 5 _2_ decimal place(s)
       _879.75_

Write the product.

5. 2.4   **6.** 1.4   **7.** $ 4.65   **8.**   357   **9.** 3.25
     × 9   × 4.2   ×   10   × 0.01   × 0.7
     ────   ─────   ──────   ──────   ─────
     21.6   5.88 $46.50   3.57   2.275

Write the product. Round dollar amounts to the nearest cent.

10. $2.15   **11.** $0.47   **12.** $7.53   **13.** $6.24   **14.** $0.58
     × 1.5   × 100   × 0.9   × 0.7   × 0.6
     ─────   ──────   ─────   ─────   ─────
     $3.23 $47.00 $6.78 $4.37 $0.35

6.10 ANOTHER LOOK

Problem Solving: Using Strategies

At a science exhibit, five different kinds of moths are on display. Their wingspans are 7.3 cm, 5 cm, 10.5 cm, 15 cm, and 6.4 cm. Find the range, or difference between the largest and smallest numbers in the set.

1. Understand

- You want to find the difference between the largest wingspan and the smallest wingspan.

- You must decide which operation you can use to find the difference in wingspans.

2. Plan

- Identify the two wingspans you need to use to solve the problem. The largest is 15 cm and the smallest is 5 cm.

- To find the difference between them, use subtraction.

3. Try It

- Subtract the smallest wingspan from the largest wingspan to find the difference.

$$\begin{array}{r} 15 \text{ cm} \\ -\ 5 \text{ cm} \\ \hline 10 \text{ cm} \end{array}$$ largest wingspan
smallest wingspan

4. Look Back

- The range is the difference between the largest and smallest numbers in a set, so the range of wingspans is 10 cm.

Use any strategy to solve.

1. A boat trip along the Mississippi River covers 750 km in 3 days. On the first and second days, the boat travels the same number of kilometers. On the third day, the boat travels 264 km. How far does the boat travel on the first day? _____ **243 km**

2. For a friend's birthday, you go to a party at a bowling alley. You bowl 3 games. The first game you score 72 points. Next, you score 91 points. Then, you score 83 points. What is the range of your scores? _____ **19 points**

6.11 ANOTHER LOOK

....

Problem Solving: Using Strategies

In May of 1986, more than 5 million people joined hands for a charity event called *Hands Across America*. From New York to California, the chain joined approximately 12 states. What is the average number of people who joined hands in each state? Round your answer to the greatest place.

1. Understand

- You want to find the average number of people who joined hands in each state.

- Decide which operation to use to find the average.

2. Plan

- Identify how many people joined hands.

- Identify the number of states the chain stretched across.

- To find the average, you will use division.

3. Try It

- Five million people joined hands across 12 states.

- Divide the number of people by the number of states. Round your answer to the greatest place.
  5,000,000 ÷ 12 = 416,667
  416,667 rounds to 400,000

4. Look Back

- The average number of people who joined hands in each state is about 400,000.

Use any strategy to solve.

1. The gas tank of your aunt's car holds 24 gallons when it is full. If the fuel gauge is on the $\frac{1}{4}$ full mark, about how much gasoline is in the gas tank? _____ **about 6 gallons** _____

2. A school has 286 students enrolled in the fifth grade. The school has 9 different fifth-grade classes. What is the average number of students in each fifth-grade class? Round your answer to the nearest whole number. _____ **32 students** _____

46 ▸ RETEACH   Correct Placement of Decimal Point

Remember to count from the right to correctly place the decimal point in the product.

Problem: | 2.77 × 0.12

```
  2.77  ◂── 2 places
× 0.12  ◂── 2 places
0.3324  ◂── 4 places   Make sure you start counting places
                       at the right.
```

Find the product. Make sure each answer appears in the Answer Box.

1.
```
  4.63  ◂── 2 places
×  1.5  ◂── 1 place
6 945   ◂── 3 places    6.945
```

2.
```
  6.55  ◂── 2 places
×  0.3  ◂── 1 place
1 965   ◂── 3 places    1.965
```

3.
```
  9.86
×  7.8
```
76.908

4.
```
  5.53
×  2.7
```
14.931

5.
```
  4.84
×  0.3
```
1.452

6.
```
  0.32
×  1.3
```
0.416

7.
```
  0.57
×  0.8
```
0.456

8.
```
 13.7
×  5.3
```
72.61

9.
```
 48.5
×    9
```
436.5

10.
```
 0.99
×  1.1
```
1.089

11.
```
 0.76
×  0.2
```
0.152

12.
```
 14.11
×   3.2
```
45.152

13. Where do you start counting to correctly place a decimal point in a multiplication product? _____ **Start from the right.** _____

Answer Box

436.5	0.456	0.416	6.945	1.965	1.089	1.452	0.152	45.152	72.61	14.931	76.908

47 **RETEACH**

Adding Regrouped Numbers after Multiplying

Always multiply the factors first. Then add any regrouped number.

Problem: | 2.6 × 6.3 |

```
    +3
    +1
     2 . 6        First multiply.
   × 6 . 3        Then add the regrouped number.
   ────────
     7 8          You can write a plus sign next to the regrouped number
 1 5 6 0          to remind yourself to add it after multiplying.
 ────────
 1 6 . 3 8
```

Write the product. Make sure each answer appears in the Answer Box.

	+②		+⑤		+①		+① +①		+④
1.	0.34	**2.**	4.9	**3.**	2.4	**4.**	0.77	**5.**	0.65
	×0.17		×0.6		×0.3		×0.22		× 0.9
	0.0578		2.94		0.72		0.1694		0.585

6.	0.45	**7.**	0.031	**8.**	3.87	**9.**	4.3	**10.**	1.18
	× 0.9		× 0.4		× 0.5		×9.4		× 3.7
	0.405		0.0124		1.935		40.42		4.366

11.	8.02	**12.**	5.66	**13.**	0.772	**14.**	44.3	**15.**	2.14
	× 25		× 0.7		× 0.5		× 5.2		× 0.9
	200.5		3.962		0.386		230.36		1.926

16.	0.112	**17.**	6.7	**18.**	29.3	**19.**	88.2	**20.**	4.012
	× 0.9		×3.3		× 8		× 2.5		× 75
	0.1008		22.11		234.4		220.5		300.9

21. How can you make sure you can tell a factor from a regrouped number? _____ Write a plus sign next to it. _____

Answer Box

40.42	0.386	1.926	22.11	230.36	0.405	0.0124	200.5	0.72	220.5	0.585	0.0578
2.94	4.366	3.962	0.1008	234.4	300.9	0.1694	1.935				

Name ________________________________ Date ______________

48 **RETEACH**

Multiplying Money

Be sure to use a dollar sign when you are writing a money amount.

Problem: $7.23 × 2

```
 ($)7.23
 ×     2
($)14.46
```

If either factor has a dollar sign, the product needs a dollar sign.

Find each product. Make sure each answer appears in the Answer Box.

1. ($)4.45 × 5 = ($)22.25
2. ($)7.73 × 3 = ($)23.19
3. 442 × ($)0.30 = ($)132.60
4. 3.76 × 42 = 157.92
5. $0.73 × 4 = $2.92
6. 32 × $0.29 = $9.28
7. 11.25 × 3 = 33.75
8. $42.75 × 3 = $128.25
9. 448 × $25.71 = $11,518.08
10. $1.79 × 14 = $25.06
11. 6.61 × 8 = 52.88
12. $0.69 × 97 = $66.93
13. $5.04 × 42 = $211.68
14. $199.86 × 5 = $999.30
15. 29.36 × 11 = 322.96
16. 48.73 × 4 = 194.92
17. 17 × $0.31 = $5.27
18. $11.11 × 65 = $722.15
19. $52.78 × 88 = $4644.64
20. How can you tell if the product of a multiplication problem needs a dollar sign? If either factor has a dollar sign, the product needs a dollar sign.

Answer Box

33.75	$132.60	$22.25	$2.92	$999.30	322.96	$5.27	$23.19	$4644.64	52.88	194.92	$66.93	157.92
$9.28	$25.06	$11,518.08	$211.68	$128.25	$722.15							

Name _____ Date _____

Always round to the nearest cent when multiplying money amounts.

Problems:

$$\$3.69 \times 1.5$$
$$\$2.31 \times 3.2$$

If the thousandths digit is 5 or greater, round the
hundredths digit **(up.)**
If the thousandths digit is less than 5, **(don't change)** the hundredths digit.

$\$3.69 \times 1.5 = \$5.53\underline{5} \longrightarrow$ 5 or greater $\longrightarrow$ round up $\longrightarrow \$5.54$
$\$2.31 \times 3.2 = \$7.39\underline{2} \longrightarrow$ less than 5 $\longrightarrow$ don't change $\longrightarrow \$7.39$

**Round these money amounts to the nearest cent. Make sure
each answer appears in the Answer Box.**

1. $\$14.35\underline{9}$ (5 or greater $\longrightarrow$ round up) _____ $\$14.36$

2. $\$34.86\underline{2}$ (less than 5 $\longrightarrow$ don't change) _____ $\$34.86$

3. $\$1.43\underline{5}$ (5 or greater $\longrightarrow$ __round up__) _____ $\$1.44$

4. $\$0.89\underline{4}$ (less than 5 $\longrightarrow$ __don't change__) _____ $\$0.89$

**Write the product to the nearest cent. Make sure each answer
appears in the Answer Box.**

5.	6.	7.	8.	9.
$\$0.70$	$\$47.37$	$\$1.82$	$\$15.39$	$\$139.82$
$\times\ 0.75$	$\times\ 0.25$	$\times\ 0.4$	$\times\ 4.4$	$\times\ 0.6$
$\$0.53$	$\$11.84$	$\$0.73$	$\$67.72$	$\$83.89$

10.	11.	12.	13.	14.
$\$2.19$	$\$25.76$	$\$171.09$	$\$6.54$	$\$12.72$
$\times\ 2.3$	$\times\ 0.8$	$\times\ 0.7$	$\times\ 1.1$	$\times\ 2.9$
$\$5.04$	$\$20.61$	$\$119.76$	$\$7.19$	$\$36.89$

15. How can you tell when to round the hundredths digit up? When the thousandths digit is
greater than or equal to 5, round the hundredths digit up.

Answer Box

$0.89	$0.53	$14.36	$5.04	$119.76	$36.89	$34.86	$7.19	$1.44	$11.84	$0.73	$20.61
$67.72	$83.89										

Name_____ Date_____

7.1 ANOTHER LOOK

Dividing by a Whole Number

You can use a model to help you divide a decimal.

Divide 1.5 by 3.

This model represents 1.5.

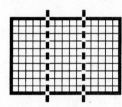

There are 15 columns of tenths. The dashed lines divide 15 tenths into 3 equal parts. Each part has 5 tenths.

$$15 \text{ tenths} \div 3 = 5 \text{ tenths}$$
$$\text{or}$$
$$1.5 \div 3 = 0.5$$

Divide 1.5 by 2.

You know that 1 = 100 hundredths.
So 1.5 = 150 hundredths.

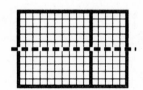

The dashed line divides 150 hundredths into 2 equal parts.

$$150 \text{ hundredths} \div 2 = 75 \text{ hundredths}$$
$$\text{or}$$
$$1.5 \div 2 = 0.75$$

Use the model to find the quotient. Draw lines to show equal parts. Lines may vary.

1. $1.2 \div 4 =$ _____ 0.3 _____

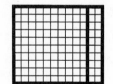

2. $3.4 \div 4 =$ _____ 0.85 _____

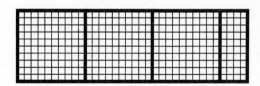

3. $1.8 \div 3 =$ _____ 0.6 _____

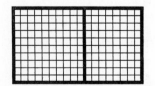

4. $2.4 \div 5 =$ _____ 0.48 _____

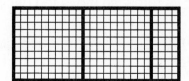

Name _____ Date _____

7.2 ANOTHER LOOK

Mental Math: **Dividing by 10, 100, and 1000**

It's easy to divide by 10, 100, or 1000 when you know the mental math rules.

Watch what happens to the decimal point when you divide by 10, by 100, and by 1000. Look for a pattern.

Divide by 10:
$455 \div 10 = 45.5$
$25.7 \div 10 = 2.57$
$564.32 \div 10 = 56.432$

Divide by 100:
$455 \div 100 = 4.55$
$25.7 \div 100 = 0.257$
$564.32 \div 100 = 5.6432$

Divide by 1000:
$455 \div 1000 = 0.455$
$25.7 \div 1000 = 0.0257$
$564.32 \div 1000 = 0.56432$

1. How does the position of the decimal point change as you divide by 10?

It moves one place to the left.

2. How does the position of the decimal point change as you divide by 100?

It moves two places to the left.

3. How does the position of the decimal point change as you divide by 1000?

It moves three places to the left.

Use a calculator to find each quotient. Look for patterns.

4. $1.4 \div 10 =$ ___0.14___
$1.4 \div 100 =$ ___0.014___
$1.4 \div 1000 =$ ___0.0014___

5. $200 \div 10 =$ ___20___
$200 \div 100 =$ ___2___
$200 \div 1000 =$ ___0.2___

6. $763.15 \div 10 =$ ___76.315___
$763.15 \div 100 =$ ___7.6315___
$763.15 \div 1000 =$ ___0.76315___

Use the patterns you discovered to complete each division rule.

7. 10 has __1__ zero, so move the decimal point __1__ place to the left.

8. 100 has __2__ zeros, so move the decimal point __2__ places to the left.

9. 1000 has __3__ zeros, so move the decimal point __3__ places to the left.

Use the mental math rules to write each quotient. Then use a calculator to check.

10. $5.2 \div 10 =$ ___0.52___

11. $12.6 \div 10 =$ ___1.26___

12. $275.5 \div 100 =$ ___2.755___

13. $0.15 \div 10 =$ ___0. 015___

14. $0.067 \div 100 =$ ___0.00067___

15. $5005 \div 1000 =$ ___5.005___

Name _____ Date _____

7.3 ANOTHER LOOK

Equivalent Metric Measures

It is easier to compare measures if they are written in the same units. You can use a table to find equivalent measurements.

1 centimeter (cm)	=	10 millimeters (mm)
1 meter (m)	=	1000 millimeters (mm)
1 meter (m)	=	100 centimeters (cm)
1 kilometer (km)	=	1000 meters (m)

Claude's pencil is 10 centimeters long. Janine's pencil is 140 millimeters long. Whose pencil is longer?

Find the equivalent measure, in centimeters, of 140mm.

140mm ÷ 10= 14cm

Look at the table. To go from millimeters to centimeters, divide by 10.

Compare measures.
10 cm < 14 cm

Janine has the longer pencil.

You multiply to write a larger unit as a smaller one.
You divide to write a smaller unit as a larger one.

___

Complete. Use the table of equivalent measures.

1. To write 175 centimeters as meters, do you multiply or divide? By what amount?   divide by 100

2. If you write centimeters as meters, will you have a greater number of centimeters or meters?   cm

3. To write 7.50 meters as millimeters, do you multiply or divide? By what amount?   multiply by 1000

4. If you write meters as millimeters, will you have a greater number of meters or millimeters?   mm

6. 1500 mm = __1.5__ m   7. 14 m = __1400__ cm   8. 5 km = __5000__ m

9. 47 cm = __470__ mm   10. 0.5 m = __50__ cm   11. 1260 m = __1.26__ km

12. 0.75 m = __750__ mm   13. 3480 mm = __3.48__ m   14. 0.530 km = __530__ m

Name _____   Date _____

7.4 ANOTHER LOOK

···

Estimating with Money

Use compatible numbers to estimate the quotient when dividing
with money.

Look at the problem: 5)$4.57   ⎰ Think of $4.57 as 457¢. ⎱

Replace $4.57, which is 457¢, with a number that you can divide
mentally by 5.

You could estimate:

$$\begin{array}{cc} 90¢ & 100¢ \\ 5)\overline{450¢} & 5)\overline{500¢} \end{array}$$

Both 90¢ and 100¢ (or $1.00) are reasonable estimates.

_____

**Tell what compatible numbers you would use. Then estimate
the quotient.**   Answers may vary.

   $3.60, 6, $0.60 $7.20, 9, $0.80 $20, 4, $5.00 $250, 5, $50
1. 6)$3.65   **2.** 9)$7.30   **3.** 4)$19.00   **4.** 5)$245

   $140, 7, $20 $1.60, 4, $0.40 $32, 8, $4 $300, 6, $50
5. 7)$143   **6.** 4)$1.76   **7.** 8)$33.15   **8.** 6)$346

Circle the most reasonable estimate.

9. $4.35 ÷ 5   **10.** $2.19 ÷ 3   **11.** $12.28 ÷ 4   **12.** $25.99 ÷ 6

    a. $0.08   **(a.)** $0.70   **(a.)** $3.00   **a.** $0.04
    (b.) $0.80   **b.** $0.07   **b.** $0.30   **(b.)** $4.00
    c. $8.00   **c.** $7.00   **c.** $0.03   **c.** $0.40

13. $4.98 ÷ 8   **14.** $36.45 ÷ 5   **15.** $250 ÷ 3   **16.** $6.98 ÷ 2

    a. $0.06   **(a.)** $7.00   **a.** $8   **(a.)** $3.00
    b. $6.00   **b.** $0.70   **(b.)** $80   **b.** $0.03
    (c.) $0.60   **c.** $0.07   **c.** $800   **c.** $0.30

Name _____ Date _____

7.5 ANOTHER LOOK

Problem Solving Decisions: Is the Answer Reasonable?

Your friend has 72 photos from her vacation. She is deciding how many pages she will need for a vacation photo album. Each page can hold 4 pictures on each side, front and back. The pages are sold in packs of 4. How many packs of pages does she need?

1. Understand
  - You know how many photos she has.
  - You know how many photos fit on a page.
  - You need to find out how many packs of pages she needs.

2. Plan
  - Find out how many pages she needs, by dividing the number of photos by the number of photos on a page.
  - Then, find out how many packs she needs, by dividing the number of pages needed by the number of pages in each pack.

3. Try It
  - Each page holds 4 photos in front and 4 in the back, or 8 photos altogether.
  - 72 photos ÷ 8 = 9. So 9 pages are needed.
  - 9 pages ÷ 4 = 2 R1. So 2 whole packs plus 1 partial pack are needed.

4. Look Back
  - Your friend needs 3 packs of pages.

Solve the problem. Tell how to use the remainder.

1. One pack of pages costs $6. You friend earns 7¢ for each newspaper she delivers on her paper route. How many newspapers must she deliver to earn enough for the pages?

  258 papers: $18 ÷ $.07 = 257 R1, so 257 is not enough.

2. Your friend wants to show the pictures to 8 friends. They have only 35 minutes at lunchtime. How long can each friend look at the pictures?

  35 min ÷ 8 = 4 R3, so each friend can look for less than $4\frac{1}{2}$ min. ($4\frac{3}{8}$ min).

3. At the end of the school year, you plan to give each of the 27 other students in your class 2 stickers. The stickers come in packs of 15. How many packs will you need?

  4 packs: 27 students × 2 = 54 stickers needed; 54 ÷ 15 = 3 R9,

  so 3 packs will not be enough.

137

50 ▸ **RETEACH**

Use models to help you decide where to place a decimal point in a quotient.

Problem: | **Divide 4.2 by 6**

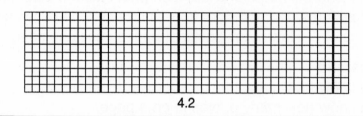

4.2

The model above represents 4.2.

1. What does each small square represent? ___1 hundredth___

2. What does each column of small squares represent? ___ten hundredths or 1 tenth___

3. How many tenths are in 4.2? Count the columns. ___42 tenths___

4. Draw lines to divide the model of 4.2 into 6 equal parts.

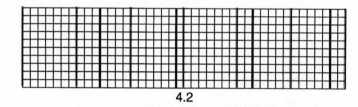

4.2

5. How many hundredths are in each part? Tenths?

___70 hundredths; 7 tenths___

6. Write a decimal to represent each part.

___0.70 or 0.7___

7. Ring the letter of the division sentence that describes dividing 42 tenths into 6 parts:

    a. $42 \div 6 = 7$ **b.** $4.2 \div 6 = 0.7$ **c.** $4.2 \div 6 = 7$ **d.** $4.2 \div 6 = 0.07$

Use a model to find each quotient.

8. $2.8 \div 4 =$ ___0.7___   **9.** $1.8 \div 3 =$ ___0.6___   **10.** $2.6 \div 4 =$ ___0.65___

▶RETEACH
51

You can follow two steps to be sure you have completed a division problem.

Problem: | $6.57 \div 6$

```
    1.095
6)6.570    ← Step 1
 -6
 ___
   57
  -54
  ___
   30
  -30
  ___
    0    ← Step 2
```

Step 1. Check to see that no digits are left in the dividend.

Step 2. Keep dividing until the remainder is 0.

Write the quotient. Make sure each answer appears in the Answer Box.

<u>0.15</u>

1.
```
8)1.20    ← Step 1
 8
 __
 40
-40
 __
  0    ← Step 2
```

<u>7.25</u>

2.
```
4)29.00    ← Step 1
 -28
 ___
  1 0
  -8
  ___
   20
  -20
  ___
    0    ← Step 2
```

<u>0.844</u>

3.
```
5)4.220    ← Step 1
 -4 0
 ____
  22
 -20
 ___
  20
 -20
 ___
   0    ← Step 2
```

4. $4.5 \div 6 =$ _____0.75_____

5. $2.2 \div 4 =$ _____0.55_____

6. $8.7 \div 2 =$ _____4.35_____

7. $3.7 \div 5 =$ _____0.74_____

8. $1.8 \div 8 =$ _____0.225_____

9. $7.5 \div 6 =$ _____1.25_____

10. How can you tell when you are finished dividing? ___when there___
___are no numbers left to bring down from the dividend and___
___the remainder is 0___

Answer Box

0.15	0.225	0.55	0.74	0.75	0.844	1.25	4.35	7.25

RETEACH

52

Equivalent Metric Measures: Multiply or Divide?

Remember to move the decimal point in the correct direction when writing equivalent metric measures.

Problem: | 0.236 km = _____ m |

When you are going from larger to smaller units, you need more units; so multiply. Move the decimal point right.	When you are going from smaller to larger units, you need fewer units; so divide. Move the decimal point left.
$0.236 \times 1000 = 236$	$236 \div 1000 = 0.236$
0.236 km = $\underline{236}$ m	236 m = $\underline{0.236}$ km

Equivalent Measures of Length
1 cm = 10 mm	1 m = 100 cm
1 m = 1000 mm	1 km = 1000 m

Solve. Use the chart to help you. Make sure each answer appears in the Answer Box.

1. 422 cm = _____ **4.22** _____ m

$422 \div 100 =$ _____ **4.22** _____

2. 42 cm = _____ **0.42** _____ m

3. 0.96 m = _____ **96** _____ cm

$0.96 \times 100 =$ _____ **96** _____

4. 9.06 m = _____ **906** _____ cm

5. 46,577 km = _____ **46,577,000** _____ m

$46,577 \times 1000 =$ _____ **46,577,000** _____

6. 29.8 km = _____ **29,800** _____ m

7. 191 mm = _____ **19.1** _____ cm

$191 \div 10 =$ _____ **19.1** _____

8. 4005 mm = _____ **400.5** _____ cm

9. How do you decide which direction to move the decimal point when writing equivalent metric measures? _____ **Move the** _____

_____ **decimal point to the right when writing larger units as** _____

_____ **smaller units and to the left when writing smaller units as** _____

_____ **larger units.** _____

Answer Box

29,800	0.42	400.5	19.1	4.22	46,577,000	906	96

53 ▲ RETEACH

Equivalent Metric Measures: Counting Zeros in the Divisor

When writing equivalent metric measures, make sure to move the decimal point the correct number of places.

Problem: | 6.8 mm = ■ cm

6.8 mm = ■ cm	Step 1: Decide whether to divide or multiply.
6.8 ÷ 10 = ■	Step 2: Count the number of zeros.
6.8 mm = 0.68 cm	Step 3: Move the decimal point that number of places.

Equivalent Metric Measures

10 mm = 1 cm   100 cm = 1 m   1000 m = 1 km

Solve. Use the chart to help you. Make sure each answer appears in the Answer Box.

1. 5.8 km = _____5800_____ m
   5.8 × 1000 = 5800

2. 15 mm = _____1.5_____ cm
   15 ÷ 10 = 1.5

3. 151 cm = _____1510_____ mm
   151 × _____10_____ = 1510

4. 5.04 m = _____504_____ cm
   5.04 × _____100_____ = 504

5. 5.171 m = _____517.1_____ cm

6. 9500 m = _____9.5_____ km

7. 5.36 mm = _____0.536_____ cm

8. 5700 km = _____5,700,000_____ m

9. 5280 cm = _____52.8_____ m

10. 0.503 mm = _____0.0503_____ cm

Answer Box

517.1	52.8	0.0503	5,700,000	1.5	5800	1510	0.536	9.5	504

Name_____ Date_____

7.6 ANOLook — **ANOTHER LOOK**

Placing the Decimal Point

How can you tell where to place the decimal point in the quotient of a decimal division problem?

Divide as you would with whole numbers. Squared paper can help you keep the digits lined up.

decimal point.

When you divide a decimal by a whole number, place the decimal point in the quotient directly above the decimal point in the dividend.

Write the quotient. Use squared paper if it helps.

1. 5)5.25 ____1.05____

2. 2)10.05 ____5.025____

3. 6)48.6 ____8.1____

4. 3)$18.99 ____6.33____

5. 7)$14.77 ____$2.11____

6. 9)180.9 ____20.1____

Write the quotient. Multiply the quotient by the divisor to check whether you have placed the decimal point correctly. Use a calculator to check.

7. 20.02 ÷ 2 = ____10.01____

8. 7.26 ÷ 6 = ____1.21____

9. $10.10 ÷ 5 = ____2.02____

10. 36.12 ÷ 6 = ____6.02____

11. 40.44 ÷ 4 = ____10.11____

12. $312.60 ÷ 3 = ____$104.20____

Circle a, b, or c to indicate the correct quotient.

13. 6)0.054
   a. 9.0
   b.) 0.009
   c. 0.09

14. 9)27.72
   a.) 3.08
   b. 30.8
   c. 0.308

15. 8)640.56
   a. 80.007
   b. 8.007
   c.) 80.07

16. 4)16.004
   a. 40.01
   b.) 4.001
   c. 400.1

Name _____ Date _____

7.7

ANOTHER LOOK

....

Decimal Quotients

When you divide a number by a greater number, the quotient will be a fraction or a decimal less than one.

Five friends were given 4 kilograms of apples for helping to rake the Thompsons' orchard. The friends divided the apples equally among themselves. How many kilograms of apples did each friend get?

Divide: 4 ÷ 5
You know that 4 is less than 5.
So, think of 4 as 40 tenths:

```
   0.8
5)4.0
   4 0
   ———
     0
```

Each friend got 0.8 kilogram of apples.

Write the quotient. Be sure the decimal point in the quotient is above the decimal point in the dividend.

1. $\overset{1.2}{5)6}$	2. $\overset{0.25}{8)2}$	3. $\overset{0.6}{5)3}$	4. $\overset{\$6.40}{5)\$32}$
5. $\overset{4.625}{8)37}$	6. $\overset{1.5}{6)9}$	7. $\overset{2.8}{5)14}$	8. $\overset{0.625}{8)5}$
9. $\overset{\$5.50}{4)\$22}$	10. $\overset{5.875}{8)47}$	11. $\overset{4.8}{5)24}$	12. $\overset{0.5}{8)4}$

13. 2 ÷ 5 __0.4__   **14.** 18 ÷ 4 __$4.50__   **15.** 12 ÷ 5 __2.4__   **16.** 43 ÷ 8 __5.375__

17. Write the exercise numbers above in which the quotient is less than one. What do you notice about the divisors and dividends in each one?

2, 3, 8, 12, 13; The divisors are greater than the dividends.

7.8 ANOTHER LOOK

Problem Solving Strategy: Work a Simpler Problem

You are taking care of a neighbor's large dogs. There are 3 bags of partially-used dog food left. The bags weigh 5.6 lb, 2.5 lb, and 8.6 lb. If the dogs eat 2 lb each day, how long will the food last?

1. Understand

- You know the dogs eat 2 lb of food each day.

- The three bags weigh 5.6 lb, 2.5 lb, and 8.6 lb.

2. Plan

- Round to get simpler numbers.

- Add the weights to find out how much dog food you have. Then, use division.

3. Try It

- Round each decimal to the nearest whole number: 5.6 to 6, 2.5 to 3, and 8.6 to 9. Add the new weights to find how much total dog food you have: 18 lb.

- Divide this by 2, the amount of dog food used each day: $18 \div 2 = 9$. You have 18 lb, enough for about 9 days. Then, follow the same steps using the original numbers.

4. Look Back

- Using simpler numbers, your answer is 9 days. Using the original numbers, your answer is about 8.35 days.

Solve. Use Work a Simpler Problem when you can.

1. You are going to make a garden. One plan is for a square with 7.2 ft of fencing on each side. Another plan is for a rectangle with 3.2 ft of fencing along the width, and 6.1 ft along the

   length. Which plan would need the least amount of fencing? _____ the rectangle _____

2. Your class is holding a poster sale to raise $150 for your school library. You have $25 left over from last year's sale that you can add to your total. If you sell 3 small posters for $1.25 each, 7 medium posters for $3.25 each, and 12 large posters for $5.75 each, will you have raised enough money? If not,

   how much more money will you need to make? _____ No; $29.50 more _____

144

Name _____ Date _____

7.9 ANOTHER LOOK

Problem Solving: **Using Strategies**

Suppose the statue in your neighborhood park has been tilting. If it tilted 1.9 cm a month for the first 6 months, 2.3 cm a month for the next 4 months, and 0.7 cm a month for the last 2 months, how much will it have tilted in one year?

1. Understand

- You know how much the statue tilts each month.

- You need to find how much the statue has tilted in one year.

2. Plan

- Multiply each amount the statue tilted by the number of months. To do this, simplify the problem.

- Use addition to find the total amount that the statue tilted.

3. Try It

- Choose Work a Simpler Problem. Round each decimal to the nearest whole number: 1.9 to 2, 2.3 to 2, and 0.7 to 1.

- Multiply the tilt by the number of months: 2×6, 2×4, and 1×2.

- Add each amount. This is the amount for one year. Now, follow the steps using the original numbers.

4. Look Back

- Using simpler numbers, your answer is 22 cm. Using the original numbers, your answer is about 20 cm. Since 22 is close to 20, your answer makes sense.

Use any strategy to solve.

1. While babysitting, you make $20 the first week, $15 the second week, $35 the third week, and $25 the fourth week. If this pattern continues, how much will you have made at the end of 12 weeks? _____ $285

2. Sarah, Juan, Marco, and Val use different colors of paint. Sarah uses the red, and Juan does not use the orange or blue. If Val does not use the orange, and Marco does not use the green, which color does Marco use? _____ orange

Name_____ Date_____

7.10 ANOTHER LOOK

Fractions and Decimals

It sometimes is difficult to compare fractions with different denominators.

For $3.00, Peri can buy any one of the following items:

$\frac{5}{8}$ lb of pecans

$\frac{2}{3}$ lb of cashews

$\frac{1}{2}$ lb of filberts

Which will give her more for her money?

By changing each fraction to a decimal it is easier to compare.

Since $\frac{5}{8}$ means 5 ÷ 8, enter that operation in your calculator.

Round quotients to the nearest thousandth:

$5 \div 8 = 0.625$ $2 \div 3 = 0.667$ $1 \div 2 = 0.500$

The greatest decimal is 0.667. So $\frac{2}{3}$ lb of cashews will give Peri the most for her money.

Divide to change the following fractions to decimals.
Round to the nearest thousandth. Use your calculator.

1. $\frac{1}{4}$ = ___0.250___

2. $\frac{1}{6}$ = ___0.167___

3. $\frac{4}{7}$ = ___0.571___

4. $\frac{5}{9}$ = ___0.555___

5. $\frac{1}{3}$ = ___.333___

6. $\frac{7}{8}$ = ___0.875___

7. $\frac{8}{15}$ = ___0.533___

8. $\frac{10}{25}$ = ___0.400___

9. $\frac{3}{5}$ = ___0.600___

10. $\frac{3}{10}$ = ___0.300___

11. $\frac{11}{13}$ = ___0.846___

12. $\frac{8}{33}$ = ___0.242___

Order the following fractions from greatest to least. Change the fraction to decimals to compare. Use your calculator.

13. $\frac{7}{8}, \frac{3}{4}, \frac{9}{10}$ _____ $\frac{9}{10}, \frac{7}{8}, \frac{3}{4}$

14. $\frac{5}{13}, \frac{6}{11}, \frac{14}{27}$ _____ $\frac{6}{11}, \frac{14}{27}, \frac{5}{13}$

15. $\frac{8}{15}, \frac{9}{17}, \frac{21}{22}$ _____ $\frac{21}{22}, \frac{8}{15}, \frac{9}{17}$

RETEACH

54

Placing Zeros in the Quotient

Be careful that zeros are placed correctly in the quotient.

Problem: | 0.084 ÷ 3

```
        2 8
3)0 . 0 8 4
  -    6 0
        2 4
      - 2 4
          0
```

1. Pretend the decimal point is not there. Divide as you would whole numbers. As you divide, keep the quotient carefully lined up with the dividend.

```
  0 . 0 2 8
3)0 . 0 8 4
  -    6 0
        2 4
      - 2 4
          0
```

2. Write the decimal point in the quotient right above the decimal point in the dividend. Write zeros in any empty places.

Write the quotient. Make sure each answer appears in the Answer Box.

1.
```
  0 . 0 9
8)0 . 7 2
  -  7 2
       0
```

2.
```
  0 . 2 0 6
4)0 . 8 2 4
  -  8 0 0
        2 4
      - 2 4
          0
```

3.
```
  0 . 0 2 9
3)0 . 0 8 7
  -    6 0
        2 7
      - 2 7
          0
```

4.
```
   0.109
2)0.218
```

5.
```
   0.04
8)0.32
```

6.
```
   0.014
6)0.084
```

7.
```
   0.021
9)0.189
```

8.
```
   0.004
4)0.016
```

9.
```
   0.209
4)0.836
```

10. How can you make sure to place zeros correctly in the quotient? ___ by keeping the quotient lined up with the dividend ___

Answer Box								
0.004	0.109	0.206	0.09	0.014	0.029	0.021	0.04	0.209

55 ▶ **RETEACH**

Subtracting When Dividing

When doing the steps of a division problem, be sure to subtract carefully.

Problem: | $0.096 \div 2$

$$
\begin{array}{r}
0.048 \\
2\overline{)0.096} \\
-80 \\
\hline
16 \\
-16 \\
\hline
0
\end{array}
$$

$16 + 80 = 96$

$0 + 16 = 16$

Subtract carefully.

Check your subtraction by adding.

Find the quotient. You can check your subtraction by adding.
Make sure each answer appears in the Answer Box.

1.
$$
\begin{array}{r}
0.0226 \\
6\overline{)0.1356} \\
-1200 \\
\hline
156 \\
-120 \\
\hline
36 \\
-36 \\
\hline
0
\end{array}
$$

$156 + 1200 = 1356$

$36 + 120 = 156$

$0 + 36 = 36$

2.
$$
\begin{array}{r}
0.279 \\
6\overline{)1.674} \\
-1\,200 \\
\hline
474 \\
-420 \\
\hline
54 \\
-54 \\
\hline
0
\end{array}
$$

$474 + 1200 = 1674$

$54 + 420 = 474$

$0 + 54 = 54$

3. $3\overline{)0.768}$ 0.256

4. $5\overline{)0.365}$ 0.073

5. $3\overline{)0.195}$ 0.065

6. $0.264 \div 6 =$ ___0.044___

7. $3.568 \div 4 =$ ___0.892___

8. $3.714 \div 6 =$ ___0.619___

9. How can you make sure you subtracted correctly in your division

problem? _____ Check your work by adding. _____

Answer Box

0.0226	0.619	0.279	0.073	0.065	0.256	0.892	0.044

RETEACH

56

When you rewrite a horizontal division problem in the $\overline{)\quad}$, make sure you copy the dividend and divisor in the proper places.

Problem: | 2 ÷ 20 |

When you copy the problem, reverse the order. The first number is the dividend, even if it is smaller than the other number. It goes inside.
The second number is the divisor. It goes outside.   2 ÷ 20
Write the problem this way: $20\overline{)2}$

$20\overline{)2}$

Write the problem. Then solve it. Make sure each answer appears in the Answer Box.

1. 3 ÷ 6 _____0.5_____

   $6\overline{)3}$

2. 7 ÷ 8 _____0.875_____

   $8\overline{)7}$

3. 6 ÷ 15 _____0.4_____

   $15\overline{)6}$

Write the quotient. Make sure each answer appears in the Answer Box.

4. 4 ÷ 5 = ____0.8____

5. 3 ÷ 4 = ____0.75____

6. 5 ÷ 8 = ____0.625____

7. 9 ÷ 10 = ____0.9____

8. 2 ÷ 8 = ____0.25____

9. 3 ÷ 15 = ____0.2____

10. How can you tell if you have rewritten a horizontal division problem correctly? ____When you read left to right, the____ ____numbers should be in reverse order. The first____ ____number must go inside the $\overline{)\quad}$.____

Answer Box

0.2	0.25	0.4	0.5	0.625	0.75	0.8	0.875	0.9

57 ▼ RETEACH   Dividing from Left to Right

When dividing, make sure you work from left to right.

Problem: | 5 ÷ 8 |

$$
\begin{array}{r}
6 \\
8\overline{)5.0} \\
-4\ 8 \\
\hline
2
\end{array}
\qquad
\begin{array}{r}
62 \\
8\overline{)5.00} \\
-4\ 8 \\
\hline
20 \\
-16 \\
\hline
4
\end{array}
\qquad
\begin{array}{r}
.625 \\
8\overline{)5.000} \\
-4\ 8 \\
\hline
20 \\
-16 \\
\hline
40 \\
-40 \\
\hline
0
\end{array}
\qquad
5 \div 8 = 0.625
$$

Write the quotient. Make sure each answer appears in the Answer Box.

1.
$$
\begin{array}{r}
5.25 \\
4\overline{)21.00} \\
-20\ 00 \\
\hline
1\ 00 \\
-80 \\
\hline
20 \\
-20 \\
\hline
0
\end{array}
$$

2.
$$
\begin{array}{r}
7.25 \\
8\overline{)58.00} \\
-56\ 00 \\
\hline
2\ 00 \\
-160 \\
\hline
40 \\
-40 \\
\hline
0
\end{array}
$$

3. $8\overline{)22}$ → 2.75

4. $6\overline{)57}$ → 9.5

5. $4\overline{)42}$ → 10.5

6. $3 \div 6 =$ ___0.5___

7. $27 \div 8 =$ ___3.375___

8. $7 \div 8 =$ ___0.875___

9. In which direction do you work in division?

_____ **left to right** _____

Answer Box

10.5	7.25	3.375	9.5	5.25	0.875	0.5	2.75

Name _____   Date _____

8.1 ▶ ANOTHER LOOK

Quadrilaterals

A **quadrilateral** is a polygon with four sides. You can make quadrilaterals using Tangram pieces.

Trace the Tangram figure at the right. Label the pieces as shown. Then cut the figure into the 7 pieces.

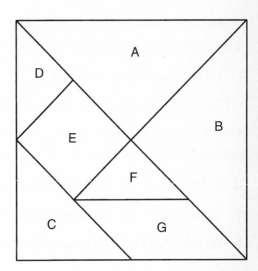

Make a **square** using pieces A and B.

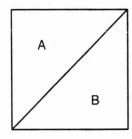

- Opposite sides are parallel. They are always the same distance apart.

- All sides are congruent. They are all the same length.

- All angles are congruent. They all have the same measure.

A **rhombus** is a figure that has two pairs of parallel sides and four congruent sides. The square is a rhombus.

A **parallelogram** is a quadrilateral with two pairs of parallel sides. Make a parallelogram that is not a square using pieces A and B.

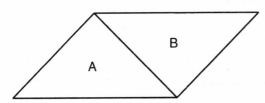

A **trapezoid** is a quadrilateral with only one pair of parallel sides. Make a trapezoid using pieces D, E, and F.

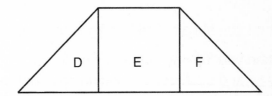

Make each figure with Tangram pieces. Then draw each figure.

1. a parallelogram with pieces D and F

2. a trapezoid with pieces G and D

3. a square with pieces D and F

8.2 ANOTHER LOOK

Slides and Flips

When you slide a figure, you move each point of the figure the same distance in the same direction.

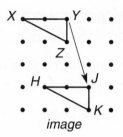

image

- The arrow shows the slide.

- The figure and its slide image are congruent.

The distance between each point of the figure and each corresponding point of the image is equal.

Use the figure above to answer each question.

1. Which segment is congruent to $\overline{YZ}$?

2. Which segment is parallel to $\overline{XY}$?

Draw and label each slide image.

3.

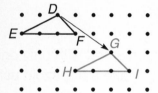

4.

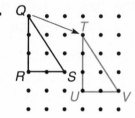

When you flip a figure, the figure and its image are congruent.

When you flip any polygon, the distance between each point of the figure and each corresponding point of the image is not equal.

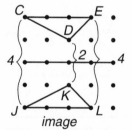

image

Use the figure of the flip to answer each question.

5. Which angle is congruent to ∠CED? ∠JLK

6. Which segment is congruent to $\overline{CD}$? _____ JK

Draw and label each flip image.

7.

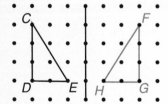

8.

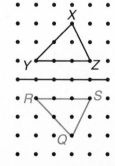

8.3 ANOTHER LOOK

....

Measuring and Drawing Angles

When you measure an angle, you can use a square corner as a guide. A square corner has a 90° angle.

- If the opening of the angle is greater than a square corner, the angle is greater than 90°.

- If the opening is less than a square corner, the angle is less than 90°.

90°

An **acute angle** measures less than 90°.

An **obtuse angle** measures more than 90° and less than 180°.

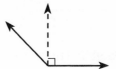

You can measure the number of degrees in an angle with a protractor.

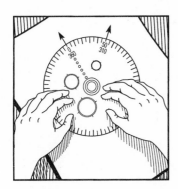

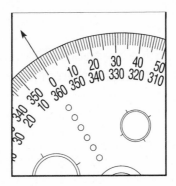

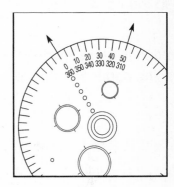

Place the center point in the red circle at the vertex of the angle. Turn the protractor so that 0 lines up with one of the rays.

Read along the scale (from 0 to 10 to 20 . . .) in the direction of the other ray.

Read the degree measure at that ray. The measure of this angle is 50°.

_____

Follow the directions. Write the measure. Ex. 1 and 2: Answers may vary.

1. Draw an acute angle. Use a protractor to measure the number of degrees in the angle.

2. Draw an obtuse angle. Use a protractor to measure the number of degrees in the angle.

3. Draw a right angle. 90°

8.4 ANOTHER LOOK

Turns

You can use what you have learned about angles to help you understand turns.

Place 2 pencils on your desk as shown at the right.

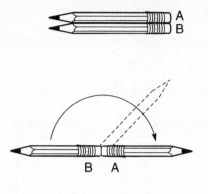

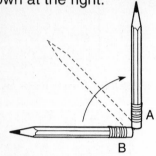

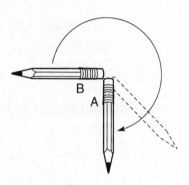

Hold pencil B still. Turn pencil A a quarter-turn around the eraser of pencil B to form a 90° angle.

Then turn pencil A as shown. Pencil A has been turned a half-turn, or 180°.

Turn pencil A once more. The turn is 270°, or a three-quarter turn.

To find the turn image of any figure, trace the figure. Then turn the tracing paper around the turn center the desired direction and amount.

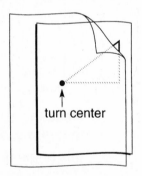

turn center

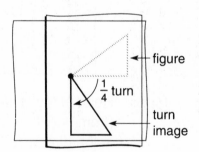

← figure

$\frac{1}{4}$ turn

turn image

The figure and its turn image are congruent.

Trace the triangle below. Then draw quarter-turn, half-turn, and three-quarter turn images of the figure in the space provided.

1. Quarter-turn

2. Half-turn

3. Three-quarter turn

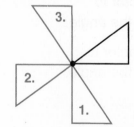

Name _____   Date _____

8.5 ▎▶ ANOTHER LOOK

Symmetry

If a figure can be turned halfway around a turn center so that it looks exactly the same, it has half-turn symmetry. You can use tracing paper to see if a figure has half-turn symmetry.

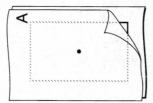

Place a sheet of tracing paper over the figure. Trace over the figure.

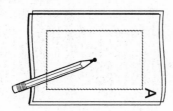

Place your pencil on the dot. Turn the tracing paper halfway around. The tracing exactly fits over the figure.

Trace each figure. Does the figure have half-turn symmetry? Write *yes* or *no*.

1.

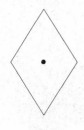

_____yes_____

2.

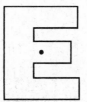

_____no_____

3.

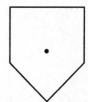

_____no_____

4.

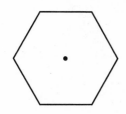

_____yes_____

5.

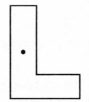

_____no_____

6.

_____yes_____

Name _____ Date _____

Problem Solving Decisions: Logical Reasoning

The words *and*, *or*, and *not* can be used to describe how numbers or objects are related.

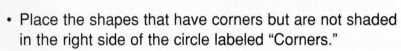

The triangle *and* the circle are shaded.

The circle *or* the square has corners.

The square is *not* shaded.

Which shapes are both shaded and have corners?

- You can use a Venn Diagram to answer the question.

- Place the shapes that are shaded but don't have corners in the left side of the circle labeled "Shaded."

- Place the shapes that have corners but are not shaded in the right side of the circle labeled "Corners."

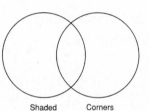

- Place the shapes that are both shaded and have corners in the middle where the two circles overlap.

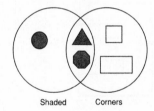

- The shapes in the intersection, or overlap, are the triangle and the octagon.

Decide which figures fit each statement.

1. Which figures are shaded or do not have corners? _____ triangle, octagon, circle _____

2. Which figures have four corners or are shaded?
   _____ square, rectangle, circle, triangle, octagon _____

3. Which figures do not have three or four corners? _____ octagon, circle _____

4. Which figures are not shaded but have corners? _____ square, rectangle _____

5. Which figures have four or eight corners? _____ square, rectangle, octagon _____

58 ◢ **RETEACH**

Quadrilaterals

You know that a **quadrilateral** is a 4-sided polygon. Special types of quadrilaterals have special names.

A **parallelogram** is a quadrilateral with opposite sides that are parallel and the same length. **Squares** and **rectangles** are examples.

A **rhombus** is a quadrilateral with parallel opposite sides and whose 4 sides are the same length. A square is a rhombus.

A **trapezoid** is a quadrilateral with only one pair of parallel sides. Figure ABCD is a trapezoid.

Circle *all* the names that apply to each figure.

1.

(quadrilateral) square rhombus
(parallelogram) rectangle trapezoid

2.

(quadrilateral) (square) (rhombus)
(parallelogram) (rectangle) trapezoid

3.

(quadrilateral) square rhombus
parallelogram rectangle trapezoid

4.

(quadrilateral) square rhombus
parallelogram rectangle (trapezoid)

5.

(quadrilateral) square rhombus
(parallelogram) rectangle trapezoid

6.

(quadrilateral) square rhombus
(parallelogram) rectangle trapezoid

7.

(quadrilateral) square rhombus
(parallelogram) (rectangle) trapezoid

8.

(quadrilateral) square rhombus
parallelogram rectangle (trapezoid)

59 **RETEACH** **Slides and Flips**

Two polygons are congruent when they have the same size and shape. You can find out if two polygons are congruent by sliding or by flipping them.

When you slide a polygon, you move it in any direction. An arrow is used to show the direction and distance of the slide.

When you flip a polygon, you reverse it. Think of an image shown in a mirror. It is a flip image. A flip image is shown on the opposite side of a flip line. A flip line is like a mirror.

SLIDE   FLIP

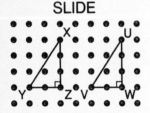 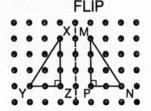

Look at the original figure and its slide image.
The corresponding sides are congruent $XY = UV$, $XZ = UW$, $YZ = VW$
The corresponding angles are congruent $\angle XYZ = \angle UVW$, $\angle YZX = \angle VWU$, $\angle ZXY = \angle WUV$

Triangle MNP is the flip image of triangle XYZ. For the slide, congruent angles XYZ and UVW both open to the right. For the flip, congruent angles XYZ and MNP open in opposite directions.

Complete. Use the figure at the right. Make sure your answers are in the Answer Box.

1. $\overline{AB} =$ _____ $\overline{LM}$ _____   2. $\overline{LN} =$ _____ $\overline{AC}$ _____

3. $\angle LMN =$ _____ $\angle ABC$ _____   4. $\overline{BC} =$ _____ $\overline{MN}$ _____

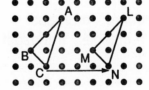

Complete. Use the figure at the right. Make sure your answers are in the Answer Box.

5. $\overline{BI} =$ _____ $\overline{HO}$ _____   6. $\angle HOP =$ _____ $\angle BIG$ _____

7. $\overline{HP} =$ _____ $\overline{BG}$ _____   8. $\angle PHO =$ _____ $\angle GBI$ _____

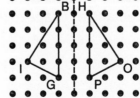

Answer Box

$\angle BIG$	$\overline{LM}$	$\overline{MN}$	$\overline{BG}$	$\angle GBI$	$\overline{HO}$	$\angle ABC$	$\overline{AC}$

Name _____ Date _____

To measure or draw an angle accurately, you need to use a protractor. To measure an angle, place the center point of the protractor on the vertex of the angle and along one side of the angle. Read the measurement counter-clockwise from 0° to 180°. Remember: angles are measured in degrees (°).

Here is how to draw a 45° angle, ∠ *ECD*. First draw one side of the angle. Label it *CD*. Place the center of the protractor on the vertex, *C*. Make a dot at 45°. Label the point *E*. Then connect points *C* and *E*. ∠ *ECD* = 45°.

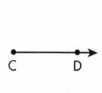
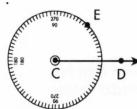
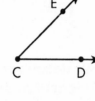

An **acute angle** is one that measures less than 90°. An **obtuse angle** is one that is greater than 90°. A **right angle** measures 90°. A **straight angle** measures 180°.

Measure each angle below. On another piece of paper draw an angle having the same measure. Write whether each is acute, obtuse, right, or straight. Angles drawn should have measures shown.

1.

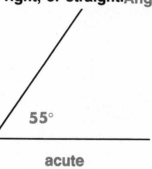

55°

_____ acute _____

2.

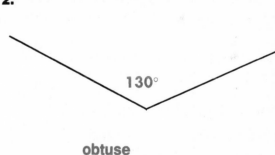

130°

_____ obtuse _____

3.

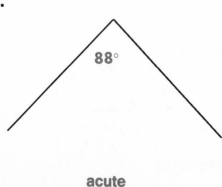

88°

_____ acute _____

4.

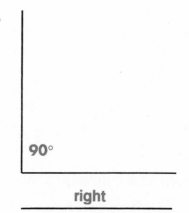

90°

_____ right _____

61 **RETEACH**   **Turns**

It may help you to think of turns as the movement of the hands on a clock.

Look at the figure below. Think of the first position as 12 o'clock.
Moving clockwise, a ¼ turn is a quarter of a circle, or a quarter of
an hour. A ½ turn is half of a circle or half an hour. A ¾ turn is
¾ of a circle, or three quarters of an hour.

**Choose the correct letter that describes the clockwise turn for
each figure. Unscramble the letters to answer the riddle below.**

1.

L $\frac{1}{4}$ turn

O $\frac{1}{2}$ turn

Ⓝ $\frac{3}{4}$ turn

2.

I $\frac{1}{4}$ turn

Ⓤ $\frac{1}{2}$ turn

C $\frac{3}{4}$ turn

3.

I $\frac{1}{4}$ turn

Ⓔ $\frac{1}{2}$ turn

P $\frac{3}{4}$ turn

4.

M $\frac{1}{4}$ turn

U $\frac{1}{2}$ turn

Ⓕ $\frac{3}{4}$ turn

5.

L $\frac{1}{4}$ turn

S $\frac{1}{2}$ turn

Ⓝ $\frac{3}{4}$ turn

6.

Ⓛ $\frac{1}{4}$ turn

T $\frac{1}{2}$ turn

A $\frac{3}{4}$ turn

Big as a biscuit, deep as a cup, even a river can't fill it up. What is it?

<u>A</u> <u>F</u> <u>U</u> <u>N</u> <u>N</u> <u>E</u> <u>L</u>

Name _____ Date _____

62 **RETEACH**   **Symmetry**

A line that divides a polygon or shape into two identical parts is called a **line of symmetry.** The dotted line shows a line of symmetry. Some figures have more than one line of symmetry.

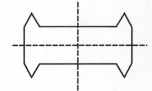

Look at the figure to the right. If you could fold it along either of its lines of symmetry, you would find that the halves match exactly. They form mirror images of one another.

There is another type of symmetry. It is made by turning the entire figure. Look at the figures below. If you put the point of your pencil on the center point of each and turn the figure clockwise a half turn, the image would fit back on the figure. Such symmetry is called **half-turn symmetry.**

Choose the correct letter that tells if all of the lines of symmetry are shown for each figure. If your answer is _no,_ draw the missing lines of symmetry. Then unscramble the letters to solve the riddle.

1.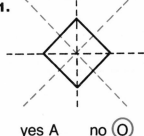

   yes A   no Ⓞ

2.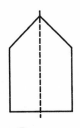

   yes Ⓛ   no T

3.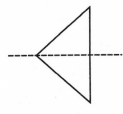

   yes Ⓔ   no Y

4.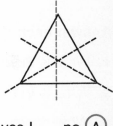

   yes I   no Ⓐ

Choose the correct letter that tells if each figure has a half-turn symmetry. Then unscramble the letters to solve the riddle.

5.

   yes B   no Ⓣ

6.

   yes Ⓥ   no O

7.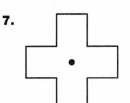

   yes Ⓡ   no E

8.

   yes L   no Ⓔ

What is shaped like a box, has no feet, and runs up and down?

AN __E__ __L__ __E__ __V__ __A__ __T__ __O__ __R__

8.7 ANOTHER LOOK

Triangles

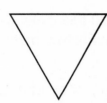

A triangle with two sides congruent is an **isosceles triangle**.

An **equilateral triangle** is a special isosceles triangle. It has all sides congruent.

A triangle with no sides congruent is a **scalene triangle**.

Trace the 3 triangles above.

• Color each triangle a different color.

• Cut out the triangles.

• Tear off the angles from one triangle and place them on the line segment around the point. Repeat for each triangle. The angles of an equilateral triangle are shown. A line segment is a straight angle and has a measure of 180°. The sum of the angles is 180°.

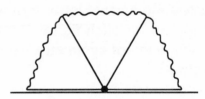

Answer each question.

1. What is the sum of the angles in an isosceles triangle? _____ 180° _____

2. What is the sum of the angles in a scalene triangle? _____ 180° _____

3. What do you notice about the sum of the angles in any triangle? ___ It is always 180°. ___

You can use what you discovered to find the missing angle measure for any triangle.

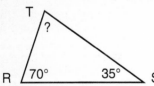

• To find the missing angle measure, add 35° + 70°. Then subtract the total from 180°.

180° − 105° = 75°   Angle T measures 75°.

Write the missing angle measure for each triangle.

4. △DEF ∠D = 50° ∠E = 70° ∠F = _60°_   5. △JKL ∠J = 25° ∠K = 65° ∠L = _90°_

6. △PQR ∠P = 86° ∠Q = 31° ∠R = _63°_   7. △GHI ∠G = 65° ∠H = 50° ∠I = _65°_

8. △STU ∠S = 105° ∠T = 35° ∠U = _40°_   9. △ABC ∠A = 90° ∠B = 45° ∠C = _45°_

10. △MNO ∠M = 62° ∠N = 48° ∠O = _70°_   11. △WXY ∠W = 97° ∠X = 52° ∠Z = _31°_

8.8 ANOTHER LOOK

Ordered Pairs

Two lines intersect at a point. You can identify that point by giving the number of each line.

To identify the location of point A, start at A and move down. Find the number of the line (2). Then, start again at A and move across. Point A is located at (2,1).

Because order is important in locating a point, the numbers are called an **ordered pair**.

- The first number in an ordered pair always tells how far to move across.

- The second number tells how far to move up.

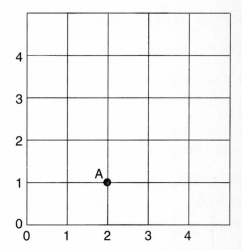

Use the grid at the right. Write the letter for each point named below.

1. (1,2) _____C_____

2. (4,2) _____A_____

3. (2,4) _____F_____

4. (0,3) _____E_____

5. (4,1) _____B_____

6. (3,0) _____D_____

7. Which letter names a point where both numbers are the same? _____G_____

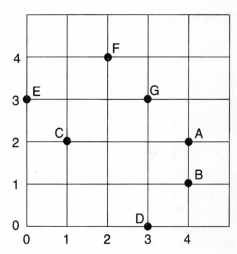

You can draw slide images on a grid.

8. First, write the ordered pair for each vertex of triangle XYZ.

   X __(1,0)__   Y __(1,1)__   Z __(0,1)__

9. Next, draw the slide image of triangle XYZ.

10. Then, write the ordered pair for each vertex of the slide image of triangle XYZ.

    image X __(3,2)__   Y __(3,3)__   Z __(2,3)__

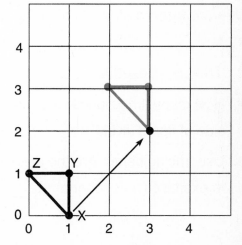

8.9 ⬛ ANOTHER LOOK

Similar Figures

Similar figures have the same shape but not necessarily the same size.

Look at the two figures on the grid at the right.

• The length of $\overline{QR}$ is 4 units. The length of $\overline{WX}$ is 2 units. $\overline{QR}$ is twice as long as $\overline{WX}$.

• The length of $\overline{RS}$ is 2 units. The length of $\overline{XY}$ is 1 unit. $\overline{RS}$ is twice as long as $\overline{XY}$.

Each side in figure QRST is twice as long as each side in figure WXYZ.

Trace over the angles in figure WXYZ. Compare the angles in figure WXYZ to the angles in figure QRST. The angles in the two figures are congruent.

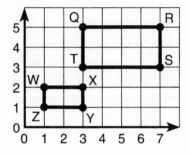

Look at each figure. Then complete the figure next to it so that the two figures are similar.

1. triangle DEF

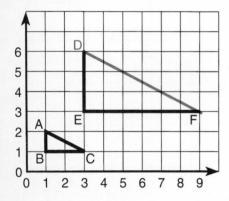

2. figure QRST

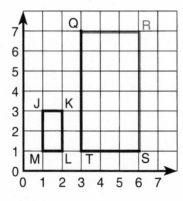

3. figure GHIJ

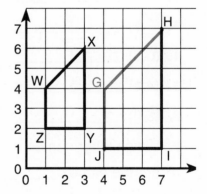

Use the figures above. Write the length.

4. $\overline{ML}$ _____1 unit_____   **5.** $\overline{MJ}$ _____2 units_____   **6.** $\overline{KL}$ _____2 units_____

  $\overline{TS}$ _____3 units_____ $\overline{TQ}$ _____6 units_____ $\overline{RS}$ _____6 units_____

7. How many times longer is each side of figure QRST than each

  side of figure JKLM? _____3 times_____

8. Use tracing paper. Are the angles of each pair of similar figures

  in exercises 1–3 congruent? _____yes_____

8.10 ANOTHER LOOK

Making Cubes

A **net** for a cube is a pattern that can be used to make a cube. To work with nets in this lesson, you will need tracing paper, scissors, and tape.

Each net shown below can be cut out along the solid lines and folded along the dotted lines to make a cube.

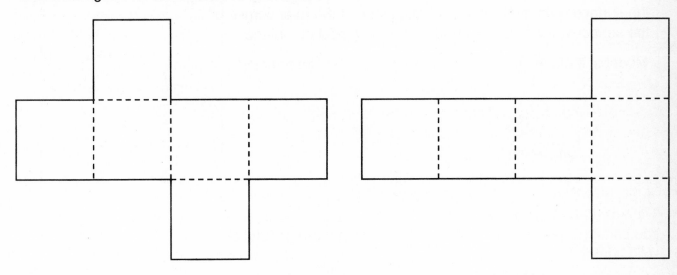

1. Trace each of the nets. Then cut, fold, and tape each net to make a cube.

2. Trace the square at the right 18 times. Cut out the 18 squares.

3. Use the cutout squares and tape to make 3 more nets for a cube. Record each net on the dot paper grid.

a. 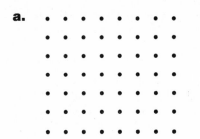   b. 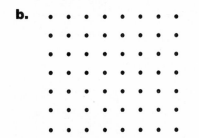   c.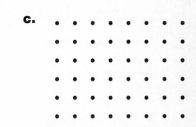

Check students' drawings.

Name _____ Date _____

8.11 ANOTHER LOOK

The Plane in Geometry

A **plane** is a flat surface that goes on forever in all directions.

Here is a way to tell if a surface is a model of a plane.

• Mark 2 points anywhere on a surface, but not too close together.

• Use a ruler to connect the 2 points. If the ruler stays on the surface, the surface is flat and is a model of a plane. If the ruler comes off the surface anywhere, the surface is not a model of a plane.

Model of a plane

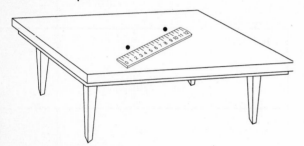

Not a model of a plane

You can find planes that intersect and planes that are parallel on solid figures.

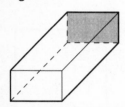

• There are 3 pairs of parallel faces on this figure.

• Four faces intersect with the face that is shaded.

• Three planes meet at each vertex.

Answer questions a, b, and c for each figure below.

a. How many pairs of parallel faces are there?

b. How many faces intersect with the shaded face?

c. How many planes meet at each vertex?

1.

a. _____ 3 _____

b. _____ 4 _____

c. _____ 3 _____

2.

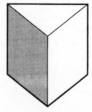

a. _____ 1 _____

b. _____ 4 _____

c. _____ 3 _____

3.

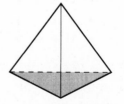

a. _____ none _____

b. _____ 3 _____

c. _____ 3 _____

8.12 ANLOTHER LOOK

Problem Solving Strategy: **Draw a Picture**

You are on your way to meet a friend at the park. Leaving your house, you walk 4 blocks north and then turn and walk 5 blocks west. Realizing you are late, you start walking faster. You walk 3 blocks south and 1 block east. Finally, you run 1 block south and 3 blocks east. As you reach the park, you realize you could have used a different route. How many blocks are you from home?

1. Understand

• You need to know how many blocks you run and walk in each direction.

• You need to be able to show this information to solve the problem.

2. Plan

• You can use Draw a Picture to solve the problem.

3. Try It

• Draw a point to represent your house.

• Draw a line to show the route you traveled. Draw a line that shows you going 4 blocks north, 5 blocks west, 3 blocks south, 1 block east, 1 block south, and 3 blocks east.

4. Look Back

• Your picture shows that your route ends 1 block west of home.

HOME

Solve. Use Draw a Picture when you can.

1. Your cousin leaves her house and rides her bike 5 blocks west, and then 1 block north. From there, she turns and rides 6 blocks east, and then 8 blocks south. How many blocks is she from her house? In which direction must she travel to get home? _____ **8 blocks; She must go 7 blocks north and 1 block west.**

2. You are cleaning a tiled floor. The floor is shaped like a rectangle. It is 4 tiles wide and 5 tiles long. If you start with the width and clean 3 rows of tiles, how many more rows will be left? _____ **2 rows**

8.13 ANOTHER LOOK

Problem Solving: Using Strategies

The *Chicago Kidz* are performing in your city. They must drive from their hotel to the theater. The theater is exactly 5 blocks north of their hotel. Leaving their hotel, they drive 3 blocks east, then 8 blocks north, and 5 blocks west. They realize they have gone the wrong way, so they drive 6 blocks east and then 3 blocks south. How many blocks are they from the theater?

1. Understand

- You know how many blocks the *Kidz* drove in each direction.
- You will find out how many blocks they are from the theater.

2. Plan

- You can use the Draw a Picture strategy to solve the problem.

3. Try It

- Draw a point to show the starting point (the hotel). Draw a point 5 blocks north of the first point to show the theatre.

- Draw a line that shows their route: 3 blocks east, 8 blocks north, 5 blocks west, 6 blocks east, then 3 blocks south.

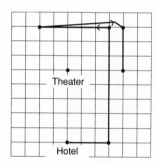

4. Look Back

- The *Kidz* end up 4 blocks east of the theater.

Use any strategy to solve.

1. You are going to see the *Chicago Kidz* perform. The show starts at 1:30 P.M. It takes you about 45 minutes to get ready, and then 30 minutes to ride your bike to the theater. You want to leave yourself an extra 30 minutes to find your seat and meet your friends. What is the latest you should start getting ready for the show? _____ **11:45 A.M.**

2. You bring $3.95 for snacks. You want to buy two hot dogs, for $1.50 each, a bottle of juice, for $1.25, and a box of popcorn, for $.65. Do you have enough money? Your friend says he will lend you a dollar if you need it. Do you need it? If so, how much will you have left over? _____ **No; Yes; $.05 left over**

63 ►RETEACH

Triangles

Remember that a triangle has 3 sides and the sum of its angles is 180°. Use a protractor to measure an angle.

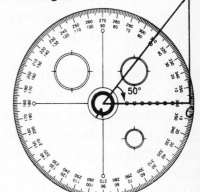

- A **right triangle** has a 90° angle, or right angle.
- An **equilateral triangle** has all congruent sides.
- An **isosceles triangle** has 2 congruent sides.
- A **scalene triangle** has no congruent sides.

Measure each angle and side of the triangles below to the nearest unit. Complete the table. Use a protractor and a centimeter ruler. Make sure each answer appears in the Answer Box.

Triangle	∠ A	∠ B	∠ C	Sum of ∠ measures (∠ A + ∠ B + ∠ C)	$\overline{AB}$	$\overline{BC}$	$\overline{CA}$
1	110°	35°	35°	180°	5 cm	8 cm	5 cm
2	60°	60°	60°	180°	4 cm	4 cm	4 cm
3	53°	90°	37°	180°	3 cm	4 cm	5 cm

Ring the correct name or names for each triangle.

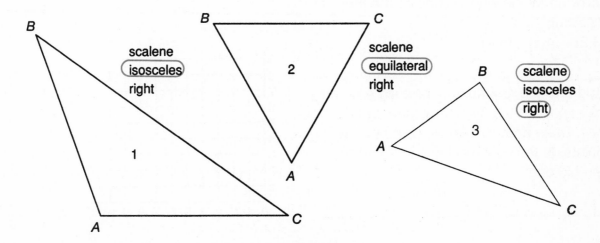

scalene
(isosceles)
right

scalene
(equilateral)
right

scalene
isosceles
(right)

Answer Box

4 cm	180°	5 cm	60°	8 cm	4 cm	180°	53°	35°	60°	37°	4 cm	60°	35°	5 cm	90°
110°	4 cm	3 cm	180°	5 cm											

64 ◣ **RETEACH** **Ordered Pairs**
....

Ordered pairs can name points on a grid. The first number tells the number of units to the right of zero. The second number tells the number of units up from zero.

Here is how to name the ordered pair for point *C* on the grid. Notice that *C* is located where a vertical line and a horizontal line cross. What is the number of the vertical line? What is the number of the horizontal line that *C* is located on? (3,5) is the ordered pair that names the location of point *C*.

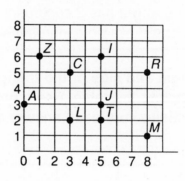

1. What letter is at point (5,3)?   *J*

Write the ordered pair for each point on the grid above.

2. *Z* _____(1,6)_____   **3.** *T* _____(5,2)_____

4. *A* _____(0,3)_____   **5.** *M* _____(8,1)_____

6. *L* _____(3,2)_____   **7.** *I* _____(5,6)_____

You can use ordered pairs to draw a figure on the grid.

8. Draw a triangle whose vertices are the following points:
(3,2)   (4,5)   (5,4)

9. Add 2 to the first number of each ordered pair and 1 to the second number in the pair. Draw another triangle using the new points. Is the new triangle congruent to the old one?

_____**yes**_____

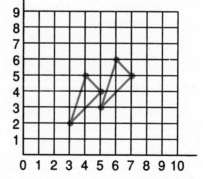

65 ⏵**RETEACH**

Look at the pair of rectangles below.

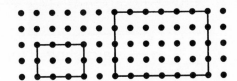

You know that the angles of both rectangles are congruent because
a rectangle has four 90° angles. You can see that each side of the
larger rectangle is two times the length of the corresponding side
of the smaller rectangle. The two rectangles are **similar.**

Use the grid to graph each pair of similar figures.

1. Fig A: (4,3) (2,1) (2,4)
    Fig B: (8,6) (4,2) (4,8)

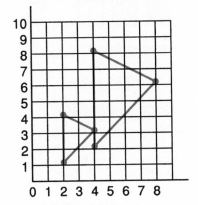

2. Fig C: (1,2) (2,2) (3,1) (2,4)
    Fig D: (2,4) (4,4) (6,2) (4,8)

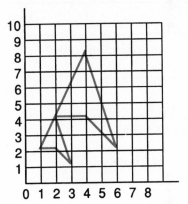

**Multiply the numbers in each ordered pair by 2. Then draw the
new figure.**

3.

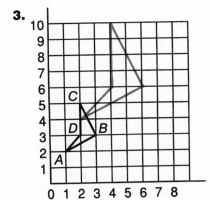

4.

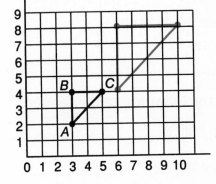

171

9.1 ANOTHER LOOK

Fractions

• This Fraction Bar has 4 equal parts:

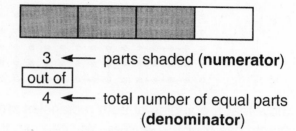

3 parts of the bar are shaded.
Word form: three fourths
Standard form: $\frac{3}{4}$

3 ← parts shaded (**numerator**)

out of

4 ← total number of equal parts
(**denominator**)

• There are 5 counters at the right:

2 out of 5 are light $\frac{2}{5}$ are light   two fifths are light

3 out of 5 are dark $\frac{3}{5}$ are dark   three fifths are dark

---

Answer each question.

1.

   a. How many parts shaded? _____1_____

   b. Total number of equal parts? ___3___

   c. Write the fraction in standard
      and word form.

          $\frac{1}{3}$, **one third**

2.

   a. How many parts shaded? ___5___

   b. Total number of equal parts? ___6___

   c. Write the fraction in standard
      and word form.

          $\frac{5}{6}$, **five sixths**

3.

   a. How many parts shaded? ___3___

   b. Total number of equal parts? ___7___

   c. Write the fraction in standard
      and word form.

          $\frac{3}{7}$, **three sevenths**

4.

   a. How many parts shaded? ___4___

   b. Total number of equal parts? ___10___

   c. Write the fraction in standard
      and word form.

          $\frac{4}{10}$, **four tenths**

Write the letter for each standard fraction next to the matching word form.

5. one half _____d_____

6. two fourths _____a_____

7. three tenths _____c_____

8. eight twelfths _____b_____

   a. $\frac{2}{4}$ **b.** $\frac{8}{12}$ **c.** $\frac{3}{10}$ **d.** $\frac{1}{2}$

9.2 ANOTHER LOOK

Problem Solving Strategy: Act It Out

There are 16 boys in your math class. Four of the boys have brown hair. Half of the remaining students have blond hair. Of the boys without brown or blond hair, $\frac{1}{3}$ have red hair, and the rest have black hair. How many students have black hair?

1. Understand

- You know how many boys are in the class.

- You know the number of boys with brown, blond, red, and black hair.

2. Plan

- You can use 16 objects to represent the number of boys.

3. Try It

- Line up the objects. Now, remove 4 objects because the problem says that 4 of the boys have brown hair. You are left with 12 objects: $16 - 4 = 12$.

- Take $\frac{1}{2}$ of 12, because $\frac{1}{2}$ of the remaining boys have blond hair: $\frac{1}{2} \times 12 = 6$.

- Take $\frac{1}{3}$ of 6, because $\frac{1}{3}$ of the boys have red hair: $\frac{1}{3} \times 6 = 2$.

- The remaining objects represent the boys with black hair: $6 - 2 = 4$.

4. Look Back

- You know that 4 is correct because the numbers of boys with each hair color add up to 16.

Solve. Use Act It Out when you can.

1. There are 25 pieces of construction paper in one package: $\frac{1}{5}$ are red, $\frac{1}{2}$ of the remaining paper is blue, 4 of the remaining pieces are yellow, and $\frac{2}{3}$ of the rest are purple. The last pieces are green. How many pieces are green? _____ 2 pieces _____

2. There are 28 pens in a metallic pen kit: $\frac{1}{2}$ have gold-colored ink, 6 pens have silver-colored ink, and 2 of the pens have bronze-colored ink. The remaining pens have copper-colored ink. How many pens have copper-colored ink? _____ 6 pens _____

9.3 ANOTHER LOOK

Equivalent Fractions

• You can make folded paper models to show equivalent fractions.

Fold a piece of paper in half. Open it and color one half.

$\frac{1}{2}$ is colored.

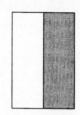

Fold the folded paper in half again.

$\frac{2}{4}$ is colored.

The same amount of paper is still colored. $\frac{1}{2}$ and $\frac{2}{4}$ are **equivalent fractions**.

• You also can use multiplication or division to find equivalent fractions. Here are two ways to find equivalent fractions:

Multiply the numerator and the denominator by the same number.	Divide the numerator and the denominator by the same number.
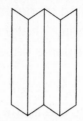 $\frac{1}{3} = \frac{\boxed{}}{\boxed{6}}$	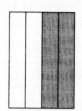 $\frac{8}{12} = \frac{\boxed{2}}{\boxed{3}}$

Complete. Multiply to make equivalent fractions.

1. $\overset{\times 4}{\frac{2}{3}} = \frac{\boxed{8}}{12}$ $\underset{\times 4}{}$

2. $\overset{\times 4}{\frac{3}{5}} = \frac{12}{\boxed{20}}$ $\underset{\times 4}{}$

3. $\overset{\times 2}{\frac{4}{7}} = \frac{\boxed{8}}{14}$ $\underset{\times 2}{}$

4. $\overset{\times 3}{\frac{8}{9}} = \frac{24}{\boxed{27}}$ $\underset{\times 3}{}$

5. $\overset{\times 5}{\frac{\boxed{1}}{2}} = \frac{5}{10}$ $\underset{\times 5}{}$

6. $\frac{1}{5} = \frac{\boxed{2}}{10}$

7. $\frac{2}{5} = \frac{4}{\boxed{10}}$

8. $\frac{\boxed{1}}{2} = \frac{3}{6}$

9. $\frac{1}{2} = \frac{6}{\boxed{12}}$

10. $\frac{3}{4} = \frac{\boxed{15}}{20}$

Complete. Divide to make equivalent fractions.

11. $\overset{\div 2}{\frac{6}{18}} = \frac{\boxed{3}}{9}$ $\underset{\div 2}{}$

12. $\overset{\div 10}{\frac{10}{20}} = \frac{1}{\boxed{2}}$ $\underset{\div 10}{}$

13. $\overset{\div 5}{\frac{25}{30}} = \frac{\boxed{5}}{6}$ $\underset{\div 5}{}$

14. $\frac{12}{20} = \frac{6}{\boxed{10}}$

15. $\frac{8}{24} = \frac{\boxed{2}}{6}$

9.4 ANOTHER LOOK

Simplest Form

• When working with fractions, you often need to find the simplest form.

$\frac{2}{3}$, $\frac{4}{6}$, and $\frac{8}{12}$ are equivalent fractions. $\frac{2}{3}$ is the simplest form of the fractions because it has the least possible number of equal parts.

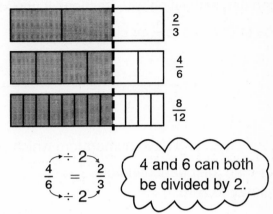

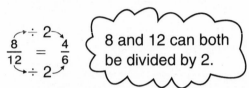

8 and 12 can both be divided by 2.

4 and 6 can both be divided by 2.

The 2 and 3 in $\frac{2}{3}$ cannot both be divided by any number but 1, so $\frac{2}{3}$ is the simplest form of the fraction.

• Another way to find the simplest form of a fraction is to divide the numerator and denominator by the greatest common factor of both.

To find the simplest form of $\frac{20}{30}$:

Write the factors for the numerator 20: 1, 2, 4, 5, 10, 20
Write the factors for the denominator 30: 1, 2, 3, 5, 6, 10, 15, 30

The greatest common factor (GCF) of 20 and 30 is 10.

$$\frac{20}{30} \overset{\div 10}{\underset{\div 10}{=}} \frac{2}{3}$$

Follow the steps below to write each fraction in simplest form.

1. $\frac{8}{14}$

    a. Write factors of 8. ___1, 2, 4, 8___

    b. Write factors of 14. ___1, 2, 7, 14___

    c. What is the GCF? ___2___

    d. Write $\frac{8}{14}$ in simplest form. ___$\frac{4}{7}$___

2. $\frac{12}{28}$

    a. Write factors of 12. ___1, 2, 3, 4, 6, 12___

    b. Write factors of 28. ___1, 2, 4, 7, 14, 28___

    c. What is the GCF? ___4___

    d. Write $\frac{12}{28}$ in simplest form. ___$\frac{3}{7}$___

Write each fraction in simplest form.

3. $\frac{18}{36}$ ___$\frac{1}{2}$___   4. $\frac{15}{25}$ ___$\frac{3}{5}$___   5. $\frac{20}{22}$ ___$\frac{10}{11}$___   6. $\frac{16}{24}$ ___$\frac{2}{3}$___   7. $\frac{12}{16}$ ___$\frac{3}{4}$___

Name _____ Date _____

Estimating Fractions

You can use estimation with fractions if you know whether a fraction is close to 0, close to $\frac{1}{2}$, or close to 1.

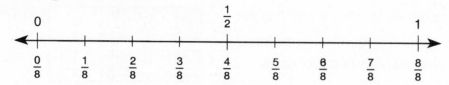

Fractions close to 0 have numerators which are much smaller than their denominators. $\frac{1}{8}$ is close to zero. $\frac{1}{16}$ would be even closer to zero.

Fractions close to $\frac{1}{2}$ have denominators that are about twice as large as their numerators. On this number line both $\frac{3}{8}$ and $\frac{5}{8}$ are close to $\frac{1}{2}$.

Fractions close to 1 have numerators and denominators that are about the same size. $\frac{7}{8}$ is close to 1. $\frac{15}{16}$ would be even closer to 1.

Circle the letter to tell whether each fraction is

   a. close to 0

   b. close to $\frac{1}{2}$

   c. close to 1

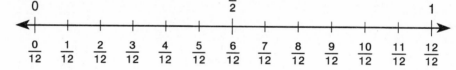

1. $\frac{5}{12}$

   a. **(b.)** **c.**

2. $\frac{2}{12}$

   (a.) **b.** **c.**

3. $\frac{8}{12}$

   a. **(b.)** **c.**

4. $\frac{11}{12}$

   a. **b.** **(c.)**

Circle the fraction that is closest to $\frac{1}{2}$.

5. $\frac{8}{9}, \frac{2}{9}, \left(\frac{4}{9}\right)$

6. $\frac{1}{6} \left(\frac{3}{8}\right) \frac{7}{8}$

7. $\frac{5}{6} \left(\frac{3}{4}\right) \frac{1}{8}$

8. $\left(\frac{5}{8}\right) \frac{9}{11}, \frac{1}{5}$

Make each fraction close to 1, but not exactly 1.

Answers may vary. Possible answer is shown.

9. $\frac{\boxed{11}}{12}$

10. $\frac{\boxed{6}}{7}$

11. $\frac{9}{\boxed{10}}$

12. $\frac{\boxed{24}}{25}$

9.6 ANOTHER LOOK

Problem Solving Decisions: **Is There Enough Information?**

You take part in a walkathon. You walk for 8 hours, from 9 A.M. until 5 P.M. By the time you finish, you have walked 23 miles. One person pledged $.50 for every mile, while another pledged $1.50 for every mile. How much money did you raise?

1. Understand

- You know the number of hours and miles you walked.
- You know the amount that was pledged for every mile.

2. Plan

- Multiply the amount pledged by the number of miles walked to find the amount each person will pay.
- Add the money contributed by each person.
- You don't need to know the number of hours you walked because you are being paid for every mile, not every hour.

3. Try It

- Find the first person's pledge. Multiply the distance walked by the amount pledged: 23 miles × $.50 = $11.50.
- Find the second person's pledge: 23 × $1.50 = $34.50.
- Add the two amounts: $11.50 + $34.50 = $46.00

4. Look Back

- You raised a total of $46.00.

Decide what information you need to solve. Then solve.

1. At a bake sale for charity, you sold 12 granola bars for $.55 each, and 43 bottles of juice for $1.50 each. How much money did you make by selling drinks? _____ $64.50 _____

2. Austin is going to change a chicken soup recipe in order to make vegetable soup. The recipe calls for $\frac{3}{4}$ cup of chopped carrots, $\frac{1}{2}$ cup of chopped onions, $\frac{1}{4}$ cup of chopped celery, and $2\frac{1}{4}$ lb of chicken. How many cups of chopped vegetables will he use in total? _____ $1\frac{1}{2}$ **cups vegetables** _____

Name _____   Date _____

66 RETEACH

Working with Numerators and Denominators

When you find equivalent fractions, make sure you multiply or divide both the numerator and denominator by the same number.

Problem: Write an equivalent fraction for $\frac{6}{10}$.

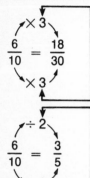

$$\overset{\times 3}{\frac{6}{10}} = \frac{18}{30} \quad \underset{\times 3}{}$$

If you multiply to find an equivalent fraction, be sure to multiply the numerator and the denominator by the same number.

$$\overset{\div 2}{\frac{6}{10}} = \frac{3}{5} \quad \underset{\div 2}{}$$

If you divide to find an equivalent fraction, be sure to divide the numerator and denominator by the same number.

Complete. Make sure each answer appears in the Answer Box.

1. $\overset{\times 5}{\frac{4}{10}} = \frac{20}{\boxed{50}} \quad \underset{\times 5}{}$

2. $\overset{\div 2}{\frac{4}{10}} = \frac{\boxed{2}}{5} \quad \underset{\div 2}{}$

3. $\overset{\times 5}{\frac{3}{9}} = \frac{\boxed{15}}{\boxed{45}} \quad \underset{\times 5}{}$

4. $\overset{\div 3}{\frac{3}{9}} = \frac{\boxed{1}}{\boxed{3}} \quad \underset{\div 3}{}$

5. $\frac{16}{24} = \frac{2}{3}$ _____

6. $\frac{7}{9} = \frac{35}{45}$ _____

7. $\frac{12}{20} = \frac{3}{5}$ _____

8. $\frac{3}{8} = \frac{12}{32}$ _____

9. $\frac{2}{3} = \frac{10}{15}$ _____

10. $\frac{8}{9} = \frac{24}{27}$ _____

11. $\frac{16}{28} = \frac{4}{7}$ _____

12. $\frac{12}{16} = \frac{3}{4}$ _____

13. $\frac{3}{8} = \frac{9}{24}$ _____

14. $\frac{2}{5} = \frac{12}{30}$ _____

15. $\frac{3}{7} = \frac{9}{21}$ _____

16. $\frac{8}{28} = \frac{2}{7}$ _____

Answer Box

| $\frac{9}{21}$ | $\frac{4}{7}$ | $\frac{2}{5}$ | $\frac{1}{3}$ | $\frac{35}{45}$ | $\frac{10}{15}$ | $\frac{24}{27}$ | $\frac{15}{45}$ | $\frac{9}{24}$ | $\frac{12}{30}$ | $\frac{3}{5}$ | $\frac{2}{3}$ | $\frac{2}{7}$ | $\frac{3}{4}$ | $\frac{20}{50}$ | $\frac{12}{32}$ |

178

RETEACH

When you find an equivalent fraction, be sure only to use multiplication or division.

Problem: | Find an equivalent fraction for $\frac{12}{16}$.

$$\overset{\div 4}{\overbrace{\frac{12}{16} = \frac{3}{4}}}_{\div 4}$$

$$\overset{\times 2}{\overbrace{\frac{12}{16} = \frac{24}{32}}}_{\times 2}$$

When finding equivalent fractions, you can either multiply or divide the numerator and the denominator by the same number.

Solve each problem. Make sure each answer appears in the Answer Box.

1.
$$\overset{\div 3}{\overbrace{\frac{6}{9} = \frac{2}{\boxed{3}}}}_{\div 3}$$

2.
$$\overset{\times 2}{\overbrace{\frac{6}{9} = \frac{12}{\boxed{18}}}}_{\times 2}$$

3.
$$\overset{\div 2}{\overbrace{\frac{4}{18} = \frac{2}{\boxed{9}}}}_{\div 2}$$

Complete. Make sure each answer appears in the Answer Box.

4. $\frac{15}{30} = \frac{5}{10}$

5. $\frac{3}{6} = \frac{9}{18}$

6. $\frac{2}{5} = \frac{4}{10}$

7. $\frac{4}{8} = \frac{12}{24}$

8. $\frac{12}{30} = \frac{2}{5}$

9. $\frac{7}{12} = \frac{21}{36}$

10. $\frac{5}{12} = \frac{10}{24}$

11. $\frac{12}{24} = \frac{3}{6}$

12. $\frac{4}{16} = \frac{1}{4}$

13. $\frac{2}{5} = \frac{8}{20}$

14. $\frac{1}{5} = \frac{3}{15}$

15. $\frac{10}{12} = \frac{5}{6}$

Answer Box

$\frac{2}{9}$	$\frac{12}{18}$	$\frac{9}{18}$	$\frac{8}{20}$	$\frac{12}{24}$	$\frac{10}{24}$	$\frac{1}{4}$	$\frac{5}{6}$	$\frac{2}{5}$	$\frac{3}{15}$	$\frac{4}{10}$	$\frac{21}{36}$	$\frac{3}{6}$	$\frac{2}{3}$	$\frac{5}{10}$

68 ▸ **RETEACH** Performing the Same Operation Twice

When you find equivalent fractions, make sure you multiply or divide both the numerator and denominator by the same number.

Problem: | Find an equivalent fraction for $\frac{4}{12}$.

$$\frac{4}{12} = \frac{1}{3} \quad (\div 4)$$

$$\frac{4}{12} = \frac{16}{48} \quad (\times 4)$$

Multiply or divide the numerator and denominator by the same number.

Complete. Make sure each answer appears in the Answer Box.

1. $\frac{2}{5} = \frac{6}{15}$ ($\times 3$)

2. $\frac{14}{20} = \frac{7}{10}$ ($\div 2$)

3. $\frac{8}{11} = \frac{16}{22}$ ($\times 2$)

4. $\frac{18}{30} = \frac{9}{15}$ ($\div 2$)

5. $\frac{4}{9} = \frac{20}{45}$

6. $\frac{1}{3} = \frac{6}{18}$

7. $\frac{14}{35} = \frac{2}{5}$

8. $\frac{9}{24} = \frac{3}{8}$

9. $\frac{4}{5} = \frac{16}{20}$

10. $\frac{10}{50} = \frac{2}{10}$

11. $\frac{3}{8} = \frac{6}{16}$

12. $\frac{6}{7} = \frac{18}{21}$

13. $\frac{8}{12} = \frac{2}{3}$

14. $\frac{2}{5} = \frac{8}{20}$

15. $\frac{12}{15} = \frac{4}{5}$

16. $\frac{1}{4} = \frac{3}{12}$

17. What must you be sure to do when multiplying or dividing to find and equivalent fraction? __Multiply or divide the numerator__

__and denominator by the same number.__

Answer Box

$\frac{9}{15}$	$\frac{6}{18}$	$\frac{2}{3}$	$\frac{7}{10}$	$\frac{2}{10}$	$\frac{3}{12}$	$\frac{20}{45}$	$\frac{2}{5}$	$\frac{16}{22}$	$\frac{6}{16}$	$\frac{4}{5}$	$\frac{18}{21}$	$\frac{16}{20}$	$\frac{8}{20}$	$\frac{6}{15}$	$\frac{3}{8}$

69 ▲ **RETEACH**

A fraction is in simplest form when the only number that will divide both the numerator and the denominator evenly is 1.

Problem: | Write $\frac{20}{24}$ in simplest form.

List the factors of 20 and 24.
20: 1, 2, ④, 5, 10, 20
24: 1, 2, 3, ④, 6, 8, 12, 24
Greatest common factor (GCF): 4
Divide both the numerator and denominator by the GCF.

$$\frac{20}{24} = \frac{5}{6}$$
÷ 4 ... ÷ 4

You know $\frac{5}{6}$ is in simplest form since 1 is the only number that will divide both the numerator and denominator evenly.

Write each fraction in simplest form. Make sure each answer appears in the Answer Box.

1. $\frac{32}{40}$
factors of 32: 1, 2, 4, ⑧, 16, 32
factors of 40: 1, 2, 4, 5, ⑧, 10, 20, 40
divide by GCF

$$\frac{32}{40} = \frac{4}{5}$$
÷ 8 ... ÷ 8

2. $\frac{8}{28}$
factors of 8: 1, 2, ④, 8
factors of 28: 1, 2, ④, 7, 14, 28
divide by GCF

$$\frac{8}{28} = \frac{2}{7}$$
÷ 4 ... ÷ 4

3. $\frac{16}{18} = \frac{8}{9}$

4. $\frac{10}{20} = \frac{1}{2}$

5. $\frac{20}{25} = \frac{4}{5}$

6. $\frac{24}{40} = \frac{3}{5}$

7. $\frac{24}{30} = \frac{4}{5}$

8. $\frac{10}{40} = \frac{1}{4}$

9. $\frac{30}{45} = \frac{2}{3}$

10. $\frac{9}{24} = \frac{3}{8}$

11. $\frac{9}{27} = \frac{1}{3}$

12. $\frac{6}{16} = \frac{3}{8}$

13. $\frac{15}{18} = \frac{5}{6}$

14. $\frac{10}{18} = \frac{5}{9}$

Answer Box

| $\frac{3}{8}$ | $\frac{4}{5}$ | $\frac{3}{8}$ | $\frac{8}{9}$ | $\frac{4}{5}$ | $\frac{1}{4}$ | $\frac{2}{3}$ | $\frac{3}{5}$ | $\frac{2}{7}$ | $\frac{5}{9}$ | $\frac{5}{6}$ | $\frac{1}{3}$ | $\frac{1}{2}$ | $\frac{4}{5}$ |

181

▶RETEACH   Writing a Fraction in Simplest Form

70

The fastest way to write a fraction in simplest form is to divide by the greatest common factor (GCF).

Problem: | Find the simplest form of $\frac{8}{12}$.

$\frac{8}{12} = \frac{2}{3}$ (÷4 top, ÷4 bottom)

Find the GCF of the numerator and the denominator.
Divide the numerator and denominator by the GCF.

Write each fraction in simplest form. Make sure each answer appears in the Answer Box.

GCF ↓

1. ÷ 3
$\frac{9}{15} = \frac{3}{5}$
÷ 3

GCF ↓

2. ÷ 4
$\frac{8}{36} = \frac{2}{9}$
÷ 4

3. $\frac{6}{22} = \frac{3}{11}$

4. $\frac{5}{20} = \frac{1}{4}$

5. $\frac{10}{12} = \frac{5}{6}$

6. $\frac{9}{27} = \frac{1}{3}$

7. $\frac{15}{30} = \frac{1}{2}$

8. $\frac{16}{24} = \frac{2}{3}$

9. $\frac{9}{15} = \frac{3}{5}$

10. $\frac{7}{21} = \frac{1}{3}$

11. $\frac{5}{30} = \frac{1}{6}$

12. $\frac{5}{45} = \frac{1}{9}$

13. $\frac{8}{16} = \frac{1}{2}$

14. $\frac{8}{12} = \frac{2}{3}$

15. What should you do after you find the greatest common factor?

   __Divide both numerator and denominator by that number.__

Answer Box

| $\frac{1}{3}$ | $\frac{2}{9}$ | $\frac{1}{4}$ | $\frac{2}{3}$ | $\frac{1}{3}$ | $\frac{3}{5}$ | $\frac{3}{5}$ | $\frac{1}{9}$ | $\frac{3}{11}$ | $\frac{1}{2}$ | $\frac{1}{6}$ | $\frac{5}{6}$ | $\frac{1}{2}$ | $\frac{2}{3}$ |

RETEACH

71

The simplest form of a fraction does not always have 1 as the numerator.

Problem: | Find the simplest form of $\frac{9}{15}$.

$\frac{9}{15} = \frac{3}{5}$ (÷3)

- Make sure to divide the numerator and the denominator by their greatest common factor.

- The GCF of 9 and 15 is 3.

$\frac{3}{9} = \frac{1}{3}$ (÷3)

- The numerator can be 1 only when the numerator is a factor of the denominator.

Write the simplest form. Make sure each answer appears in the Answer Box.

1. (÷4) $\frac{8}{12} = \frac{\boxed{2}}{\boxed{3}}$ (÷4)

2. (÷3) $\frac{6}{15} = \frac{\boxed{2}}{\boxed{5}}$ (÷3)

3. (÷3) $\frac{3}{12} = \frac{\boxed{1}}{\boxed{4}}$ (÷3)

4. $\frac{6}{8} = \frac{3}{4}$

5. $\frac{8}{20} = \frac{2}{5}$

6. $\frac{14}{21} = \frac{2}{3}$

7. $\frac{8}{10} = \frac{4}{5}$

8. $\frac{18}{30} = \frac{3}{5}$

9. $\frac{15}{24} = \frac{5}{8}$

10. $\frac{16}{20} = \frac{4}{5}$

11. $\frac{8}{14} = \frac{4}{7}$

12. $\frac{15}{27} = \frac{5}{9}$

13. $\frac{15}{21} = \frac{5}{7}$

14. $\frac{10}{12} = \frac{5}{6}$

15. $\frac{4}{10} = \frac{2}{5}$

Answer Box

| $\frac{2}{5}$ | $\frac{2}{3}$ | $\frac{1}{4}$ | $\frac{5}{7}$ | $\frac{4}{5}$ | $\frac{3}{4}$ | $\frac{4}{7}$ | $\frac{2}{3}$ | $\frac{5}{6}$ | $\frac{2}{5}$ | $\frac{5}{8}$ | $\frac{5}{9}$ | $\frac{3}{5}$ | $\frac{2}{5}$ | $\frac{4}{5}$ |

9.7 ANOTHER LOOK

Whole Numbers and Mixed Numbers

All whole numbers and mixed numbers can be written as fractions.
Look at these four examples:

- Three parts of the thirds Fraction Bar are shaded. Three thirds equal 1 whole bar.

  You can write this as 1 or $\frac{3}{3}$.

  $$1 = \frac{3}{3}$$

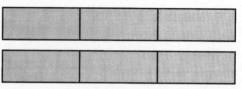

- Six parts of the thirds Fraction Bars are shaded. Six thirds equal 2 whole bars.

  You can write this as 2 or $\frac{6}{3}$.

  $$2 = \frac{6}{3}$$

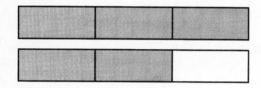

- Five parts of the thirds Fraction Bars are shaded. You can write this as $1\frac{2}{3}$ or $\frac{5}{3}$.

  $$1\frac{2}{3} = \frac{5}{3}$$

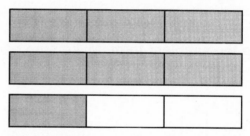

- Seven parts of the thirds Fraction Bars are shaded. You can write this as $2\frac{1}{3}$ or $\frac{7}{3}$.

  $$2\frac{1}{3} = \frac{7}{3}$$

**Use Fraction Bars to show the whole number or mixed number.
Then complete.**

1. $1 = \frac{\boxed{5}}{5}$

2. $4 = \frac{\boxed{20}}{5}$

3. $2\frac{3}{5} = \frac{\boxed{13}}{5}$

4. $3\frac{4}{5} = \frac{\boxed{19}}{5}$

5. $2 = \frac{\boxed{12}}{6}$

6. $10 = \frac{\boxed{60}}{6}$

7. $3\frac{5}{6} = \frac{\boxed{23}}{6}$

8. $5\frac{1}{6} = \frac{\boxed{31}}{6}$

9. $2 = \frac{\boxed{16}}{8}$

10. $6 = \frac{\boxed{48}}{8}$

11. $4\frac{3}{8} = \frac{\boxed{35}}{8}$

12. $5\frac{1}{8} = \frac{\boxed{41}}{8}$

9.8 ► ANOTHER LOOK

Writing Fractions

All whole numbers can be written as fractions. For example,
look at these Fraction Bars:

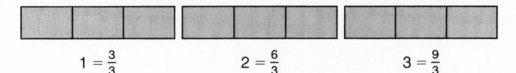

$$1 = \frac{3}{3} \qquad\qquad 2 = \frac{6}{3} \qquad\qquad 3 = \frac{9}{3}$$

You can think of 1 Fraction Bar as $\frac{3}{3}$, 2 Fraction Bars as $\frac{6}{3}$,
and 3 Fraction Bars as $\frac{9}{3}$.

To write a whole number as a fraction with a given denominator,
multiply the denominator by the whole number to find the numerator.

$$4 = \frac{\square}{5} \qquad \boxed{5 \times 4 = 20} \qquad 4 = \frac{20}{5} \qquad\bigg|\qquad 6 = \frac{\square}{2} \qquad \boxed{2 \times 6 = 12} \qquad 6 = \frac{12}{2}$$

$$2 = \frac{\square}{7} \qquad \boxed{7 \times 2 = 14} \qquad 2 = \frac{14}{7} \qquad\bigg|\qquad 1 = \frac{\square}{9} \qquad \boxed{9 \times 1 = 9} \qquad 1 = \frac{9}{9}$$

Complete each fraction equivalent.

1. $2 = \dfrac{\boxed{8}}{4}$

2. $3 = \dfrac{\boxed{36}}{12}$

3. $4 = \dfrac{\boxed{40}}{10}$

4. $7 = \dfrac{\boxed{14}}{2}$

5. $5 = \dfrac{\boxed{35}}{7}$

6. $9 = \dfrac{\boxed{27}}{3}$

7. $20 = \dfrac{\boxed{100}}{5}$

8. $2 = \dfrac{\boxed{22}}{11}$

9. $12 = \dfrac{\boxed{60}}{5}$

10. $4 = \dfrac{\boxed{32}}{8}$

9.9 ► ANOTHER LOOK

Writing Mixed Numbers

You can write a fraction greater than 1 as a whole number or as a mixed number.

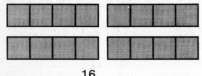

$$\frac{16}{4} = 4$$

The fraction is written as a whole number because 16 can be divided by 4 evenly.

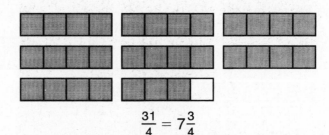

$$\frac{31}{4} = 7\frac{3}{4}$$

The fraction is written as a mixed number because 31 ÷ 4 leaves a remainder of 3.

Color the circles to show each fraction. Answer each question.

1.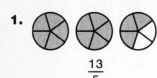

$$\frac{13}{5}$$

   a. Have you colored all whole circles? _____**No**_____

   b. Write this fraction as a mixed number. _____$2\frac{3}{5}$_____

2.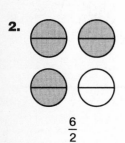

$$\frac{6}{2}$$

   a. Have you colored all whole circles? _____**Yes**_____

   b. Write this fraction as whole number. _____**3**_____

Write each fraction as a mixed number.

3. $\frac{12}{5}$

   12 ÷ 5 = $\boxed{2}$ R $\boxed{2}$

   $\boxed{2}\dfrac{\boxed{2}}{5}$

4. $\frac{19}{6}$

   19 ÷ 6 = $\boxed{3}$ R $\boxed{1}$

   $\boxed{3}\dfrac{\boxed{1}}{6}$

5. $\frac{27}{4}$

   27 ÷ 4 = $\boxed{6}$ R $\boxed{3}$

   $\boxed{6}\dfrac{\boxed{3}}{4}$

6. $\frac{31}{9}$

   31 ÷ 9 = $\boxed{3}$ R $\boxed{4}$

   $\boxed{3}\dfrac{\boxed{4}}{9}$

Name_____ Date_____

9.10 ANOTHER LOOK

Comparing and Ordering

You can use Fraction Bars to compare and order unlike fractions.

• Here is a way to compare $\frac{2}{3}$, $\frac{5}{6}$, and $\frac{1}{2}$.

Line up the Fraction Bars to see which bar has the least amount shaded and which has the greatest amount shaded. You can see that the $\frac{1}{2}$ bar has the least amount shaded, and the $\frac{5}{6}$ bar has the greatest amount shaded. So, $\frac{1}{2} < \frac{2}{3} < \frac{5}{6}$.

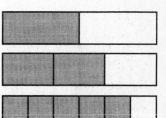

• Here is another way to compare $\frac{2}{3}$, $\frac{5}{6}$, and $\frac{1}{2}$.

Find the least common multiple (LCM) of the denominators.

2: 2, 4, **6**, 8 . . . . . .
6: **6**, 12, 18 . . . . . .
3: 3, **6**, 9, 12 . . . . .

The LCM of 2, 6, and 3 is 6. Write equivalent fractions with the least common denominator. $\frac{1}{2} = \frac{3}{6}$ $\frac{2}{3} = \frac{4}{6}$

Order from least to greatest: $\frac{3}{6} < \frac{4}{6} < \frac{5}{6}$. So, $\frac{1}{2} < \frac{2}{3} < \frac{5}{6}$.

Compare. Write >, <, or =. Use Fraction Bars if it helps.

1. $\frac{2}{8}$ $\boxed{<}$ $\frac{3}{4}$ **2.** $2\frac{1}{2}$ $\boxed{=}$ $2\frac{6}{12}$ **3.** $\frac{4}{5}$ $\boxed{>}$ $\frac{7}{10}$ **4.** $5\frac{1}{3}$ $\boxed{<}$ $5\frac{5}{12}$

Write the least common denominator for each pair of numbers.

5. $\frac{1}{3}$ and $\frac{2}{9}$ ___9___   **6.** $\frac{1}{2}$ and $\frac{2}{7}$ ___14___   **7.** $\frac{2}{3}$ and $\frac{3}{4}$ ___12___   **8.** $\frac{8}{27}$ and $\frac{4}{9}$ ___27___

Write the numbers in order from least to greatest.

9. $\frac{2}{5}$, $\frac{3}{10}$, $\frac{1}{2}$ **10.** $\frac{5}{6}$, $\frac{8}{12}$, $\frac{3}{4}$ **11.** $\frac{7}{8}$, $\frac{1}{4}$, $\frac{3}{8}$ **12.** $\frac{1}{2}$, $\frac{1}{3}$, $\frac{4}{6}$

$\frac{3}{10}, \frac{2}{5}, \frac{1}{2}$ $\frac{8}{12}, \frac{3}{4}, \frac{5}{6}$ $\frac{1}{4}, \frac{3}{8}, \frac{7}{8}$ $\frac{1}{3}, \frac{1}{2}, \frac{4}{6}$

Name_____ Date_____

9.11 ANOTHER LOOK

··

Equivalent Forms

You can write any fraction as a decimal.

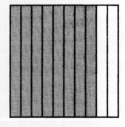

$$\frac{8}{10} = 0.8$$

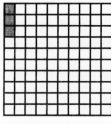

$$\frac{3}{100} = 0.03$$

Some fractions can be rewritten as equivalent fractions with

denominators of 10, 100, or 1000. For example, $\frac{3}{50}$.

• Multiply the numerator and the
denominator by the same number to find
an equivalent fraction with a denominator
of 10, 100, or 1000.

$$\overset{\times 2}{\underset{\times 2}{\frac{3}{50}}} = \frac{6}{100}$$

• Write the equivalent fraction as a decimal.

$$\frac{6}{100} = 0.06$$

──

Write each fraction as a decimal. The first one is done for you.

1. $\frac{1}{2} =$ ___0.5___

$$\overset{\times 5}{\underset{\times 5}{\frac{1}{2}}} = \frac{5}{10}$$

2. $\frac{3}{4} =$ ___0.75___

$$\overset{\times \boxed{25}}{\underset{\times \boxed{25}}{\frac{3}{4}}} = \frac{\boxed{75}}{100}$$

3. $\frac{6}{25} =$ ___0.24___

$$\overset{\times \boxed{4}}{\underset{\times \boxed{4}}{\frac{6}{25}}} = \frac{\boxed{24}}{100}$$

4. $\frac{70}{200} =$ ___0.350___

$$\overset{\times \boxed{5}}{\underset{\times \boxed{5}}{\frac{70}{200}}} = \frac{\boxed{350}}{1000}$$

5. $\frac{4}{20} =$ ___0.20___

6. $\frac{2}{5} =$ ___0.4___

7. $\frac{5}{200} =$ ___0.025___

8. $\frac{30}{250} =$ ___0.120___

Circle the letter of the decimal equivalent for each fraction.

9. $\frac{3}{10}$

   a. 3.0

   b. 0.03

   c. 0.3 ⬅circled

10. $\frac{9}{20}$

   a. 0.45 ⬅circled

   b. 4.5

   c. 0.045

11. $\frac{3}{5}$

   a. 0.6 ⬅circled

   b. 0.06

   c. 6.0

12. $\frac{6}{100}$

   a. 0.6

   b. 0.06 ⬅circled

   c. 0.006

9.12 ANOTHER LOOK

Fractions and Decimals

You can write a fraction as a decimal or a decimal as a fraction.

- One way to write equivalent decimals for fractions and mixed numbers is by dividing.

Write $\frac{1}{4}$ as a decimal. Divide the numerator by the denominator.

$$\begin{array}{r} 0.25 \\ 4\overline{)1.00} \\ -\ 80 \\ \hline 20 \\ -\ 20 \\ \hline 0 \end{array}$$

so, $\frac{1}{4} = 0.25$

Write $1\frac{3}{5}$ as a decimal. Find the decimal equivalent of the fractional part of the number. Add it to the whole number.

$$\begin{array}{r} 0.6 \\ 5\overline{)3.0} \\ -\ 30 \\ \hline 0 \end{array}$$

$1 + 0.6 = 1.6$

so, $1\frac{3}{5} = 1.6$

- You can also write a decimal as a fraction or a mixed number.

Write 0.75 as a fraction.

$0.75 = \frac{75}{100} = \frac{3}{4}$

Write 4.3 as a mixed number.

$4.3 = 4\frac{3}{10}$

Write each number as a decimal.

1. $\frac{2}{5} = $ ___0.4___

$$\begin{array}{r} 0.4 \\ 5\overline{)2.0} \\ -2\ 0 \\ \hline 0 \end{array}$$

2. $2\frac{3}{4} = $ ___2.75___

$$\begin{array}{r} 0.75 \\ 4\overline{)3.0\ 0} \\ -2\ 8 \\ \hline 2\ 0 \\ -2\ 0 \\ \hline 0 \end{array}$$

3. $\frac{7}{8} = $ ___0.875___

$$\begin{array}{r} 0.875 \\ 8\overline{)7.0\ 0\ 0} \\ -6\ 4 \\ \hline 6\ 0 \\ -5\ 6 \\ \hline 4\ 0 \\ -4\ 0 \\ \hline 0 \end{array}$$

4. $3\frac{1}{2} = $ ___3.5___

$$\begin{array}{r} 0.5 \\ 2\overline{)1.0} \\ -1\ 0 \\ \hline 0 \end{array}$$

Write the decimal as a fraction or mixed number in simplest form.

5. $0.15 = $ ___$\frac{3}{20}$___

6. $4.4 = $ ___$4\frac{2}{5}$___

7. $7.6 = $ ___$7\frac{3}{5}$___

8. $0.045 = $ ___$\frac{9}{200}$___

Name _____ Date _____

9.13 ANOTHER LOOK

Problem Solving: **Using Strategies**

You are studying reptiles. Your book features 35 different reptiles. Five are lizards, $\frac{1}{2}$ of the remaining reptiles are turtles, 2 are crocodiles, and 3 are dinosaurs. The reptiles that are left are snakes. How many snakes are featured in the book?

1. Understand

- You know the total number of reptiles in the book.
- You know the number of lizards, turtles, crocodiles, and dinosaurs.

2. Plan

- You can use an object to represent each reptile.
- You need a total of 35 objects to represent the reptiles.

3. Try It

- Line up the 35 objects. Remove 5 because 5 of the reptiles are lizards. You are left with 30 objects: $35 - 5 = 30$.
- Take $\frac{1}{2}$ of 30, because $\frac{1}{2}$ of the remaining reptiles are turtles: $\frac{1}{2} \times 30 = 15$. You have 15 remaining objects: $30 - 15 = 15$.
- Remove 2 objects from the 15, because 2 of the reptiles are crocodiles: $15 - 2 = 13$.
- Remove 3 more, because 3 are dinosaurs: $13 - 3 = 10$.

4. Look Back

- There are 10 objects remaining, so 10 reptiles are snakes.

Use any strategy to solve.

1. You have 7 h today for activities. You spend 1 h riding your bike. You spend 2 h at the movies. Half of the remaining time is spent doing homework. Half of the rest of your day is spent weeding the garden. How much time do you have left? _____ **1 h** _____

2. You have 6 weeks to get in shape. The first week, you swim 15 laps a day. The second week, you swim 20 laps a day. The third week, you swim 25 laps a day. If you continue this pattern for the next 3 weeks, how many total laps will you have swum over the entire 6 weeks? _____ **1155 laps** _____

190

72 **RETEACH**   **Writing Mixed Numbers as Fractions**

There are three steps used to write a mixed number as a fraction.

Problem: | Write $4\frac{6}{7}$ as a fraction.

$$4\frac{6}{7} = \frac{34}{7}$$

- Multiply the denominator by the whole number.
- Add the numerator to that product.
- Write that sum over the denominator.

Write each mixed number as a fraction. Make sure each answer appears in the Answer Box.

1. $9\frac{1}{3} = \dfrac{28}{3}$ _____

2. $6\frac{2}{4} = \dfrac{26}{4}$ _____

3. $7\frac{5}{6} = \dfrac{47}{6}$ _____

4. $2\frac{1}{3} = \dfrac{7}{3}$ _____

5. $6\frac{1}{2} = \dfrac{13}{2}$ _____

6. $4\frac{1}{5} = \dfrac{21}{5}$ _____

7. $3\frac{1}{5} = \dfrac{16}{5}$ _____

8. $3\frac{1}{2} = \dfrac{7}{2}$ _____

9. $3\frac{4}{5} = \dfrac{19}{5}$ _____

10. $4\frac{3}{5} = \dfrac{23}{5}$ _____

11. $3\frac{3}{4} = \dfrac{15}{4}$ _____

12. $2\frac{3}{4} = \dfrac{11}{4}$ _____

13. What are the three steps necessary when writing a mixed number as a fraction? _____ Multiply the whole number and denominator, add the numerator, and write the sum over the denominator.

Answer Box

$\frac{7}{2}$	$\frac{7}{3}$	$\frac{47}{6}$	$\frac{19}{5}$	$\frac{23}{5}$	$\frac{26}{4}$	$\frac{28}{3}$	$\frac{21}{5}$	$\frac{11}{4}$	$\frac{15}{4}$	$\frac{13}{2}$	$\frac{16}{5}$

191

RETEACH
73

Sometimes it is necessary to write a mixed number as a fraction greater than 1.

Problem: Write $4\frac{6}{7}$ as a fraction.

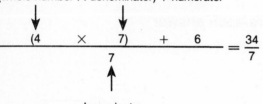

$4\frac{6}{7} = ?$

$$\frac{(4 \times 7) + 6}{7} = \frac{34}{7}$$

(whole number × denominator) + numerator

denominator

- Multiply the whole number by the denominator.
- Add the numerator to the product.
- Write the sum over the denominator.

$4\frac{6}{7} = \frac{34}{7}$

Write each number as a mixed fraction. Make sure each answer appears in the Answer Box.

1. $9\frac{1}{3} = \frac{(9 \times 3) + 1}{3} = \underline{\frac{28}{3}}$

2. $6\frac{2}{4} = \frac{(6 \times 4) + 2}{4} = \underline{\frac{26}{4}}$

3. $4\frac{1}{2} = \underline{\frac{9}{2}}$

4. $4\frac{2}{3} = \underline{\frac{14}{3}}$

5. $2\frac{1}{3} = \underline{\frac{7}{3}}$

6. $2\frac{3}{5} = \underline{\frac{13}{5}}$

7. $7\frac{1}{4} = \underline{\frac{29}{4}}$

8. $3\frac{2}{5} = \underline{\frac{17}{5}}$

9. $4\frac{3}{4} = \underline{\frac{19}{4}}$

10. $5\frac{1}{6} = \underline{\frac{31}{6}}$

11. $4\frac{3}{8} = \underline{\frac{35}{8}}$

12. $8\frac{1}{3} = \underline{\frac{25}{3}}$

13. $9\frac{2}{3} = \underline{\frac{29}{3}}$

14. $3\frac{2}{3} = \underline{\frac{11}{3}}$

Answer Box

$\frac{14}{3}$	$\frac{26}{4}$	$\frac{7}{3}$	$\frac{9}{2}$	$\frac{29}{4}$	$\frac{28}{3}$	$\frac{19}{4}$	$\frac{35}{8}$	$\frac{29}{3}$	$\frac{17}{5}$	$\frac{31}{6}$	$\frac{11}{3}$	$\frac{13}{5}$	$\frac{25}{3}$

74 ► **RETEACH**   Writing Fractions as Mixed Numbers

Remember that the way to change a fraction greater than 1 to a mixed number is to divide.

Problem: Write $\frac{23}{7}$ as a mixed number.

$\frac{23}{7}$ ◄— ÷   Remember that the fraction bar means divide.

$$
\begin{array}{r}
3 \\
7\overline{)23} \\
-21 \\
\hline
2
\end{array}
$$
Divide the numerator by the denominator.
Write the quotient as the whole number part of the mixed number.

$\frac{23}{7} = 3\frac{2}{7}$ Write the remainder over the divisor for the fraction part.

Change each fraction to a mixed number. Make sure each answer appears in the Answer Box.

1. $\frac{15}{8}$ ◄— ÷ $8\overline{)15}$
$$
\begin{array}{r}
1 \\
8\overline{)15} \\
8 \\
\hline
7
\end{array}
$$
$\frac{15}{8} =$ __$1\frac{7}{8}$__

2. $\frac{27}{8}$ ◄— ÷ $8\overline{)27}$
$$
\begin{array}{r}
3 \\
8\overline{)27} \\
24 \\
\hline
3
\end{array}
$$
$\frac{27}{8} =$ __$3\frac{3}{8}$__

3. $\frac{17}{4}$ ◄— ÷ $4\overline{)17}$
$$
\begin{array}{r}
4 \\
4\overline{)17} \\
16 \\
\hline
1
\end{array}
$$
$\frac{17}{4} =$ __$4\frac{1}{4}$__

4. $\frac{21}{5} =$ __$4\frac{1}{5}$__   5. $\frac{7}{3} =$ __$2\frac{1}{3}$__   6. $\frac{9}{5} =$ __$1\frac{4}{5}$__   7. $\frac{11}{6} =$ __$1\frac{5}{6}$__   8. $\frac{28}{5} =$ __$5\frac{3}{5}$__

9. $\frac{16}{9} =$ __$1\frac{7}{9}$__   10. $\frac{12}{5} =$ __$2\frac{2}{5}$__   11. $\frac{16}{3} =$ __$5\frac{1}{3}$__   12. $\frac{33}{8} =$ __$4\frac{1}{8}$__   13. $\frac{8}{3} =$ __$2\frac{2}{3}$__

14. When changing a fraction to a mixed number, what do you do with the remainder?
    __Use it as the numerator of the fraction part.__

Answer Box

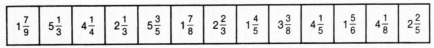

| $1\frac{7}{9}$ | $5\frac{1}{3}$ | $4\frac{1}{4}$ | $2\frac{1}{3}$ | $5\frac{3}{5}$ | $1\frac{7}{8}$ | $2\frac{2}{3}$ | $1\frac{4}{5}$ | $3\frac{3}{8}$ | $4\frac{1}{5}$ | $1\frac{5}{6}$ | $4\frac{1}{8}$ | $2\frac{2}{5}$ |

RETEACH
75

Be sure a mixed number is in simplest form when you write it.

Problem: Write $\frac{56}{12}$ as a mixed number in simplest form.

• Write the mixed number. $\frac{56}{12} = 4\frac{8}{12}$

• Then look at the fraction part. Do the numerator and denominator have any common factors?

(8 and 12 are both divisible by 2 and 4.)

• Divide the numerator and the denominator by the greatest common factor.

$$\frac{8}{12} \overset{\div 4}{\underset{\div 4}{=}} \frac{2}{3}$$

• So, $\frac{56}{12} = 4\frac{8}{12} = 4\frac{2}{3}$

Write each mixed number in simplest form. Make sure each answer appears in the Answer Box.

1. $3\frac{6}{9}$ $\frac{6}{9} \overset{\div 3}{\underset{\div 3}{=}} \frac{\boxed{2}}{\boxed{3}}$ **Mixed number:** $3\frac{2}{3}$

2. $4\frac{15}{20}$ $\frac{15}{20} \overset{\div 5}{\underset{\div 5}{=}} \frac{\boxed{3}}{\boxed{4}}$ **Mixed number:** $4\frac{3}{4}$

3. $2\frac{2}{4}$ $\frac{2}{4} \overset{\div 2}{\underset{\div 2}{=}} \frac{\boxed{1}}{\boxed{2}}$ **Mixed number:** $2\frac{1}{2}$

4. $6\frac{5}{10}$ $\frac{5}{10} \overset{\div 5}{\underset{\div 5}{=}} \frac{\boxed{1}}{\boxed{2}}$ **Mixed number:** $6\frac{1}{2}$

5. $7\frac{3}{12}$ $7\frac{1}{4}$ _____

6. $4\frac{3}{9}$ $4\frac{1}{3}$ _____

7. $9\frac{6}{8}$ $9\frac{3}{4}$ _____

8. $2\frac{5}{20}$ $2\frac{1}{4}$ _____

9. $8\frac{3}{12}$ $8\frac{1}{4}$ _____

10. $9\frac{2}{8}$ $9\frac{1}{4}$ _____

11. $5\frac{3}{6}$ $5\frac{1}{2}$ _____

12. $8\frac{4}{6}$ $8\frac{2}{3}$ _____

13. $9\frac{4}{12}$ $9\frac{1}{3}$ _____

14. $3\frac{8}{10}$ $3\frac{4}{5}$ _____

15. $1\frac{6}{12}$ $1\frac{1}{2}$ _____

16. $7\frac{2}{6}$ $7\frac{1}{3}$ _____

Answer Box

| $3\frac{4}{5}$ | $4\frac{1}{3}$ | $5\frac{1}{2}$ | $2\frac{1}{4}$ | $3\frac{2}{3}$ | $9\frac{1}{4}$ | $8\frac{2}{3}$ | $1\frac{1}{2}$ | $7\frac{1}{3}$ | $4\frac{3}{4}$ | $8\frac{1}{4}$ | $9\frac{1}{3}$ | $7\frac{1}{4}$ | $2\frac{1}{2}$ | $9\frac{3}{4}$ | $6\frac{1}{2}$ |

76 RETEACH

Comparing and Ordering

To compare or order fractions that have different denominators, such as $\frac{3}{4}$ and $\frac{4}{5}$, use equivalent fractions.

Problem: | Which is greater, $\frac{3}{4}$ or $\frac{4}{5}$?

multiples of 4: 4, 8, 12, 16, ⓪20 | The first step is to find the **least common multiple** of the denominators.
multiples of 5: 5, 10, 15, ⓪20

$\frac{3}{4} = \frac{?}{20}$

$\frac{3 \times 5}{4 \times 5} = \frac{15}{⑳20}$

Use the least common multiple as the **least common denominator.**
Write equivalent fractions with the least common denominator.

$\frac{4}{5} = \frac{?}{20}$ $\quad \frac{4 \times 4}{5 \times 4} = \frac{16}{⑳20}$

$16 > 15$, so $\frac{16}{20} > \frac{15}{20}$ and $\frac{4}{5} > \frac{3}{4}$. | Now compare the numerators.

Compare these fractions. Use >, <, or =.

1. $\frac{2}{3} \underline{<} \frac{3}{4}$

multiples of 3: 3, 6, 9, ⑫12
multiples of 4: 4, 8, ⑫12, 16

$\frac{2}{3} = \frac{8}{⑫12} \quad \frac{3}{4} = \frac{9}{⑫12}$

2. $\frac{2}{5} \underline{>} \frac{1}{8}$

multiples of 5: 5, 10, 15, 20, 25, 30, 35, ㊵40

multiples of 8: 8, 16, 24, 32, ㊵40

$\frac{2}{5} = \frac{16}{40} \quad \frac{1}{8} = \frac{5}{40}$

3. $\frac{4}{6} \underline{>} \frac{3}{5}$

4. $\frac{3}{4} \underline{<} \frac{4}{5}$

5. $\frac{5}{12} \underline{>} \frac{3}{10}$

6. $\frac{4}{5} \underline{>} \frac{3}{8}$

7. $\frac{5}{8} \underline{<} \frac{4}{5}$

8. $\frac{7}{10} \underline{>} \frac{2}{3}$

9. $\frac{3}{4} \underline{=} \frac{6}{8}$

10. $\frac{6}{9} \underline{<} \frac{4}{5}$

Subtract the number of = you wrote from the number of > you wrote in exercises 3–10. The answer will be the number of wheels on a tricycle. _____ **3 wheels** _____

To compare a mixed number and a decimal, you can write the mixed number as a decimal.

Problem: | Write an equivalent decimal for $\frac{4}{5}$.

$$\begin{array}{r} 0\,.\,8 \\ 5\overline{)4\,.\,0} \\ \underline{4\;\;0} \\ 0 \end{array}$$

To write an equivalent decimal for a fraction, divide the numerator by the denominator.

Keep dividing until there is no remainder.

$\frac{4}{5} = 0.8$

$2\frac{4}{5} = 2.8$

If you have a mixed number, you only need to write an equivalent decimal for the fraction part. The whole number stays the same.

Write an equivalent decimal for each fraction. Make sure each answer appears in the Answer Box.

1. $\frac{3}{4} =$ __0.75__

$$\begin{array}{r} 0\,.\,75 \\ 4\overline{)3.00} \\ -2\;8 \\ \hline 20 \\ -20 \\ \hline 0 \end{array}$$

2. $\frac{7}{8} =$ __0.875__

$$\begin{array}{r} 0\,.\,875 \\ 8\overline{)7.0} \\ -6\;4 \\ \hline 60 \\ -56 \\ \hline 40 \\ -40 \\ \hline 0 \end{array}$$

3. $1\frac{1}{2} =$ __1.5__

$$\begin{array}{r} 0\,.\,5 \\ 2\overline{)1.0} \\ -1\;0 \\ \hline 0 \end{array}$$

4. $2\frac{2}{5} =$ __2.4__

5. $\frac{5}{8} =$ __0.625__

6. $\frac{1}{8} =$ __0.125__

7. $3\frac{1}{4} =$ __3.25__

8. $1\frac{3}{10} =$ __1.3__

9. $\frac{4}{5} =$ __0.8__

10. $\frac{3}{8} =$ __0.375__

11. $5\frac{1}{5} =$ __5.2__

Answer Box

1.3	0.875	2.4	0.625	0.75	3.25	0.125	0.375	1.5	5.2	0.8

10.1 ANOTHER LOOK

Fractions with Like Denominators

You can model addition and subtraction of fractions
with the same denominators.

Add: $\frac{4}{10} + \frac{2}{10}$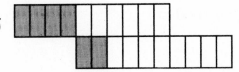

• Check that the denominators are the same.	• Add the numerators.	• Simplify if you can.
$\frac{4}{10} + \frac{2}{10}$	$\frac{4}{10} + \frac{2}{10} = \frac{6}{10}$	$\frac{6}{10} = \frac{3}{5}$

Subtract: $\frac{4}{10} - \frac{2}{10}$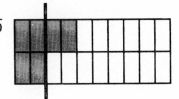

• Check that the denominators are the same.	• Subtract the numerators.	• Simplify if you can.
$\frac{4}{10} - \frac{2}{10}$	$\frac{4}{10} - \frac{2}{10} = \frac{2}{10}$	$\frac{2}{10} = \frac{1}{5}$

Write the answer in simplest form. Use Fraction Bars when it helps.

1. $\frac{2}{5} + \frac{1}{5} = \underline{\frac{3}{5}}$

2. $\frac{5}{6} - \frac{2}{6} = \underline{\frac{1}{2}}$

3. $\frac{3}{9} + \frac{2}{9} = \underline{\frac{5}{9}}$

4. $\frac{7}{8} - \frac{4}{8} = \underline{\frac{3}{8}}$

5. $\frac{4}{10} + \frac{5}{10} = \underline{\frac{9}{10}}$

6. $\frac{6}{7} - \frac{5}{7} = \underline{\frac{1}{7}}$

7. $\frac{3}{4} + \frac{3}{4} = \underline{1\frac{1}{2}}$

8. $\frac{9}{12} - \frac{5}{12} = \underline{\frac{1}{3}}$

9. $\frac{3}{8} + \frac{7}{8} = \underline{1\frac{1}{4}}$

10. $\frac{15}{16} - \frac{3}{16} = \underline{\frac{3}{4}}$

11. $\frac{8}{9} + \frac{7}{9} = \underline{1\frac{2}{3}}$

12. $\frac{7}{10} - \frac{5}{10} = \underline{\frac{1}{5}}$

13. $\frac{5}{8} + \frac{7}{8} = \underline{1\frac{1}{2}}$

14. $\frac{9}{10} - \frac{3}{10} = \underline{\frac{3}{5}}$

15. $\frac{5}{12} + \frac{11}{12} = \underline{1\frac{1}{3}}$

16. $\frac{8}{9} - \frac{2}{9} = \underline{\frac{2}{3}}$

10.2 ANOTHER LOOK

Estimating Fractions

You do not always need an exact answer to a problem. Sometimes an estimate is enough.

To estimate sums and differences of fractions, you need to know whether a fraction is close to 0, $\frac{1}{2}$, or 1.

Look at the Fraction Bars below.

- This bar shows $\frac{1}{12}$.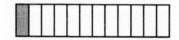

The denominator, 12, is much larger than the numerator, 1. When the denominator of a fraction is much larger than the numerator, the fraction is close to 0.

- This bar shows $\frac{7}{12}$.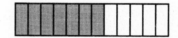

The numerator, 7, is about one half the denominator, 12. The fraction is close to $\frac{1}{2}$.

- This bar shows $\frac{10}{12}$.

The numerator, 10, and the denominator, 12, are close to each other. When the numerator and denominator of a fraction are close in value, the fraction is close to 1. This is true even if the numerator is larger than the denominator.

Estimate the fraction as close to 0, $\frac{1}{2}$, or 1. Use Fraction Bars when it helps.

1. $\frac{5}{6}$ _____ 1 _____   2. $\frac{7}{12}$ _____ $\frac{1}{2}$ _____   3. $\frac{9}{16}$ _____ $\frac{1}{2}$ _____   4. $\frac{3}{50}$ _____ 0 _____

5. $\frac{2}{10}$ _____ 0 _____   6. $\frac{1}{5}$ _____ 0 _____   7. $\frac{17}{20}$ _____ 1 _____   8. $\frac{46}{100}$ _____ $\frac{1}{2}$ _____

Estimate the answer. Use Fraction Bars when it helps.

9. $\frac{2}{12} + \frac{3}{5}$ _____ $\frac{1}{2}$ 10. $\frac{2}{10} + \frac{10}{12}$ _____ 1   11. $\frac{9}{20} + \frac{5}{6}$ _____ $1\frac{1}{2}$ 12. $\frac{18}{20} + \frac{4}{10}$ _____ $1\frac{1}{2}$

13. $\frac{5}{6} - \frac{6}{10}$ _____ $\frac{1}{2}$ 14. $\frac{13}{12} - \frac{1}{6}$ _____ 1   15. $\frac{14}{25} - \frac{2}{9}$ _____ $\frac{1}{2}$ 16. $\frac{17}{30} + \frac{2}{11}$ _____ $\frac{1}{2}$

Name_____ Date_____

Fractions with Unlike Denominators

To add or subtract fractions with unlike denominators, you need to rewrite the fractions so they have like denominators. You can use Fraction Bars to find equivalent fractions.

Add $\frac{1}{2} + \frac{5}{8}$:

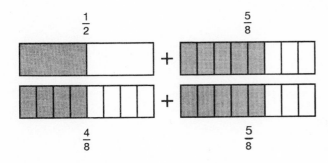

Remember, LCD means least common denominator.

• Find the LCD of $\frac{1}{2}$ and $\frac{5}{8}$.

• Write equivalent fractions using the LCD.

• Add. Simplify if you can:

$\frac{4}{8} + \frac{5}{8} = \frac{9}{8}$, or $1\frac{1}{8}$

Subtract $\frac{1}{3} - \frac{1}{4}$:

• Find the LCD of $\frac{1}{3}$ and $\frac{1}{4}$.

• Write equivalent fractions with the LCD.

• Subtract. Simplify if you can:

$\frac{4}{12} - \frac{3}{12} = \frac{1}{12}$

Write the answer in simplest form. Use Fraction Bars if it helps.

1. $\frac{2}{5}$
    $+ \frac{11}{20}$
    _____
    $\frac{19}{20}$

2. $\frac{3}{4}$
    $+ \frac{7}{16}$
    _____
    $1\frac{3}{16}$

3. $\frac{1}{2}$
    $+ \frac{4}{5}$
    _____
    $1\frac{3}{10}$

4. $\frac{2}{3}$
    $+ \frac{1}{2}$
    _____
    $1\frac{1}{6}$

5. $\frac{3}{5}$
    $+ \frac{13}{15}$
    _____
    $1\frac{7}{15}$

6. $\frac{3}{4}$
    $- \frac{1}{5}$
    _____
    $\frac{11}{20}$

7. $\frac{2}{3}$
    $- \frac{3}{10}$
    _____
    $\frac{11}{30}$

8. $\frac{5}{6}$
    $- \frac{1}{4}$
    _____
    $\frac{7}{12}$

9. $\frac{7}{9}$
    $- \frac{1}{2}$
    _____
    $\frac{5}{18}$

10. $\frac{7}{8}$
    $- \frac{2}{3}$
    _____
    $\frac{5}{24}$

10.4 ANOTHER LOOK

Problem Solving Decisions: Is the Answer Reasonable?

Thirty-five students went to the museum. They rode on two small buses. A friend told you that $\frac{1}{2}$ of the students took one bus and $\frac{1}{2}$ took the other bus. Does this statement make sense?

1. Understand

- You know how many students went on the trip.
- Find the number of students on each bus.

2. Plan

- You will need to use division to find $\frac{1}{2}$ of 35.
- Then, compare your answer to the statement.

3. Try It

- Multiply: $\frac{1}{2} \times 35 = 17.5$.

4. Look Back

- The statement is not reasonable. The number 17.5 is not a whole number, so it cannot represent people.

Decide whether the statement or answer is reasonable. Explain.

1. The pizza chef is running out of mushroom topping. He has $\frac{3}{4}$ cup of mushrooms left. You order two pizzas. He tells you he has put $\frac{1}{2}$ cup of mushrooms on each pizza. Is this statement reasonable?

   No; $\frac{1}{2} + \frac{1}{2} = 1$, so the 2 pizzas would take 1 cup mushrooms.

2. You order a super-duper extra large pizza with only one item on each piece. The pizza chef tells you that $\frac{1}{3}$ of the pizza has pepperoni, $\frac{1}{3}$ of the pizza has mushroom, and $\frac{2}{3}$ of the pizza has broccoli. Does this make sense?

   No; $\frac{1}{3} + \frac{1}{3} + \frac{2}{3} = \frac{4}{3}$, which is more than 1.

3. You and your cousin are sharing a bag of trail mix. You eat $\frac{1}{2}$ of the bag, and your cousin eats $\frac{3}{4}$ of the bag. Is this statement reasonable?

   No; $\frac{1}{2} + \frac{3}{4} = \frac{5}{4} = 1\frac{1}{4}$ and $1\frac{1}{4}$ bag is more than 1 bag.

RETEACH

Adding and Subtracting with Like Denominators

When adding or subtracting fractions with the same denominator, add or subtract only the numerators.

Problem: $\dfrac{3}{6} + \dfrac{5}{6}$

$\dfrac{3}{6} + \dfrac{5}{6}$ 1. Are the denominators the same?

$\dfrac{\boxed{3 + 5}}{6 \quad 6} = \dfrac{8}{6}$ 2. The denominators are the same, so you can add. Remember to add *only* the numerators.

$\dfrac{8}{6} = 1\dfrac{2}{6} = 1\dfrac{1}{3}$ 3. Write the answer in simplest form.

Write the answer in simplest form. Make sure each answer appears in the Answer Box.

1. $\dfrac{1}{12} + \dfrac{6}{12} = \dfrac{\boxed{1 + 6}}{12 \quad 12} = \dfrac{7}{12}$ _____

2. $\dfrac{5}{8} - \dfrac{2}{8} = \dfrac{\boxed{5 - 2}}{8 \quad 8} = \dfrac{3}{8}$ _____

3. $\dfrac{3}{4} - \dfrac{2}{4} = \dfrac{1}{4}$ _____

4. $\dfrac{7}{9} + \dfrac{5}{9} = 1\dfrac{1}{3}$ _____

5. $\dfrac{1}{3} + \dfrac{2}{3} = \underline{\quad 1 \quad}$

6. $\dfrac{5}{14} + \dfrac{8}{14} = \dfrac{13}{14}$ _____

7. $\dfrac{9}{10} - \dfrac{4}{10} = \dfrac{1}{2}$ _____

8. $\dfrac{7}{12} + \dfrac{7}{12} = 1\dfrac{1}{6}$ _____

9. $\dfrac{2}{7} + \dfrac{4}{7} = \dfrac{6}{7}$ _____

10. $\dfrac{7}{16} - \dfrac{3}{16} = \dfrac{1}{4}$ _____

11. $\dfrac{1}{5} + \dfrac{3}{5} = \dfrac{4}{5}$ _____

12. What can you remember that will help you when you add or subtract fractions with the same denominator?

   Add or subtract only the numerators. _____

   _____

Answer Box

$1\dfrac{1}{3}$	$\dfrac{1}{4}$	$\dfrac{3}{8}$	$\dfrac{1}{2}$	$\dfrac{7}{12}$	$\dfrac{4}{5}$	1	$\dfrac{6}{7}$	$\dfrac{13}{14}$	$\dfrac{1}{4}$	$1\dfrac{1}{6}$

79 ◤ RETEACH

Simplest Form

When you add or subtract fractions or mixed numbers, give your answer in simplest form.

Problem: $\dfrac{4}{6} + \dfrac{3}{6}$

$\dfrac{4}{6} + \dfrac{3}{6} = \dfrac{7}{6}$

$\dfrac{7}{6} = 1\dfrac{1}{6}$ If your answer is a fraction greater than one, rewrite it as a mixed number.

$\dfrac{5}{6} - \dfrac{3}{6} = \dfrac{2}{6}$ If your answer is a fraction less than one or a

$\dfrac{2}{6} = \dfrac{1}{3}$ mixed number with a fraction part, be sure the fraction is in simplest form.

Write each fraction in simplest form. Make sure each answer appears in the Answer Box.

1. $\dfrac{12}{16} = \underline{\dfrac{3}{4}}$ Fraction is less than one.

2. $\dfrac{8}{5} = \underline{1\dfrac{3}{5}}$ Fraction is greater than one.

3. $\dfrac{2}{8} = \underline{\dfrac{1}{4}}$

4. $\dfrac{6}{4} = \underline{1\dfrac{1}{2}}$

Write the sum or difference in simplest form. Make sure each answer appears in the Answer Box.

5. $\dfrac{4}{5} + \dfrac{3}{5} = \underline{1\dfrac{2}{5}}$

6. $\dfrac{7}{10} + \dfrac{4}{10} = \underline{1\dfrac{1}{10}}$

7. $\dfrac{6}{12} + \dfrac{4}{12} = \underline{\dfrac{5}{6}}$

8. $1\dfrac{2}{3} + \dfrac{2}{3} = \underline{2\dfrac{1}{3}}$

9. $\dfrac{5}{8} - \dfrac{1}{8} = \underline{\dfrac{1}{2}}$

10. $1\dfrac{3}{5} + 2\dfrac{4}{5} = \underline{4\dfrac{2}{5}}$

11. What is the first thing to look for when you are about to simplify an answer that is a fraction? __Look to see if the fraction__ __is greater than one.__

Answer Box

| $1\dfrac{1}{10}$ | $1\dfrac{3}{5}$ | $\dfrac{1}{2}$ | $\dfrac{3}{4}$ | $4\dfrac{2}{5}$ | $1\dfrac{1}{2}$ | $1\dfrac{2}{5}$ | $\dfrac{5}{6}$ | $2\dfrac{1}{3}$ | $\dfrac{1}{4}$ |

RETEACH 80

Adding and Subtracting with Unlike Denominators

When adding or subtracting fractions with unlike denominators, rewrite each fraction using the least common denominator.

Problem: $\dfrac{3}{4} - \dfrac{2}{3}$

Are the denominators the same? If not, rewrite the fractions as equivalent fractions.

Find the least common multiple (LCM). This is also the least common denominator (LCD).

multiples of 4: 4, 8, $\boxed{12}$

multiples of 3: 3, 6, 9, $\boxed{12}$

Rewrite each fraction using the LCM as the denominator.

$\overset{\times 3}{\dfrac{3}{4}} = \dfrac{9}{\boxed{12}} \quad \overset{\times 4}{\dfrac{2}{3}} = \dfrac{8}{\boxed{12}}$

Subtract. Remember to subtract only the numerators.

$\dfrac{9}{12} - \dfrac{8}{12} = \dfrac{1}{12}$

Write the answer. Make sure each answer appears in the Answer Box.

1. $\dfrac{4}{5} - \dfrac{2}{3} = \dfrac{2}{15}$

multiples of 5: 5, 10, $\boxed{15}$

multiples of 3: 3, 6, 9, 12, $\boxed{15}$

$\dfrac{4}{5} = \dfrac{12}{\boxed{15}} \quad \dfrac{2}{3} = \dfrac{10}{\boxed{15}}$

2. $\dfrac{1}{2} + \dfrac{1}{3} = \dfrac{5}{6}$

multiples of 2: 2, 4, $\boxed{6}$

multiples of 3: 3, $\boxed{6}$

$\dfrac{1}{2} = \dfrac{3}{\boxed{6}} \quad \dfrac{1}{3} = \dfrac{2}{\boxed{6}}$

3. $\dfrac{1}{2} + \dfrac{3}{7} = \dfrac{13}{14}$

4. $\dfrac{7}{8} - \dfrac{2}{3} = \dfrac{5}{24}$

5. $\dfrac{2}{3} + \dfrac{1}{5} = \dfrac{13}{15}$

6. $\dfrac{5}{6} - \dfrac{2}{9} = \dfrac{11}{18}$

7. $\dfrac{11}{12} - \dfrac{7}{8} = \dfrac{1}{24}$

8. $\dfrac{2}{7} + \dfrac{2}{9} = \dfrac{32}{63}$

Answer Box

$\frac{13}{14}$	$\frac{5}{24}$	$\frac{2}{15}$	$\frac{13}{15}$	$\frac{5}{6}$	$\frac{32}{63}$	$\frac{1}{24}$	$\frac{11}{18}$

81 ◣ RETEACH

Zero Property

Remember the zero property when you add zero to any fraction.

Problem: $\boxed{\dfrac{3}{8} + 0}$

When you add zero to any other number, the sum is the other number.

$\dfrac{3}{7} + \cancel{0} = \dfrac{3}{7}$ You can cross out the zero to remind you.

Find the sum. Make sure each answer appears in the Answer Box.

1. $\dfrac{2}{9} + \cancel{0} = \underline{\dfrac{2}{9}}$

2. $\cancel{0} + \dfrac{1}{4} = \underline{\dfrac{1}{4}}$

3. $\dfrac{2}{3} + \cancel{0} = \underline{\dfrac{2}{3}}$

4. $\dfrac{17}{20} + 0 = \underline{\dfrac{17}{20}}$

5. $\dfrac{5}{15} + 0 = \underline{\dfrac{5}{15}}$

6. $0 + \dfrac{3}{8} = \underline{\dfrac{3}{8}}$

7. $\dfrac{4}{5} + 0 = \underline{\dfrac{4}{5}}$

8. $\dfrac{2}{19} + 0 = \underline{\dfrac{2}{19}}$

9. $0 + \dfrac{5}{7} = \underline{\dfrac{5}{7}}$

10. $0 + \dfrac{1}{2} = \underline{\dfrac{1}{2}}$

11. $\dfrac{3}{4} + 0 = \underline{\dfrac{3}{4}}$

12. $\dfrac{1}{6} + 0 = \underline{\dfrac{1}{6}}$

13. $\dfrac{12}{13} + 0 = \underline{\dfrac{12}{13}}$

14. $\dfrac{3}{7} + 0 = \underline{\dfrac{3}{7}}$

15. $0 + \dfrac{9}{17} = \underline{\dfrac{9}{17}}$

16. $0 + \dfrac{14}{23} = \underline{\dfrac{14}{23}}$

17. $0 + \dfrac{6}{13} = \underline{\dfrac{6}{13}}$

18. $\dfrac{17}{24} + 0 = \underline{\dfrac{17}{24}}$

19. $\dfrac{9}{15} + 0 = \underline{\dfrac{9}{15}}$

20. $\dfrac{7}{19} + 0 = \underline{\dfrac{7}{19}}$

21. $0 + \dfrac{3}{5} = \underline{\dfrac{3}{5}}$

22. $0 + \dfrac{13}{20} = \underline{\dfrac{13}{20}}$

23. $\dfrac{4}{9} + 0 = \underline{\dfrac{4}{9}}$

24. $\dfrac{1}{3} + 0 = \underline{\dfrac{1}{3}}$

Answer Box

$\dfrac{17}{20}$	$\dfrac{1}{4}$	$\dfrac{3}{8}$	$\dfrac{2}{9}$	$\dfrac{1}{2}$	$\dfrac{5}{15}$	$\dfrac{2}{3}$	$\dfrac{5}{7}$	$\dfrac{1}{6}$	$\dfrac{3}{4}$	$\dfrac{4}{5}$	$\dfrac{2}{19}$	$\dfrac{9}{17}$	$\dfrac{7}{19}$	$\dfrac{6}{13}$	$\dfrac{13}{20}$	$\dfrac{12}{13}$	$\dfrac{9}{15}$	$\dfrac{14}{23}$	$\dfrac{4}{9}$	$\dfrac{3}{7}$	$\dfrac{1}{3}$	$\dfrac{3}{5}$	$\dfrac{17}{24}$

Name _____ Date _____

10.5 ANOTHER LOOK

Mixed Numbers With Like Denominators

When adding or subtracting mixed numbers, add or subtract the fractions and the whole numbers.

Add: $1\frac{2}{6} + 2\frac{2}{6}$.

• Check that the denominators are the same.

$$1\frac{2}{6}$$
$$+\ 2\frac{2}{6}$$

• Add the fractions.

$$1\frac{2}{6}$$
$$+\ 2\frac{2}{6}$$
$$\overline{\quad\frac{4}{6}}$$

• Then add the whole numbers. Simplify.

$$1\frac{2}{6}$$
$$+\ 2\frac{2}{6}$$
$$\overline{3\frac{4}{6} = 3\frac{2}{3}}$$

Subtract: $2\frac{3}{4} - 1\frac{1}{4}$.

• Check that the denominators are the same.

$$2\frac{3}{4}$$
$$-\ 1\frac{1}{4}$$

• Subtract the fractions.

$$2\frac{3}{4}$$
$$-\ 1\frac{1}{4}$$
$$\overline{\quad\frac{2}{4}}$$

• Then subtract the whole numbers. Simplify.

$$2\frac{3}{4}$$
$$-\ 1\frac{1}{4}$$
$$\overline{1\frac{2}{4} = 1\frac{1}{2}}$$

Write the answer in simplest form.

1. $4\frac{1}{2} - 2\frac{1}{2} = $ ___2___

2. $2\frac{1}{4} + 3\frac{2}{4} = $ ___$5\frac{3}{4}$___

3. $3\frac{1}{3} + 2\frac{1}{3} = $ ___$5\frac{2}{3}$___

4. $5\frac{7}{8} - 3 = $ ___$2\frac{7}{8}$___

5. $6\frac{5}{8} - 4\frac{1}{8} = $ ___$2\frac{1}{2}$___

6. $3\frac{1}{6} + 1\frac{4}{6} = $ ___$4\frac{5}{6}$___

7. $4\frac{5}{6} - \frac{1}{6} = $ ___$4\frac{2}{3}$___

8. $3\frac{3}{4} + 1 = $ ___$4\frac{3}{4}$___

9. $4\frac{1}{2} + 3 = $ ___$7\frac{1}{2}$___

10. $3\frac{5}{6} - 1\frac{5}{6} = $ ___2___

11. $3\frac{7}{8} - 3\frac{5}{8} = $ ___$\frac{1}{4}$___

12. $5\frac{1}{6} - 2 = $ ___$3\frac{1}{6}$___

Name _____ Date _____

10.6 ANOTHER LOOK

·····································

Estimation: Mixed Numbers

You can estimate sums and differences with mixed numbers the same way you did with fractions. You only need to know whether each fraction is close to 0, $\frac{1}{2}$, or 1.

Add: $3\frac{1}{5} + 2\frac{9}{10}$

Estimate the size of the fractions.

$\frac{1}{5}$

The denominator is much larger than the numerator. The fraction is close to 0.

$\frac{9}{10}$

The numerator and denominator are about the same size. The fraction is close to 1.

So, $3\frac{1}{5}$ is close to 3 and $2\frac{9}{10}$ is close to 3. $3 + 3 = 6$.
A reasonable estimate for the sum is 6.

Estimate differences the same way. Subtract: $7\frac{3}{15} - 4\frac{1}{8}$

In each fraction, the denominator is much larger than the numerator. Each fraction is close to 0.

So, $7\frac{3}{15}$ is close to 7, and $4\frac{1}{8}$ is close to 4. A reasonable estimate for the difference is $7 - 4 = 3$.

Write your estimate.   Answers may vary.

1. $1\frac{1}{6} + 4\frac{5}{8}$ _____ $5\frac{1}{2}$ _____

2. $3\frac{5}{6} - 1\frac{1}{8}$ _____ 3 _____

3. $2\frac{1}{5} + \frac{9}{10}$ _____ 3 _____

4. $5\frac{7}{10} - \frac{3}{8}$ _____ 5 _____

5. $6\frac{1}{5} - 3\frac{7}{8}$ _____ 2 _____

6. $5\frac{2}{10} + 1\frac{4}{6}$ _____ $6\frac{1}{2}$ _____

7. $6\frac{7}{10} - 1\frac{3}{8}$ _____ 5 _____

8. $2\frac{1}{6} + \frac{4}{10}$ _____ $2\frac{1}{2}$ _____

9. $2\frac{2}{12} + 7\frac{2}{10}$ _____ 9 _____

10. $4\frac{9}{10} - \frac{7}{8}$ _____ 4 _____

11. $5\frac{10}{12} - 5$ _____ 1 _____

12. $3\frac{8}{10} + \frac{2}{12}$ _____ 4 _____

13. $8\frac{3}{10} - 1\frac{3}{8}$ _____ 7 _____

14. $5\frac{11}{12} + 3\frac{5}{6}$ _____ 10 _____

15. $9\frac{5}{12} - 7\frac{3}{6}$ _____ 2 _____

16. $8\frac{2}{12} + 1\frac{1}{10}$ _____ 9 _____

10.7 ANOTHER LOOK

Adding Mixed Numbers

To add mixed numbers with unlike denominators, you need to rewrite the fractions using like denominators.

Fraction Bars can help you find equivalent fractions with like denominators.

Add: $2\frac{1}{2} + 1\frac{2}{3}$

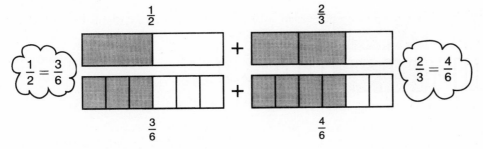

- Rewrite the mixed numbers.

$$2\frac{1}{2} = 2\frac{3}{6} \text{ and } 1\frac{2}{3} = 1\frac{4}{6}$$

- Add the fractions. Then add the whole numbers. Simplify if you can.

$$2\frac{3}{6} + 1\frac{4}{6} = 3\frac{7}{6} = 4\frac{1}{6}$$

**Rewrite the fractions with like denominators.
Use Fraction Bars if it helps.** Answers may vary.

1. $\frac{2}{3}, \frac{3}{5}$ $\underline{\frac{10}{15}, \frac{9}{15}}$ 2. $\frac{1}{4}, \frac{5}{6}$ $\underline{\frac{3}{12}, \frac{10}{12}}$ 3. $\frac{1}{4}, \frac{3}{10}$ $\underline{\frac{5}{20}, \frac{6}{20}}$ 4. $\frac{1}{2}, \frac{5}{12}$ $\underline{\frac{6}{12}, \frac{5}{12}}$

Write the sum in simplest form. Use Fraction Bars if it helps.

5. $4\frac{1}{3} + \frac{5}{6} = $ _____ $5\frac{1}{6}$ 6. $3\frac{3}{4} + 5 = $ _____ $8\frac{3}{4}$

7. $2\frac{1}{4} + 3\frac{1}{6} = $ _____ $5\frac{5}{12}$ 8. $3\frac{3}{10} + 5\frac{1}{4} = $ _____ $8\frac{11}{20}$

9. $3\frac{1}{2} + 5\frac{9}{10} = $ _____ $9\frac{2}{5}$ 10. $4\frac{1}{3} + 1\frac{3}{4} = $ _____ $6\frac{1}{12}$

11. $1\frac{5}{12} + 6\frac{1}{6} = $ _____ $7\frac{7}{12}$ 12. $4\frac{2}{3} + \frac{3}{5} = $ _____ $5\frac{4}{15}$

13. $2\frac{7}{10} + \frac{3}{5} = $ _____ $3\frac{3}{10}$ 14. $6\frac{5}{9} + 3 = $ _____ $9\frac{5}{9}$

15. $2\frac{1}{3} + 2\frac{1}{6} = $ _____ $4\frac{1}{2}$ 16. $1\frac{1}{2} + 5\frac{7}{8} = $ _____ $7\frac{3}{8}$

Name_____ Date_____

10.8 ANOTHER LOOK

Subtracting Mixed Numbers

To subtract mixed numbers with unlike denominators,
find equivalent fractions with like denominators.

Subtract: $3\frac{3}{4} - 1\frac{2}{3}$

Fraction Bars can help you rewrite the fractions with like denominators.

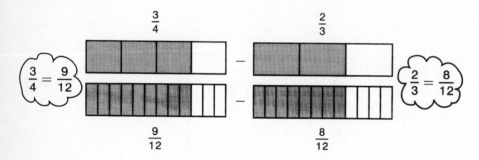

• Rewrite the mixed numbers.

$$3\frac{3}{4} = 3\frac{9}{12} \text{ and } 1\frac{2}{3} = 1\frac{8}{12}$$

• Subtract the fractions. Then subtract the whole numbers. Simplify if you can.

$$3\frac{9}{12} - 1\frac{8}{12} = 2\frac{1}{12}$$

Write the difference in simplest form. Use Fraction Bars if it helps.

1. $3\frac{1}{2} - 1\frac{1}{6} =$ _____ $2\frac{1}{3}$

2. $5\frac{3}{4} - 3\frac{3}{10} =$ _____ $2\frac{9}{20}$

3. $2\frac{2}{5} - \frac{1}{10} =$ _____ $2\frac{3}{10}$

4. $6\frac{7}{12} - 2\frac{1}{3} =$ _____ $4\frac{1}{4}$

5. $4\frac{2}{3} - 1\frac{1}{6} =$ _____ $3\frac{1}{2}$

6. $6\frac{4}{5} - 5\frac{1}{4} =$ _____ $1\frac{11}{20}$

7. $5\frac{5}{12} - 3 =$ _____ $2\frac{5}{12}$

8. $7\frac{9}{10} - 4\frac{2}{3} =$ _____ $3\frac{7}{30}$

9. $\begin{array}{r} 7\frac{3}{5} \\ -5\frac{1}{10} \\ \hline 2\frac{1}{2} \end{array}$

10. $\begin{array}{r} 6\frac{2}{3} \\ -3\frac{1}{4} \\ \hline 3\frac{5}{12} \end{array}$

11. $\begin{array}{r} 8\frac{11}{12} \\ -5\frac{3}{4} \\ \hline 3\frac{1}{6} \end{array}$

12. $\begin{array}{r} 6\frac{3}{5} \\ -\frac{1}{4} \\ \hline 6\frac{7}{20} \end{array}$

13. $\begin{array}{r} 5\frac{9}{10} \\ -3\frac{5}{6} \\ \hline 2\frac{1}{15} \end{array}$

Name_____   Date_____

10.9 ANOTHER LOOK

Renaming for Subtraction

Sometimes when you subtract fractions or mixed numbers, you need to rename fractions.

Subtract: $3\frac{2}{5} - 1\frac{1}{2}$

Use Fraction Bars to find the common denominator for $\frac{2}{5}$ and $\frac{1}{2}$.

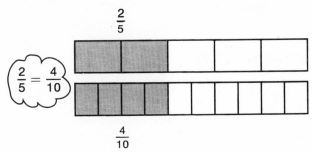
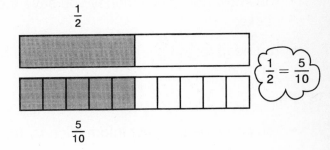

Here is a set of steps to follow:

• Rewrite the mixed numbers.	• Is $\frac{4}{10}$ large enough to subtract $\frac{5}{10}$ from it? If not, rename.	• Subtract. Simplify if you can.
$3\frac{2}{5} = 3\frac{4}{10}$ $1\frac{1}{2} = 1\frac{5}{10}$	$3\frac{4}{10} = 2\frac{14}{10}$	$2\frac{14}{10}$ $-1\frac{5}{10}$ $1\frac{9}{10}$

Write the difference in simplest form. Use Fraction Bars if it helps.

1. $4\frac{1}{4} - 1\frac{3}{4} = \underline{2\frac{1}{2}}$ 2. $5\frac{2}{5} - 2\frac{4}{5} = \underline{2\frac{3}{5}}$ 3. $6 - \frac{5}{6} = \underline{5\frac{1}{6}}$

4. $4\frac{1}{6} - 3\frac{5}{6} = \underline{\frac{1}{3}}$ 5. $6\frac{1}{2} - 3\frac{7}{10} = \underline{2\frac{4}{5}}$ 6. $5\frac{1}{3} - 3\frac{7}{10} = \underline{1\frac{19}{30}}$

7. $9\frac{1}{9}$ $-\frac{7}{9}$ $8\frac{1}{3}$ 8. 8 $-2\frac{3}{5}$ $5\frac{2}{5}$ 9. $5\frac{1}{4}$ $-1\frac{5}{6}$ $3\frac{5}{12}$ 10. $4\frac{1}{12}$ $-3\frac{7}{12}$ $\frac{1}{2}$ 11. $9\frac{5}{12}$ $-3\frac{3}{4}$ $5\frac{2}{3}$

12. $6\frac{1}{8}$ $-3\frac{5}{8}$ $2\frac{1}{2}$ 13. $7\frac{1}{3}$ $-3\frac{1}{2}$ $3\frac{5}{6}$ 14. $8\frac{9}{10}$ $-3\frac{2}{5}$ $5\frac{1}{2}$ 15. $6\frac{2}{3}$ $-5\frac{3}{10}$ $1\frac{11}{30}$ 16. $7\frac{5}{6}$ -5 $2\frac{5}{6}$

209

10.10 ANOTHER LOOK

Problem Solving Strategy: **Make a Table**

You are saving money to buy a new bicycle. The first week, you save $4, the second week you save $5, and the third week you save $6. If this pattern continues, how much will you have saved by the end of 10 weeks?

1. Understand

- You know how much money you save the first, second, third weeks.

- You need to find out how much you will have saved at the end of ten weeks.

2. Plan

- You can organize your information by making a table.

3. Try it

- Find the amount saved each week. Remember to add $1 to the amount saved the week before.

- Add the amount saved each week to find the total.

4. Look Back

- You will save $85 after 10 weeks.

Week	Amount Saved
Week 1	$4
Week 2	$5
Week 3	$6
Week 4	$7
Week 5	$8
Week 6	$9
Week 7	$10
Week 8	$11
Week 9	$12
Week 10	$13

Solve. Use Make a Table when you can.

1. Suppose you have 12 weeks to get into shape for a bicycle race. You ride 5 miles the first week and $5\frac{1}{2}$ miles the second week. Every week for the next 10 weeks, you ride $\frac{1}{2}$ mile more than you did the week before. At the end of the 12 weeks, how many total miles have you ridden?

   _____ **93 miles** _____

2. A train travels $10\frac{1}{4}$ miles before the first stop, another $15\frac{1}{2}$ miles before the second stop, and another $20\frac{3}{4}$ miles before the third stop. If this pattern continues, how many miles

   will the train have traveled when it reaches the fifth stop? _____ $103\frac{3}{4}$ **miles** _____

10.11 ANOTHER LOOK

Problem Solving: **Using Strategies**

At the zoo, your friend watches a trainer feeding seals. In the first 15 minutes, the trainer gives the seals 25 fish. Each 15 minutes after that, she gives them 10 more than she did the previous 15 minutes. If your friend sees the seals eat a total of 480 fish, how long was he watching the seals?

1. Understand

• You know how many fish the seals ate in the first 15 minutes.

• You know that every 15 minutes, the seals eat 10 more fish than they did in the previous 15 minutes.

• You know the total number of fish the seals eat.

• You need to find out the total amount of time your friend watched the seals.

2. Plan

• You can organize your information by making a table.

3. Try It

• Use addition to find the amount of fish eaten every 15 minutes. Remember to add 10 to your total each time. Fill in the table to keep track of your information.

• Keep writing columns until your total is 480. You should have a total of 8 columns.

• Figure out how long your friend watched the seals by multiplying the number of minutes, 15, by the number of columns, 8: 15 minutes × 8 = 120 minutes.

Time	Number of Fish
15 minutes	25 fish
15 minutes	35 fish
15 minutes	45 fish
15 minutes	55 fish
15 minutes	65 fish
15 minutes	75 fish

4. Look Back

• Your answer is 120 minutes. Your friend watched the seals for 2 hours.

Use any strategy to solve.

1. There are 35 glass beads in a bead kit. Two-fifths of the beads are blue, five of the beads are red, one-fourth of the remaining beads are yellow, and the rest of the beads are purple. How many beads are purple? _____ **12 beads** _____

◢RETEACH

82

Adding and Subtracting Mixed Numbers

When you add or subtract mixed numbers, be sure to add or subtract both fractions and whole numbers.

Problems: $5\frac{1}{3} + 6\frac{1}{3}$ and $6\frac{2}{3} - 5\frac{1}{3}$

Add.	Subtract.
$5\frac{1}{3}$	$6\frac{2}{3}$
$+\ 6\frac{1}{3}$	$-\ 5\frac{1}{3}$
$11\frac{2}{3}$	$1\frac{1}{3}$

1. Are the denominators the same?
2. Add or subtract the fractions. Then add or subtract the whole numbers. Draw columns to help you. Make sure your answer is in simplest form.

Write the sum or difference in simplest form. Make sure each answer appears in the Answer Box.

1.
$$6\frac{2}{8}$$
$$+\ 7\frac{1}{8}$$
$$13\frac{3}{8}$$

2.
$$4\frac{4}{5}$$
$$-\ 2\frac{1}{5}$$
$$2\frac{3}{5}$$

3.
$$5\frac{2}{7}$$
$$+\ 8\frac{4}{7}$$
$$13\frac{6}{7}$$

4.
$$2\frac{2}{3}$$
$$-\ 1\frac{1}{3}$$
$$1\frac{1}{3}$$

4.
$$8\frac{5}{12}$$
$$+\ 4\frac{6}{12}$$
$$12\frac{11}{12}$$

5.
$$4\frac{3}{5}$$
$$-\ 1\frac{2}{5}$$
$$3\frac{1}{5}$$

6.
$$5\frac{1}{3}$$
$$+\ 4\frac{1}{3}$$
$$9\frac{2}{3}$$

7.
$$1\frac{7}{9}$$
$$-\ \frac{2}{9}$$
$$1\frac{5}{9}$$

8.
$$3\frac{4}{9}$$
$$+\ \frac{3}{9}$$
$$3\frac{7}{9}$$

9.
$$12\frac{6}{7}$$
$$-\ 5\frac{5}{7}$$
$$7\frac{1}{7}$$

10.
$$6\frac{14}{15}$$
$$-\ 2\frac{1}{15}$$
$$4\frac{13}{15}$$

11.
$$4\frac{2}{11}$$
$$+\ 1\frac{3}{11}$$
$$5\frac{5}{11}$$

Answer Box

$4\frac{13}{15}$	$1\frac{5}{9}$	$5\frac{5}{11}$	$13\frac{6}{7}$	$7\frac{1}{7}$	$13\frac{3}{8}$	$2\frac{3}{5}$	$3\frac{7}{9}$	$9\frac{2}{3}$	$12\frac{11}{12}$	$1\frac{1}{3}$	$3\frac{1}{5}$

Name _____   Date _____

83 ▸RETEACH   Finding a Common Denominator

When you add or subtract two mixed numbers with unlike denominators, you must first find a common denominator for the fraction parts.

Problem: $5\frac{2}{3} + 6\frac{1}{4}$

$5\frac{2}{3} \longrightarrow 3, 6, 9, \boxed{12}$

$+6\frac{1}{4} \longrightarrow 4, 8, \boxed{12}$

Use the least common multiple for the denominators when writing equivalent fractions.

$5\frac{2}{3} = \frac{8}{12} \longrightarrow 5\frac{8}{12}$ (×4)

$+6\frac{1}{4} = \frac{3}{12} \longrightarrow +6\frac{3}{12}$ (×3)

$11\frac{11}{12}$

Add or subtract the mixed numbers.

Make sure your answer is in simplest form.

Write the sum or difference in simplest form. Make sure each answer appears in the Answer Box.

1. $3\frac{4}{5} \longrightarrow 3\frac{24}{30}$
   $-2\frac{1}{6} \longrightarrow -2\frac{5}{30}$
   $1\frac{19}{30}$

2. $5\frac{2}{3} \longrightarrow 5\frac{16}{24}$
   $+4\frac{1}{8} \longrightarrow +4\frac{3}{24}$
   $9\frac{19}{24}$

3. $5\frac{2}{5} - 4\frac{1}{4} = \underline{1\frac{3}{20}}$

4. $7\frac{1}{2} + 10\frac{1}{3} = \underline{17\frac{5}{6}}$

5. $1\frac{1}{6} - 1\frac{1}{9} = \underline{\frac{1}{18}}$

6. $3\frac{3}{5} - 2\frac{7}{12} = \underline{1\frac{1}{60}}$

7. $3\frac{1}{6} + 4\frac{3}{4} = \underline{7\frac{11}{12}}$

8. $2\frac{3}{11} + \frac{1}{2} = \underline{2\frac{17}{22}}$

9. $1\frac{1}{4} + 3\frac{3}{5} = \underline{4\frac{17}{20}}$

10. $8\frac{2}{3} - 2\frac{3}{5} = \underline{6\frac{1}{15}}$

11. $7\frac{1}{8} + 6\frac{1}{3} = \underline{13\frac{11}{24}}$

12. What can you remember to help you write equivalent fractions? __Use the LCM for the denominator and multiply numerator and denominator by the same number.__

Answer Box

| $17\frac{5}{6}$ | $4\frac{17}{20}$ | $7\frac{11}{12}$ | $9\frac{19}{24}$ | $\frac{1}{18}$ | $2\frac{17}{22}$ | $13\frac{11}{24}$ | $1\frac{1}{60}$ | $1\frac{19}{30}$ | $1\frac{3}{20}$ | $6\frac{1}{15}$ |

Name _____   Date _____

84 ▸ RETEACH   Writing the Answer in Simplest Form

When you add or subtract fractions, write the answer in simplest form. Sometimes this is a mixed number, and sometimes it is a fraction.

Problem: $6\frac{5}{8} - 3\frac{1}{8}$

Find the difference.   Then write the difference in simplest form.

$$6\frac{5}{8}$$
$$-3\frac{1}{8}$$
$$\overline{\quad 3\frac{4}{8}}$$

Divide the numerator and denominator by the greatest common factor.
The GCF of 8 and 4 is 4.

$$\frac{\div 4}{\frac{4}{8}} = \frac{1}{2}$$
$$\div 4$$

So, $6\frac{5}{8} - 3\frac{1}{8} = 3\frac{1}{2}$

Rewrite each answer in simplest form. Make sure each answer appears in the Answer Box.

1. $7\frac{7}{8}$
    $-1\frac{5}{8}$
    $\overline{6\frac{2}{8}} = \underline{6\frac{1}{4}}$

2. $2\frac{1}{4}$
    $+4\frac{1}{4}$
    $\overline{6\frac{2}{4}} = \underline{6\frac{1}{2}}$

3. $8\frac{7}{12}$
    $-3\frac{1}{12}$
    $\overline{5\frac{6}{12}} = \underline{5\frac{1}{2}}$

Write each answer in simplest form. Make sure each answer appears in the Answer Box.

4. $9\frac{3}{4} - 6\frac{1}{4} = \underline{3\frac{1}{2}}$

5. $7\frac{1}{8} + 6\frac{5}{8} = \underline{13\frac{3}{4}}$

6. $8\frac{7}{9} - 5\frac{1}{9} = \underline{3\frac{2}{3}}$

7. $5\frac{1}{12} + 6\frac{7}{12} = \underline{11\frac{2}{3}}$

8. $2\frac{7}{8} - \frac{3}{8} = \underline{2\frac{1}{2}}$

9. $3\frac{1}{10} + 4\frac{3}{10} = \underline{7\frac{2}{5}}$

10. $7\frac{1}{6} + 3\frac{1}{6} = \underline{10\frac{1}{3}}$

11. $6\frac{5}{12} - 2\frac{1}{12} = \underline{4\frac{1}{3}}$

12. $5\frac{1}{8} + 2\frac{1}{8} = \underline{7\frac{1}{4}}$

Answer Box

| $2\frac{1}{2}$ | $6\frac{1}{4}$ | $11\frac{2}{3}$ | $3\frac{1}{2}$ | $6\frac{1}{2}$ | $5\frac{1}{2}$ | $13\frac{3}{4}$ | $3\frac{2}{3}$ | $10\frac{1}{3}$ | $7\frac{2}{5}$ | $4\frac{1}{3}$ | $7\frac{1}{4}$ |

85 **RETEACH** **Renaming Before Subtracting**

Sometimes when you subtract mixed numbers, you have to rename.

Problem: $\boxed{10\dfrac{5}{12} - 3\dfrac{11}{12}}$

Since $\dfrac{11}{12}$ is greater than $\dfrac{5}{12}$, you need to rename $10\dfrac{5}{12}$ before you can subtract.

$10\dfrac{5}{12} = 9\dfrac{17}{12}$

1. Take 1 from the 10. Rename the 1 as an equivalent fraction with a denominator of twelve. Add this fraction to $\dfrac{5}{12}$.

$9\dfrac{17}{12}$

$-3\dfrac{11}{12}$

─────────

$6\dfrac{6}{12} = 6\dfrac{1}{2}$

2. Subtract. Write the difference in simplest form.

So, $10\dfrac{5}{12} - 3\dfrac{11}{12} = 6\dfrac{1}{2}$

Write the difference in simplest form. Make sure each answer appears in the Answer Box.

1.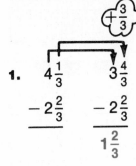

$4\dfrac{1}{3} \qquad 3\dfrac{4}{3}$

$-2\dfrac{2}{3} \qquad -2\dfrac{2}{3}$

──────────────

$\qquad\qquad 1\dfrac{2}{3}$

2.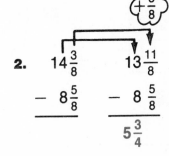

$14\dfrac{3}{8} \qquad 13\dfrac{11}{8}$

$-8\dfrac{5}{8} \qquad -8\dfrac{5}{8}$

──────────────

$\qquad\qquad 5\dfrac{3}{4}$

3.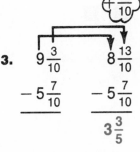

$9\dfrac{3}{10} \qquad 8\dfrac{13}{10}$

$-5\dfrac{7}{10} \qquad -5\dfrac{7}{10}$

──────────────

$\qquad\qquad 3\dfrac{3}{5}$

4. $4\dfrac{2}{7}$

$-2\dfrac{4}{7}$

─────

$1\dfrac{5}{7}$

5. $6\dfrac{1}{4}$

$-2\dfrac{3}{4}$

─────

$3\dfrac{1}{2}$

6. $7\dfrac{1}{5}$

$-1\dfrac{3}{5}$

─────

$5\dfrac{3}{5}$

7. $8\dfrac{5}{8}$

$-3\dfrac{7}{8}$

─────

$4\dfrac{3}{4}$

Answer Box

$4\dfrac{3}{4}$	$1\dfrac{5}{7}$	$5\dfrac{3}{4}$	$3\dfrac{3}{5}$	$1\dfrac{2}{3}$	$5\dfrac{3}{5}$	$3\dfrac{1}{2}$

Name_____ Date_____

11.1 ANOTHER LOOK

Fraction Factors

To play one game of checkers will take $\frac{1}{2}$ hour. How long will it take to play 5 games?

- You can use Fraction Bars to solve this problem:

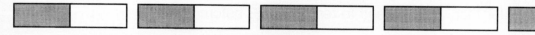

- You can write a repeated addition sentence:

$$\frac{1}{2} + \frac{1}{2} + \frac{1}{2} + \frac{1}{2} + \frac{1}{2} = \frac{5}{2} \longleftarrow \quad \frac{5}{2} = 2\frac{1}{2}$$

- Also, you can write a multiplication sentence:

$$5 \times \frac{1}{2} = \frac{5}{2}$$

You need $\frac{5}{2}$ hours, or $2\frac{1}{2}$ hours, to play 5 games.

Write a multiplication sentence for each model. Write the product.
Change fractions greater than one to mixed numbers.

1.

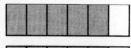

■×■=■

$2 \times \frac{5}{6} = \frac{10}{6}$, or $1\frac{2}{3}$

2.

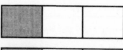
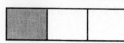

■×■=■

$4 \times \frac{1}{3} = \frac{4}{3}$, or $1\frac{1}{3}$

3.

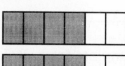

■×■=■

$2 \times \frac{4}{6} = \frac{8}{6}$, or $1\frac{1}{3}$

4.

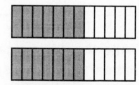

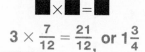

■×■=■

$3 \times \frac{7}{12} = \frac{21}{12}$, or $1\frac{3}{4}$

Write a multiplication sentence for each repeated addition.
Write the product. Change fractions greater than one to mixed numbers.

6. $\frac{4}{5} + \frac{4}{5} =$

■×■=■

$2 \times \frac{4}{5} = \frac{8}{5}$, or $1\frac{3}{5}$

6. $\frac{3}{7} + \frac{3}{7} + \frac{3}{7} =$

■×■=■

$3 \times \frac{3}{7} = \frac{9}{7}$, or $1\frac{2}{7}$

7. $\frac{1}{4} + \frac{1}{4} + \frac{1}{4} + \frac{1}{4} + \frac{1}{4} =$

■×■=■

$5 \times \frac{1}{4} = \frac{5}{4}$, or $1\frac{1}{4}$

8. $\frac{7}{8} + \frac{7}{8} =$

■×■=■

$2 \times \frac{7}{8} = \frac{14}{8}$, or $1\frac{3}{4}$

11.2 ANOTHER LOOK

Multiplying with Fractions

You can use a model to help you find a fraction of a number.

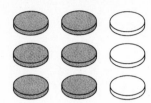
What is $\frac{2}{3}$ of 9?

Multiply: $\frac{2}{3} \times \frac{9}{1}$

$\frac{2}{3} \times \frac{9}{1} = \frac{18}{3}$, or 6.

So, $\frac{2}{3}$ of 9 is 6.

Write the multiplication sentence for each model. Write the product as a whole or mixed number.

1.

$\frac{1}{2}$ of 6

$\frac{1}{2} \times 6 = \frac{6}{2}$, or 3

2.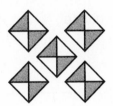

$\frac{2}{4}$ of 5

$\frac{2}{4} \times 5 = \frac{10}{4}$, or $2\frac{1}{2}$

3.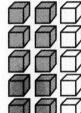

$\frac{2}{3}$ of 15

$\frac{2}{3} \times 15 = \frac{30}{3}$, or 10

4.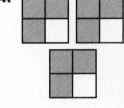

$\frac{3}{4}$ of 3

$\frac{3}{4} \times 3 = \frac{9}{4}$, or $2\frac{1}{4}$

Write the product in the simplest form. Use a model if it helps.

5.

$\frac{1}{3}$ of 18

$\frac{1}{3} \times 18 = \frac{18}{3}$, or 6

6.

$\frac{2}{5}$ of 10

$\frac{2}{5} \times 10 = \frac{20}{5}$, or 4

7.

$\frac{3}{6}$ of 12

$\frac{3}{6} \times 12 = \frac{36}{6}$, or 6

8.

$\frac{3}{8}$ of 24

$\frac{3}{8} \times 24 = \frac{72}{8}$, or 9

9. $\frac{1}{2}$ of 8   4

10. $\frac{1}{4}$ of 12   3

11. $\frac{2}{5} \times 15$ 6

12. $\frac{3}{7}$ of 21   9

13. $\frac{3}{4}$ of 16   12

14. $\frac{5}{6} \times 24$ 20

15. $\frac{3}{10}$ of 20   6

16. $\frac{2}{5} \times 100$ 40

11.3 ANOTHER LOOK

Estimation: Finding a Fraction of a Number

- Sometimes you can use mental math to find a fraction of a number.

What is $\frac{1}{3}$ of 15?

Divide 15 in 3 equal parts.

$15 \div 3 = 5$

So, $\frac{1}{3}$ of 15 is 5.

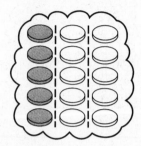

- You also can estimate a fraction of a number.

Find $\frac{1}{6}$ of $25.

Choose an amount close to $25 that you can divide mentally by 6. Try $24.

Estimate: $\frac{1}{6}$ of $25 is about $4.

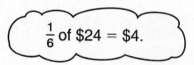

$\frac{1}{6}$ of $24 = $4.

Use mental math to solve.

1. $\frac{1}{2}$ of 30 ___15___

2. $\frac{1}{4}$ of 48 ___12___

3. $\frac{1}{5}$ of 250 ___50___

4. $\frac{1}{3}$ of 120 ___40___

5. $\frac{1}{8}$ of 400 ___50___

6. $\frac{1}{6}$ of 54 ___9___

7. $\frac{1}{7}$ of 560 ___80___

8. $\frac{1}{5}$ of $2000 ___$400___

Estimate. Choose amounts that you can divide easily. Answers may vary; accept answers within the range given.

9. $\frac{1}{2}$ of 21 → $\frac{1}{2}$ of 20 = ___10___

10. $\frac{1}{3}$ of $122 → $\frac{1}{3}$ of ___120___ = ___40___

11. $\frac{1}{8}$ of 28 → $\frac{1}{7}$ of 28 = ___4___

12. $\frac{1}{5}$ of 286 → $\frac{1}{5}$ of ___300___ = ___60___

13. $\frac{1}{5}$ of 26 ___5–6___

14. $\frac{1}{8}$ of 59 ___7–8___

15. $\frac{1}{6}$ of 38 ___6–7___

16. $\frac{1}{4}$ of 38 ___9–10___

17. $\frac{1}{3}$ of 70 ___20–30___

18. $\frac{1}{6}$ of 256 ___40–50___

Name _____ Date _____

Problem Solving Strategy: Guess and Check

Your class is going hiking. There are lunches for the hike. Half of the lunches have apple juice. Four of the lunches have cranberry juice. A third of the remaining lunches have lemonade. Eight other lunches have orange juice. How many lunches are there in all?

1. Understand

- You know the number of lunches with different juices.

- You need to find out how many lunches were packed in total.

2. Plan

- You can start by guessing the number of students in a class.

- Pick an even number because half have apple juice.

3. Try It

- Try 30 as your first guess.

- Half of 30 is 15. Subtract 4. That leaves 11 lunches.

- You can't take a third of 11. Your next possible answer should be higher. Try 32.

- Half of 32 is 16. Subtract 4. That leaves 12. One third of 12 is 4.

4. Look Back

- Check your guess. $16 + 4 + 4 + 8 = 32$. 32 is correct.

Solve. Use Guess and Check when you can.

1. To make cookies, you use 6 different kinds of sprinkles, and 4 different colors of icing. How many different combinations can you make if each cookie has both icing and sprinkles?

   24 different combinations

2. You are buying school supplies. You spend $\frac{1}{4}$ of your money on folders. Then, you spend $1 on a marker. You spend $\frac{1}{2}$ of the remaining money on paper, and then spend $2 on a ruler. If you have $2 left, how much money did you have? _____ **$12**

Name _____   Date _____

11.5 ANOTHER LOOK

Fractions and Multiplication

You can make a model that may help you multiply a fraction by a fraction.

Find $\frac{2}{3}$ of $\frac{1}{2}$.

One fraction is $\frac{1}{2}$. Fold a piece of paper into halves the long way. Open it and color one of the halves blue.

The other fraction is $\frac{2}{3}$. Fold the paper in thirds the short way. Open it and color two of the thirds red.

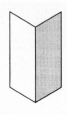

Notice that 2 of the 6 equal parts are colored both blue and red.

So, $\frac{2}{3}$ of $\frac{1}{2} = \frac{2}{6}$.　　Multiply: $\frac{2}{3} \times \frac{1}{2} = \frac{2}{6}$.

Color the models. Write the products.

1.

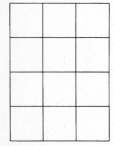

$\frac{3}{4}$ of $\frac{1}{3}$

Color $\frac{1}{3}$ blue. Color $\frac{3}{4}$ red.

How many parts altogether? _____ 12 _____

What fraction is both red and blue? _____ $\frac{3}{12}$ _____

$\frac{3}{4} \times \frac{1}{3} =$ _____ $\frac{3}{12}$ _____

2.

$\frac{3}{5}$ of $\frac{1}{2}$

Color $\frac{1}{2}$ blue. Color $\frac{3}{5}$ red.

How many parts altogether? _____ 10 _____

What fraction is both red and blue? _____ $\frac{3}{10}$ _____

$\frac{3}{5} \times \frac{1}{2} =$ _____ $\frac{3}{10}$ _____

3.

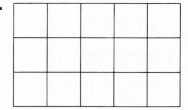

$\frac{2}{3}$ of $\frac{2}{5}$

Color $\frac{2}{5}$ blue. Color $\frac{2}{3}$ red.

How many parts altogether? _____ 15 _____

What fraction is both red and blue? _____ $\frac{4}{15}$ _____

$\frac{2}{3} \times \frac{2}{5} =$ _____ $\frac{4}{15}$ _____

220

Copyright © Houghton Mifflin Company. All rights reserved.

Name _____ Date _____

11.6 ANNOTHER LOOK

11.6 ANOTHER LOOK

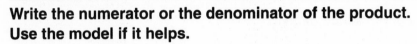

Multiplying Fractions

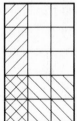

- You can use a model to help you multiply fractions.

    Multiply: $\frac{3}{4} \times \frac{2}{5}$

- You also can find the product without using a model.

- First, multiply the numerators.

    $\frac{3}{4} \times \frac{2}{5} = \frac{6}{}$

    6 is the numerator of the product.

- Second, multiply the denominators.

    $\frac{3}{4} \times \frac{2}{5} = \frac{6}{20}$

    20 is the denominator of the product.

- Third, simplify the product if you can.

    $\frac{6}{20} = \frac{3}{10}$

Write the numerator or the denominator of the product.
Use the model if it helps.

1. $\frac{1}{4} \times \frac{2}{3} = \frac{\boxed{2}}{12}$

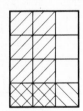

2. $\frac{1}{2} \times \frac{3}{5} = \frac{3}{\boxed{10}}$

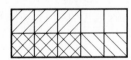

3. $\frac{2}{5} \times \frac{1}{3} = \frac{\boxed{2}}{15}$

Write the product in simplest form. Use the model if it helps.

4. $\frac{4}{5} \times \frac{1}{4} = \frac{\boxed{1}}{\boxed{5}}$

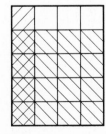

5. $\frac{1}{2} \times \frac{3}{4} = \frac{\boxed{3}}{\boxed{8}}$

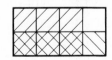

6. $\frac{2}{3} \times \frac{1}{2} = \frac{\boxed{1}}{\boxed{3}}$

Name _____ Date _____

11.7 ANOTHER LOOK

Choose a Computation Method

You have $20 in your wallet. You want to buy several T-shirts. They are on sale for $3.99 each. How many T-shirts can you buy with the $20?

- You know how much money you have to spend.

- You know the price of each T-shirt.

- You need to find out how many T-shirts you can buy.

- Decide whether to estimate or find an exact answer. You can estimate because the price of each T-shirt can easily be rounded to the nearest dollar. Your estimated answer will be close to the actual answer.

- Divide the amount of money you have by the rounded price of one T-shirt.

- Round the price of each T-shirt: $3.99 rounds to $4.

- Divide $20 by $4: 20 ÷ 4 = 5.

- You can buy 5 T-shirts.

- You can tell the answer is correct because you rounded up. If $20 will buy 5 T-shirts at $4 each, then $20 will buy 5 T-shirts at $3.99 each. You have enough money.

Decide whether you need an estimate or an exact answer. Then solve.

1. You buy 3 notebooks for school. They cost $2.53 each. The cashier says you owe $7.89. Is he correct?

   <u>**exact answer; No: $2.53 × 3 = $7.59**</u>

2. You see gym shorts on sale for $4.89 a pair. What is the greatest number of shorts you can buy with $20?

   <u>**estimate; 4 pairs: $5 × 4 = $20**</u>

3. You are getting ready to feed your dog. You see there are four bags of dog food left, and each bag weighs 5.9 lb. If your dog eats 2 lb of food each day, how many days will the dog food last?

   <u>**estimate; about 12 days: 6 lb × 4 = 24 lb, and 24 ÷ 2 = 12**</u>

86 ► **RETEACH**

When you multiply a whole number and a fraction, it helps to write the whole number as a fraction.

Problem: $\frac{3}{4} \times 6$

Write the whole number over a denominator of 1.

$$\frac{3}{4} \times 6 = \frac{3}{4} \times \frac{6}{1}$$

Multiply the 2 numerators.

Write in simplest form.

$$\frac{3}{4} \times \frac{6}{1} = \frac{18}{4} = 4\frac{2}{4} = 4\frac{1}{2}$$

Multiply the 2 denominators.

So, $\frac{3}{4} \times 6 = 4\frac{1}{2}$.

Rewrite each whole number as a fraction. Write the product in simplest form. Make sure each answer appears in the Answer Box.

1. $\frac{1}{2} \times 9$

$\frac{1}{2} \times \frac{9}{1} = 4\frac{1}{2}$

2. $3 \times \frac{4}{9}$

$\frac{3}{1} \times \frac{4}{9} = 1\frac{1}{3}$

3. $\frac{6}{7} \times 6$

$\frac{6}{7} \times \frac{6}{1} = 5\frac{1}{7}$

4. $\frac{2}{3} \times 9$

$\frac{2}{3} \times \frac{9}{1} = 6$

5. $\frac{3}{4} \times 5$

$\frac{3}{4} \times \frac{5}{1} = 3\frac{3}{4}$

6. $3 \times \frac{2}{5}$

$\frac{3}{1} \times \frac{2}{5} = 1\frac{1}{5}$

7. $4 \times \frac{2}{3}$

$\frac{4}{1} \times \frac{2}{3} = 2\frac{2}{3}$

8. $\frac{1}{8} \times 7$

$\frac{1}{8} \times \frac{7}{1} = \frac{7}{8}$

9. $8 \times \frac{7}{10}$

$\frac{8}{1} \times \frac{7}{10} = 5\frac{3}{5}$

10. $\frac{5}{6} \times 4$

$\frac{5}{6} \times \frac{4}{1} = 3\frac{1}{3}$

11. $8 \times \frac{1}{4}$

$\frac{8}{1} \times \frac{1}{4} = 2$

12. $\frac{5}{8} \times 9$

$\frac{5}{8} \times \frac{9}{1} = 5\frac{5}{8}$

Answer Box

$\frac{7}{8}$	$1\frac{1}{5}$	$1\frac{1}{3}$	$2\frac{2}{3}$	2	$3\frac{1}{3}$	$3\frac{3}{4}$	$4\frac{1}{2}$	$5\frac{3}{5}$	$5\frac{5}{8}$	6	$5\frac{1}{7}$

87 ▸RETEACH

Multiplying Fractions

When you multiply fractions, multiply numerators only by numerators. Multiply denominators only by denominators.

Problem: $\boxed{\dfrac{4}{10} \times \dfrac{3}{4}}$

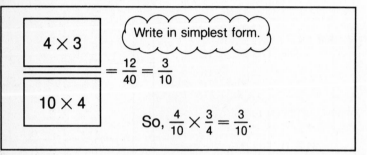

$$\frac{4 \times 3}{10 \times 4} = \frac{12}{40} = \frac{3}{10}$$

Write in simplest form.

So, $\dfrac{4}{10} \times \dfrac{3}{4} = \dfrac{3}{10}$.

Write the product in simplest form. Make sure each answer appears in the Answer Box.

1. $7 \times \dfrac{2}{5} \longrightarrow \dfrac{\boxed{7 \times 2}}{\boxed{1 \times 5}}$

$2\dfrac{4}{5}$

2. $\dfrac{4}{9} \times \dfrac{1}{4} \longrightarrow \dfrac{\boxed{4 \times 1}}{\boxed{9 \times 4}}$

$\dfrac{1}{9}$

3. $\dfrac{2}{5} \times \dfrac{2}{5} \longrightarrow \dfrac{\boxed{2 \times 2}}{\boxed{5 \times 5}}$

$\dfrac{4}{25}$

4. $\dfrac{3}{8} \times 4$

$1\dfrac{1}{2}$

5. $\dfrac{1}{2} \times \dfrac{5}{6}$

$\dfrac{5}{12}$

6. $6 \times \dfrac{1}{3}$

2

7. $\dfrac{3}{4} \times \dfrac{4}{3}$

1

8. $\dfrac{2}{3} \times 8$

$5\dfrac{1}{3}$

9. $\dfrac{7}{10} \times 5$

$3\dfrac{1}{2}$

10. $\dfrac{3}{8} \times \dfrac{1}{2}$

$\dfrac{3}{16}$

11. $\dfrac{2}{5} \times \dfrac{6}{4}$

$\dfrac{3}{5}$

12. $\dfrac{5}{9} \times 3$

$1\dfrac{2}{3}$

13. $\dfrac{5}{6} \times 7$

$5\dfrac{5}{6}$

14. $\dfrac{2}{3} \times \dfrac{5}{8}$

$\dfrac{5}{12}$

15. $\dfrac{7}{8} \times 9$

$7\dfrac{7}{8}$

Answer Box

| $\dfrac{3}{16}$ | $\dfrac{5}{12}$ | $3\dfrac{1}{2}$ | $5\dfrac{5}{6}$ | $1\dfrac{1}{2}$ | $\dfrac{5}{12}$ | $\dfrac{1}{9}$ | 1 | 2 | $\dfrac{4}{25}$ | $7\dfrac{7}{8}$ | $2\dfrac{4}{5}$ | $5\dfrac{1}{3}$ | $\dfrac{3}{5}$ | $1\dfrac{2}{3}$ |

Name _____ Date _____

88 ◣ **RETEACH**   **Writing Products in Simplest Form**

....

When you multiply fractions, write the product in simplest form.
Sometimes this is a mixed number, and sometimes it is a fraction.

Problem: $\boxed{\dfrac{3}{4} \times 6}$

Find the product.

Write the product as a mixed number.

$\dfrac{3}{4} \times \dfrac{6}{1} = \dfrac{18}{4}$ ⟹ $\dfrac{18}{4} = 4\dfrac{2}{4}$

Write the fraction in simplest form.

Divide the numerator and denominator by the greatest common factor.
The greatest common factor of 2 and 4 is 2.

$\dfrac{2}{4} \overset{\div 2}{\underset{\div 2}{=}} \dfrac{1}{2}$

So, $\dfrac{3}{4} \times 6 = 4\dfrac{1}{2}$.

Rewrite each product in simplest form. Make sure each answer appears in the Answer Box.

1. $\dfrac{3}{4} \times \dfrac{2}{3} = \dfrac{6}{12}$ $\dfrac{1}{2}$

2. $\dfrac{7}{8} \times \dfrac{4}{3} = \dfrac{28}{24}$ $1\dfrac{1}{6}$

3. $\dfrac{1}{4} \times 8 = \dfrac{8}{4}$ 2

_____   _____   _____

4. $\dfrac{1}{4} \times \dfrac{6}{7} = \dfrac{6}{28}$ $\dfrac{3}{14}$

5. $4 \times \dfrac{5}{12} = \dfrac{20}{12}$ $1\dfrac{2}{3}$

6. $\dfrac{5}{6} \times \dfrac{2}{3} = \dfrac{10}{18}$ $\dfrac{5}{9}$

_____   _____   _____

Write each product in simplest form. Make sure each answer appears in the Answer Box.

7. $\dfrac{1}{4} \times \dfrac{8}{9}$ $\dfrac{2}{9}$

8. $\dfrac{3}{8} \times \dfrac{2}{3}$ $\dfrac{1}{4}$

9. $6 \times \dfrac{5}{12}$ $2\dfrac{1}{2}$

_____   _____   _____

Answer Box

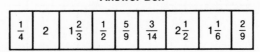

| $\dfrac{1}{4}$ | 2 | $1\dfrac{2}{3}$ | $\dfrac{1}{2}$ | $\dfrac{5}{9}$ | $\dfrac{3}{14}$ | $2\dfrac{1}{2}$ | $1\dfrac{1}{6}$ | $\dfrac{2}{9}$ |

225

Name _____ Date _____

11.8 ▸ ANOTHER LOOK

Exploring Fractions and Division

You can use a number line to find the quotient when dividing
by fractions.

Divide: $2 \div \frac{1}{4}$

How many fourths in 2?

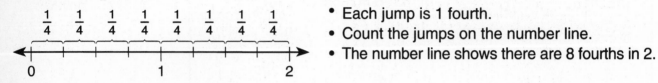

- Each jump is 1 fourth.
- Count the jumps on the number line.
- The number line shows there are 8 fourths in 2.

So, $2 \div \frac{1}{4} = 8$

Use the number line to write each quotient.

1. How many thirds in 3? ___9___

$3 \div \frac{1}{3} = $ ___9___

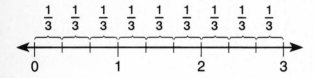

2. How many fourths in 3? ___12___

$3 \div \frac{1}{4} = $ ___12___

3. How many two fifths in 4? ___10___

$4 \div \frac{2}{5} = $ ___10___

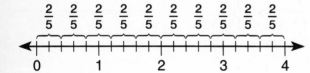

4. How many two thirds in 4? ___6___

$4 \div \frac{2}{3} = $ ___6___

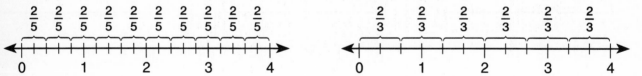

5. How many three fourths in 6? ___8___

$6 \div \frac{3}{4} = $ ___8___

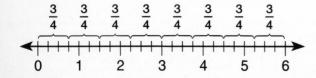

6. How many three fifths in 3? ___5___

$3 \div \frac{3}{5} = $ ___5___

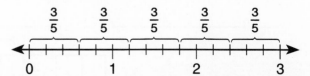

Name_____   Date_____

Reciprocals

You can write the number 1 as a fraction in many different ways.

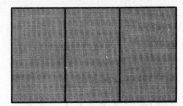

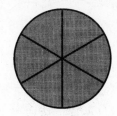

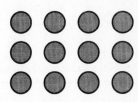

3 thirds are shaded.

$\frac{3}{3} = 1$

6 sixths are shaded.

$\frac{6}{6} = 1$

12 twelfths are shaded.

$\frac{12}{12} = 1$

When two fractions have a product of 1, they are reciprocals of each other.

$\frac{3}{4} \times \frac{4}{3} = \frac{12}{12} = 1$ $\frac{3}{4}$ and $\frac{4}{3}$ are reciprocals.

$\frac{5}{2} \times \frac{2}{5} = \frac{10}{10} = 1$ $\frac{5}{2}$ and $\frac{2}{5}$ are reciprocals.

Write the reciprocal of 4.

First write 4 as a fraction.

$4 = \frac{4}{1}.$ $\frac{4}{1} \times \frac{1}{4} = 1.$

The reciprocal of 4 is $\frac{1}{4}$.

Write the reciprocal of $2\frac{1}{3}$.

First write $2\frac{1}{3}$ as a fraction.

$2\frac{1}{3} = \frac{7}{3}.$ $\frac{7}{3} \times \frac{3}{7} = 1.$

The reciprocal of $2\frac{1}{3}$ is $\frac{3}{7}$.

Circle the sentences in which the numbers are reciprocals.

1. $\frac{1}{4} \times \frac{1}{4}$ **2.** $\frac{3}{5} \times \frac{5}{3}$ **3.** $\frac{1}{6} \times 1$ **4.** $\frac{1}{7} \times 7$

5. $\frac{8}{3} \times \frac{3}{8}$ **6.** $3\frac{1}{4} \times \frac{4}{13}$ **7.** $\frac{7}{9} \times \frac{9}{7}$ **8.** $5 \times \frac{5}{15}$

Make these reciprocals by writing the missing number.

9. $\frac{\boxed{1}}{2}$ and $\frac{2}{1}$ **10.** $\frac{2}{3}$ and $\frac{3}{\boxed{2}}$ **11.** $\frac{10}{\boxed{7}}$ and $\frac{7}{10}$ **12.** $\frac{5}{4}$ and $\frac{\boxed{4}}{5}$

13. $1\frac{3}{4}$ and $\frac{\boxed{4}}{7}$ **14.** $\frac{12}{5}$ and $\frac{5}{\boxed{12}}$ **15.** $4\frac{2}{3}$ and $\frac{3}{\boxed{14}}$ **16.** $\frac{\boxed{4}}{9}$ and $2\frac{1}{4}$

11.10 ANOTHER LOOK

··

Dividing by Fractions

Here is how you can divide by fractions.

• Divide: $5 \div \frac{1}{4}$

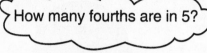
How many fourths are in 5?

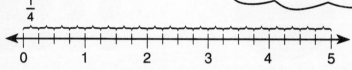

$\frac{1}{4}$

There are 20 fourths in 5. So, $5 \div \frac{1}{4} = 20$

$\frac{1}{4}$ and $\frac{4}{1}$ are reciprocals.

The related multiplication sentence is $5 \times 4 = 20$.

• Divide: $8 \div \frac{2}{3}$

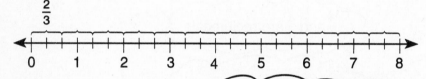

$\frac{2}{3}$

$8 \div \frac{2}{3} = 12$

$\frac{2}{3}$ and $\frac{3}{2}$ are reciprocals.

The related multiplication sentence is $8 \times \frac{3}{2} = \frac{24}{2} = 12$.

For each division sentence write the reciprocal for the fraction, the related multiplication sentence, and the product.

division sentence	reciprocal for fraction	multiplication sentence	product
1. $3 \div \frac{1}{6}$	$\frac{6}{1}$	$3 \times \frac{6}{1}$	18
2. $4 \div \frac{1}{5}$	$\frac{5}{1}$	$4 \times \frac{5}{1}$	20
3. $2 \div \frac{1}{8}$	$\frac{8}{1}$	$2 \times \frac{8}{1}$	16
4. $6 \div \frac{2}{3}$	$\frac{3}{2}$	$6 \times \frac{3}{2}$	9
5. $5 \div \frac{3}{6}$	$\frac{6}{3}$	$5 \times \frac{6}{3}$	10
6. $30 \div \frac{5}{6}$	$\frac{6}{5}$	$30 \times \frac{6}{5}$	36

11.11 ANOTHER LOOK

....

Problem Solving: Using Strategies

You are making holiday cards. You color $\frac{1}{2}$ of the cards with red marker. Three other cards are colored with pink pastel. You color one-fourth of the remaining cards blue. You color the nine cards left with a silver pen. How many cards are there in all?

1. Understand

• You know the number of cards that have different colors.

2. Plan

• Use Guess and Check.

• Guess the total number of cards. Then, check and see if the guess works. If it does not work, guess again.

3. Try it

• Try 35 as your first guess.

• The problem tells you to take half of 35. If you divide 35 by 2, you will get a remainder. Guess again.

• Try 30 as your next guess. Half of 30 is 15. You now have 15 cards. Take away 3. This leaves you with 12 cards. Now, take $\frac{1}{4}$ of the remaining cards: $12 \div 4 = 3$. It says there are 9 cards left, and that's the same number you show left.

4. Look Back

• You have a total of 30 cards.

Use any strategy to solve.

1. You are getting in shape for your school's fitness contest. The first week, you do 25 pushups. The second week, you do 30 pushups. The third week, you do 35 pushups. If you continue this pattern for the next 7 weeks, how many pushups will you do during the tenth week? _____ **70 pushups**

2. Your neighbor has 52 ft of fencing. He can fence in a square-shaped garden that is 13 ft long on each side, or a rectangular-shaped garden with a width of 10 ft and a length of 16 ft. Which shape would have the largest possible planting area? _____ **the square**

89 **RETEACH**   **Dividing with Number Lines**
....

You can use a number line to divide a whole number by a fraction.

Problem: $3 \div \frac{3}{4}$

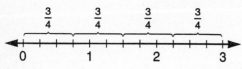

1. The denominator tells you to divide each whole number into fourths.

2. You want to see how many $\frac{3}{4}$ there are in 3. Count sets of 3 fourths.

There are 4 sets of 3 fourths in 3.

So, $3 \div \frac{3}{4} = 4$.

Write the quotient. Make sure each answer appears in the Answer Box.

1. $3 \div \frac{3}{5} =$ _____ 5 _____   2. $4 \div \frac{2}{5} =$ _____ 10 _____

   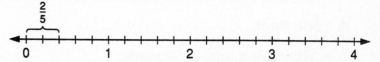

Write the quotient. Use a number line if you need to. Make sure each answer appears in the Answer Box.

3. $6 \div \frac{3}{5} =$ ___ 10 ___   4. $4 \div \frac{4}{5} =$ ___ 5 ___   5. $3 \div \frac{1}{6} =$ ___ 18 ___

6. $6 \div \frac{2}{3} =$ ___ 9 ___   7. $8 \div \frac{4}{5} =$ ___ 10 ___   8. $9 \div \frac{3}{4} =$ ___ 12 ___

9. $5 \div \frac{1}{4} =$ ___ 20 ___   10. $2 \div \frac{2}{9} =$ ___ 9 ___   11. $4 \div \frac{4}{7} =$ ___ 7 ___

Answer Box

10	12	20	10	5	7	9	18	10	5	9

90 ▶**RETEACH**

Reciprocals

Reciprocals are two numbers whose product equals 1.

$\frac{3}{4} \times \frac{4}{3} = \frac{12}{12} = 1$	$\frac{3}{4}$ is the reciprocal of $\frac{4}{3}$.

These numbers are the same. $\frac{3}{2} \times \frac{2}{3} = \frac{6}{6} = 1$ These numbers are the same.	The reciprocal of a fraction switches its numerator and denominator.

$7 \times \frac{1}{7} = \frac{7}{1} \times \frac{1}{7} = \frac{7}{7} = 1$ $\frac{1}{7}$ is the reciprocal of 7.	The reciprocal of a whole number has 1 as the numerator, and the whole number as the denominator.

$2\frac{1}{2} = \frac{5}{2}$ $\frac{5}{2} \times \frac{2}{5} = \frac{10}{10} = 1$	To find the reciprocal of a mixed number, change it to a fraction first.

Write the reciprocal. Make sure each answer appears in the Answer Box.

1. $\frac{1}{2}$ ___ $\frac{2}{1}$

2. $\frac{9}{10}$ ___ $\frac{10}{9}$

3. $\frac{4}{5}$ ___ $\frac{5}{4}$

4. 12 ___ $\frac{1}{12}$

5. $3\frac{1}{3}$ ___ $\frac{3}{10}$

6. $1\frac{1}{5}$ ___ $\frac{5}{6}$

7. $2\frac{1}{4}$ ___ $\frac{4}{9}$

8. $6\frac{5}{7}$ ___ $\frac{7}{47}$

Write the missing number in each equation. Make sure each answer appears in the Answer Box.

9. $\frac{2}{3} \times \frac{\boxed{3}}{2} = \frac{6}{6} = 1$

10. $\frac{8}{9} \times \frac{9}{\boxed{8}} = \frac{72}{72} = 1$

11. $\frac{4}{5} \times \frac{\boxed{5}}{4} = \frac{20}{20} = 1$

12. $\frac{7}{8} \times \frac{\boxed{8}}{\boxed{7}} = \frac{56}{56} = 1$

13. $2\frac{1}{3} \times \frac{3}{7} = \frac{\boxed{7}}{\boxed{3}} \times \frac{3}{7} = 1$

14. $13 \times \frac{1}{13} = \frac{\boxed{13}}{\boxed{1}} \times \frac{1}{13} = 1$

Answer Box

$\frac{2}{1}$	8	$\frac{4}{9}$	$\frac{8}{7}$	$\frac{1}{12}$	$\frac{7}{47}$	3	$\frac{10}{9}$	$\frac{5}{6}$	$\frac{7}{3}$	$\frac{13}{1}$	5	$\frac{3}{10}$	$\frac{5}{4}$

91 ▸ RETEACH   Dividing by Fractions

When dividing a number by a fraction, you can use a number line or multiply the number by the reciprocal of the fraction.

Problem: $\boxed{6 \div \frac{2}{3}}$

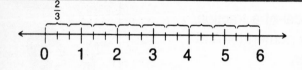

1. Use a number line. $6 \div \frac{2}{3} = 9$

OR

$6 \div \frac{2}{3} = \frac{6}{1} \div \frac{2}{3}$

$\frac{6}{1} \div \frac{2}{3} = \frac{6}{1} \times \frac{3}{2}$

$\frac{6}{1} \div \frac{2}{3} = \frac{6}{1} \times \frac{3}{2} = \frac{18}{2} = 9$

1. Write both numbers as fractions.

2. Write a multiplication problem with the reciprocal of the divisor.

3. Multiply. Write your answer in simplest form.

Use the number line to divide. Then use the reciprocal of the divisor to write a multiplication sentence. Write your answer in simplest form.

1. $9 \div \frac{3}{4} = 12$

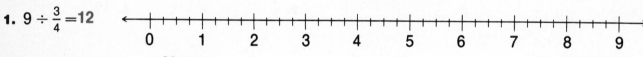

$\frac{9}{1} \div \frac{3}{4} = \frac{9}{1} \times \frac{4}{3} = \underline{\quad} \frac{36}{3} = 12$

2. $5 \div \frac{1}{4} = 20$

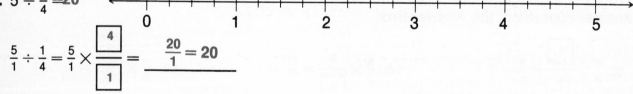

$\frac{5}{1} \div \frac{1}{4} = \frac{5}{1} \times \frac{\boxed{4}}{\boxed{1}} = \underline{\quad} \frac{20}{1} = 20$

3. $10 \div \frac{2}{5} = 25$

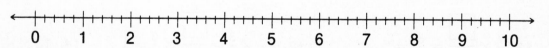

$\frac{\boxed{10}}{\boxed{1}} \div \frac{2}{5} = \frac{\boxed{10}}{\boxed{1}} \times \frac{\boxed{5}}{\boxed{2}} = \underline{\quad} \frac{50}{2} = 25$

12.1 ANHER LOOK

Exploring Ratio

Look at Bag 1. There are 6 cubes. There are 4 red and 2 green cubes. Another way to describe the contents of the bag is to use a ratio. A **ratio** compares two quantities. The ratio of red cubes to green cubes is 4 to 2.

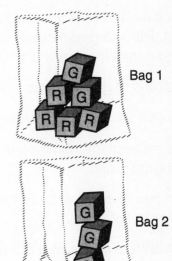

Bag 1

In Bag 2, there are 1 red and 2 green cubes. The ratio of red to green is 1 to 2.

If you pick from each bag without looking, you should expect to pick a red cube more often than a green cube from Bag 1. You should expect to pick a green cube more often than a red cube from Bag 2.

Bag 2

Write the ratio of red cubes (R) to green cubes (G) for each bag.

1. ___2 to 4___

2. ___3 to 3___

3. ___4 to 1___

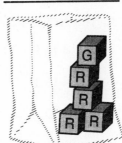

4. ___2 to 3___

For each pair of bags, tell which bag gives you a better chance of picking a red cube. Use ratios to explain your choice.

5. ___Bag 2; 4 to 1 is better than 2 to 1___

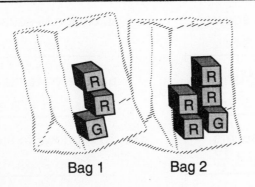

Bag 1   Bag 2

6. ___Bag 1; 1 to 2 is better than 1 to 3___

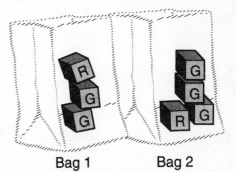

Bag 1   Bag 2

Name_____ Date_____

12.2 ANOTHER LOOK

Ratios

Place centimeter cubes in the squares at the right. Place 5 green cubes in square A. Place 3 red cubes in square B.

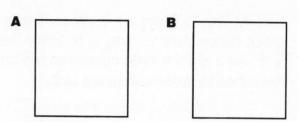

A   B

The ratio of green cubes to red cubes is 5 to 3.

You can also write this same ratio as 5:3 and $\frac{5}{3}$.

The order of the numbers is important. Since green is named first, you write 5 first.

Remove all the cubes. Place 2 red cubes in square A and 4 blue cubes in square B.

The ratio of red to blue is 2 to 4 or $\frac{2}{4}$.

Circle the correct ratio for each picture.

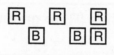

1. green to blue

   a. 2 to 3

   b. 3 to 2

   c. 3 to 5

2. red to green

   a. 4 to 5

   b. 4 to 1

   c. 1 to 4

3. blue to red

   a. 4 to 2

   b. 4 to 6

   c. 2 to 4

4. green to red

   a. 4 to 2

   b. 2 to 4

   c. 4 to 6

Write each ratio three different ways.

5.

   a. circles to triangles

      3 to 4; 3:4; $\frac{3}{4}$

   b. triangles to circles

      4 to 3; 4:3; $\frac{4}{3}$

6.

   a. triangles to squares

      3 to 5; 3:5; $\frac{3}{5}$

   b. squares to triangles

      5 to 3; 5:3; $\frac{5}{3}$

7.

   a. circles to squares

      3 to 3; 3:3; $\frac{3}{3}$

   b. squares to triangles

      3 to 4; 3:4; $\frac{3}{4}$

8. 6 baseballs to 8 footballs

    6 to 8; 6:8; $\frac{6}{8}$

9. 10 cups to 5 saucers

    10 to 5; 10:5; $\frac{10}{5}$

10. 15 windows to 9 doors

    15 to 9; 15:9; $\frac{15}{9}$

12.3 ANOTHER LOOK

Understanding Equal Ratios

You can use play money to show equal ratios.

Four quarters are equal in value to 1 dollar. You can write the ratio of quarters to dollars as $\frac{4}{1}$.

Multiply both quarters and dollars by 2.

Eight quarters are equal in value to 2 dollars.

$\frac{4}{1} = \frac{8}{2}$ These are equal ratios.

You can use a table to help you see equal ratios.

A sweater manufacturer uses 1 pound of yarn and 3 buttons for each sweater.

Number of sweaters	1	2	3	4	5	6
Pounds of yarn	1	2	3	4	5	6
Number of buttons	3	6	9	12	15	18

The ratio of pounds of yarn to the number of buttons for one sweater is $\frac{1}{3}$. For 2 sweaters the ratio is $\frac{2}{6}$. The ratio of pounds of yarn to number of buttons stays the same for any number of sweaters. So, $\frac{1}{3} = \frac{2}{6} = \frac{3}{9} = \frac{4}{12} = \frac{5}{15} = \frac{6}{18}$.

Complete the table by writing the equal ratios.

1.

Number of coats	1	2	3	4	5	6
Yards of fabric	5	10	15	20	25	30
Number of snaps	10	20	30	40	50	60

Write two equal ratios for each. Use a table if it helps. Answers may vary.

2. $\frac{1}{4}$ _____ $\frac{2}{8}, \frac{3}{12}$ _____

3. $\frac{2}{3}$ _____ $\frac{4}{6}, \frac{6}{9}$ _____

4. $\frac{7}{10}$ _____ $\frac{14}{20}, \frac{21}{30}$ _____

5. $\frac{5}{8}$ _____ $\frac{10}{16}, \frac{15}{24}$ _____

12.4 ANOTHER LOOK

Equal Ratios

The ratio of two numbers does not change when both numbers are multiplied or divided by the same number.

To find out if two ratios are equal, write each ratio as a fraction. Then compare the two ratios, using multiplication or division. Be sure to multiply or divide the numerator and denominator by the same number.

Does $\frac{3}{4} = \frac{12}{16}$?

Multiply:

$$\overset{\times 4}{\underset{\times 4}{\frac{3}{4} = \frac{12}{16}}}$$

The ratios $\frac{3}{4}$ and $\frac{12}{16}$ are equal.

Does $\frac{18}{6} = \frac{3}{1}$?

Divide:

$$\overset{\div 6}{\underset{\div 6}{\frac{18}{6} = \frac{3}{1}}}$$

The ratios $\frac{18}{6}$ and $\frac{3}{1}$ are equal.

Decide if the ratios are equal. Write *yes* or *no*.

1. 3 to 4 and 6 to 10 ___no___

2. 5:2 and 15:6 ___yes___

3. 3 to 1 and 12 to 6 ___no___

4. $\frac{9}{12}$ and $\frac{4}{3}$ ___no___

5. $\frac{8}{10}$ and $\frac{4}{5}$ ___yes___

6. 2:3 and $\frac{10}{5}$ ___no___

Write the letter of the equal ratio.

7. 1:5 ___b.___   **a.** 5:1   **b.** 3:15   **c.** 2:5   **d.** 1:10

8. $\frac{1}{8}$ ___c.___   **a.** $\frac{8}{16}$ **b.** $\frac{2}{8}$ **c.** $\frac{5}{40}$ **d.** $\frac{10}{18}$

9. 4 to 3 ___a.___   **a.** 20 to 15   **b.** 4 to 6   **c.** 8 to 3   **d.** 20 to 6

10. $\frac{3}{15}$ ___c.___   **a.** $\frac{15}{32}$ **b.** $\frac{6}{45}$ **c.** $\frac{1}{5}$ **d.** $\frac{5}{1}$

11. 2 to 7 ___c.___   **a.** 12 to 49   **b.** 6 to 14   **c.** 6 to 21   **d.** 8 to 35

12. $\frac{2}{4}$ ___d.___   **a.** $\frac{2}{8}$ **b.** $\frac{6}{20}$ **c.** $\frac{10}{40}$ **d.** $\frac{1}{2}$

12.5 ANOTHER LOOK

Problem Solving Strategy: **Write an Equation**

A standard videotape lasts four hours. 90 feet of tape lasts 60 seconds. How many feet of tape are on the standard videotape?

1. Understand

- You know that 90 feet of tape lasts 60 seconds.

- You know that the entire tape lasts four hours.

- You need to find out how many feet of tape are on the standard videotape.

2. Plan

- Write an equation about equal ratios to solve the problem.

3. Try It

- Write the equation using the information you have.

$$\frac{\text{amount of tape for part of video}}{\text{amount of time for part of video}} = \frac{\text{amount of tape for whole video}}{\text{amount of time for whole video}}$$

- Change both time amounts to minutes. You know that 60 seconds equals one minute, so you can say that 90 feet of tape will last 1 minute. You know that four hours converted into minutes is 240 minutes.

- Replace each part of the equation with the numbers you know.

$$\frac{90 \text{ feet}}{1 \text{ minute}} \xrightarrow[\times 240]{\times 240} = \frac{\text{amount of tape for whole video}}{240 \text{ minutes}}$$

4. Look Back

- There are 21, 600 ft of tape on a videotape.

Solve. Use Write an Equation when you can.

1. You find that your family has used up 3 tubes of toothpaste in 4 months. How many tubes of toothpaste will your family use in a year?

9 tubes

2. Jack is doing math homework. He has 46 problems in all. He finds that he can do 2 problems in one minute. How long will it take him to solve all of the problems?

23 minutes

Name _____ Date _____

12.6 ANOTHER LOOK

Exploring Percent

Percent is a ratio based on the number 100.

Remember that percent means "per 100" or "out of 100."

Look at the grid. There are exactly 100 squares.
Out of 100, 37 are shaded.

• You can write this as a ratio: $\frac{37}{100}$

• You can also write this as a percent: 37 percent or 37%

Shade each grid below.

1. Shade 30 squares.

2. Shade 42 squares.

3. Shade 45 squares.

4. Shade 54 squares.

5. Shade 71 squares.

6. Shade 80 squares.

Complete the chart using the grids in exercises 1–6.

	Number of squares shaded	Total number of squares	Ratio of shaded to total squares	Percent shaded
Grid 1	30	100	$\frac{30}{100}$	30%
Grid 2	42	100	$\frac{42}{100}$	42%
Grid 3	45	100	$\frac{45}{100}$	45%
Grid 4	54	100	$\frac{54}{100}$	54%
Grid 5	71	100	$\frac{71}{100}$	71%
Grid 6	80	100	$\frac{80}{100}$	80%

Name _____ Date _____

Estimating Percent

You can estimate percents using a geoboard.

Look at the figures on the geoboards below.

Section A = $\frac{1}{4}$ or 25%   Section B = $\frac{1}{2}$ or 50%   Section C = $\frac{3}{4}$ or 75%

Look at figure D at the right. Estimate the percent of the geoboard represented by figure D.

Section D is greater than 25%.

Section D is less than 50%.

Section D is about halfway between 25% and 50%.

Since 35 is about halfway between 25 and 50, 35% is a reasonable estimate.

Write the letter of the most reasonable estimate for the percent shaded.

1.   **b.**

a. 50 %

b. 25 %

c. 70 %

2.   **c.**

a. 25 %

b. 75 %

c. 45 %

3. 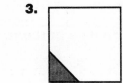   **a.**

a. 10 %

b. 30 %

c. 40 %

4.   **c.**

a. 75 %

b. 30 %

c. 50 %

Estimate what percent of each figure the shaded area represents. Accept estimates within the given range.

5.

10% to 25%

6.

60% to 75%

7.

20% to 25%

8.

80% to 90%

12.8 ANOTHER LOOK

Equivalent Forms

When you write the same value in more than one way, you are using equivalent forms.

Write 0.8 as a percent: $0.8 = \blacksquare$ %

- Write the decimal as hundredths.

    $0.8 = 0.80 = 80$ hundredths

    80 hundredths $= \frac{80}{100}$

- Write the fraction as a percent.

    $\frac{80}{100} = 80\%$

Write $\frac{4}{5}$ as a percent: $\frac{4}{5} = \blacksquare$ %

- Write an equivalent fraction with a denominator of 100.

$$\overset{\times 20}{\frac{4}{5}} = \underset{\times 20}{\frac{80}{100}}$$

- Write the fraction as a percent.

    $\frac{80}{100} = 80\%$

Write 25% as a decimal:

- Write the percent as a fraction with a denominator of 100.

    $25\% = \frac{25}{100}$

- Write the equivalent decimal.

    $\frac{25}{100} = 0.25$

Write each decimal or fraction as a percent.

1. 0.45 **45%**	2. 0.72 **72%**	3. 0.30 **30%**
4. 0.63 **63%**	5. 0.18 **18%**	6. 0.08 **8%**
7. $\frac{2}{5}$ **40%**	8. $\frac{7}{10}$ **70%**	9. $\frac{4}{20}$ **20%**
10. $\frac{6}{25}$ **24%**	11. $\frac{1}{4}$ **25%**	12. $\frac{19}{20}$ **95%**
13. 0.9 **90%**	14. $\frac{12}{25}$ **48%**	15. $\frac{3}{5}$ **60%**
16. $\frac{9}{10}$ **90%**	17. 0.1 **10%**	18. $\frac{11}{20}$ **55%**

Write each percent as a decimal.

19. 50% **0.50**	20. 15% **0.15**	21. 4% **0.04**
22. 67% **0.67**	23. 75% **0.75**	24. 9% **0.09**

Name _____ Date _____

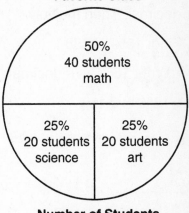

12.9 ANOTHER LOOK

Mental Math: **Finding Percent**

Favorite Class

Some percent problems can be solved mentally.

To find 50% of a number divide the number by 2.

To find 25% of a number divide the number by 4.

The whole circle represents 80 students. So, 50% represents 50% of 80, or $\frac{1}{2}$ of 80.

$$80 \div 2 = 40 \text{ students}$$

Since the whole circle represents 80 students, 25% represents 25% of 80, or $\frac{1}{4}$ of 80.

$$80 \div 4 = 20 \text{ students}$$

Number of Students Asked: 80

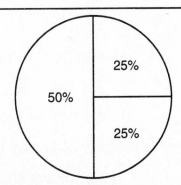

1. If the graph above represents 40 students, how many students are represented by 50%? _____ **20 students** _____

    How many are represented by 25%? _____ **10 students** _____

2. If the graph represents 200 students, how many are represented by 50%? _____ **100 students** _____

    How many are represented by 25%? _____ **50 students** _____

Write the answer. Use mental math.

3. 25% of 24 = ___6___	**4.** 50% of 18 = ___9___	**5.** 25% of 32 = ___8___
6. 50% of 60 = ___30___	**7.** 25% of 160 = ___40___	**8.** 25% of 36 = ___9___
9. 25% of 800 = ___200___	**10.** 50% of 12 = ___6___	**11.** 25% of 28 = ___7___
12. 50% of 70 = ___35___	**13.** 25% of 20 = ___5___	**14.** 50% of 240 = ___120___

12.10 ANOTHER LOOK

Percent of a Number

One way to find a percent of a number is to write the percent as a decimal. Then multiply.

Find: 15% of 288

• Write 15% as a decimal.

$15\% = 0.15$

• Multiply: 288×0.15

$$\begin{array}{r} 288 \\ \times\ 0.15 \\ \hline 1440 \\ +2880 \\ \hline 43.20 \end{array}$$ So, 15% of 288 $= 43.20$.

Another way to find the percent of a number is to write the percent as a fraction. Then multiply.

Find: 20% of 125.

• Write 20% as a fraction.

$20\% = \frac{20}{100}$, or $\frac{1}{5}$

• Multiply: $\frac{1}{5} \times 125$

$\frac{1}{5} \times 125 = \frac{125}{5}$, or 25.

So, 20% of 125 $= 25$.

You may be able to find some percents mentally by finding 10% first.

Find: 20% of 60.

10% of 60 = 6
20% of 60 = 2 × 6

So, 20% of 60 = 12

Find: 40% of 80.

10% of 80 = 8
40% of 80 = 4 × 8

So, 40% of 80 = 32

Write the percent of the number. Use mental math when you can.

1. 40% of 80 = ___32___
2. 20% of 60 = ___12___
3. 30% of 50 = ___15___

4. 10% of 90 = ___9___
5. 12% of 20 = ___2.40___
6. 35% of 70 = ___24.50___

7. 46% of 80 = ___36.80___
8. 3% of 101 = ___3.03___
9. 70% of 400 = ___280___

10. 1% of 500 = ___5___
11. 30% of 20 = ___6___
12. 65% of 90 = ___58.5___

13. 80% of 40 = ___32___
14. 65% of 300 = ___195___
15. 4% of 50 = ___2___

16. 16% of 300 = ___48___
17. 25% of 60 = ___15___
18. 75% of 24 = ___18___

Name _____ Date _____

12.11 ANOTHER LOOK

Problem Solving: **Choose a Computation Method**

You practice the piano for 2 h a day for 6 days. If you spend 25% of your time practicing new pieces, how many total hours are you practicing new pieces during those 6 days?

1. Understand

- You know how many days and how many hours a day you spend practicing.

- You know what percent of your time is spent practicing new pieces.

2. Plan

- Decide whether you will use a calculator or mental math. You will have to multiply the hours per day by the number of days.

- Take 25% of that number. Try using mental math to solve.

3. Try It

- Multiply 2 by 6 to get the total number of hours that you spent practicing: $2 \times 6 = 12$.

- Now, take 25% of this number. Think about 25% as the fraction $\frac{1}{4}$.

- Multiply $\frac{1}{4}$ by the total practice hours: $\frac{1}{4} \times 12 = 3$.

4. Look Back

- Three hours will be spent practicing new pieces.

Decide whether to use a calculator or mental math. Then solve.

1. You practice your trombone 20 h a week. You practice 3 h a day on the first three days, 5 hours on the 5th day, and 6 hours on the 6th day. You do not practice on the seventh day. Did you meet your goal of 20 h? _____**Yes.**_____

2. You spend $\frac{1}{3}$ as much time riding your skateboard as you spend doing homework. If you spend 7 hours a week riding your skateboard, how much time do you spend a week doing homework? _____**21 hours**_____

92 ▸ **RETEACH**   **Ratios**

··

You can use a ratio to compare two amounts.

What is the ratio of striped balloons to starred balloons?	What is the ratio of starred balloons to all the balloons?
3 striped balloons	2 starred balloons
2 starred balloons	10 balloons in all
The ratio is 3 to 2,	The ratio is 2 to 10,
or 3:2, or $\frac{3}{2}$.	or 2:10, or $\frac{2}{10}$.

You can write the same ratio in three ways.

Circle the letter of the correct ratio.

1. triangles to squares   **a.** $\frac{3}{4}$ **b.** $\frac{3}{7}$ **c.** $\frac{4}{3}$ **d.** $\frac{4}{7}$

2. squares to polygons   **a.** 3 to 10   **b.** 4 to 10   **c.** 3 to 2   **d.** 3 to 1

3. baseballs to footballs   **a.** 2:5   **b.** 5:7   **c.** 2:7   **d.** 5:2

4. cats to all the animals   **a.** $\frac{6}{1}$ **b.** $\frac{2}{6}$ **c.** $\frac{1}{6}$ **d.** $\frac{1}{4}$

5. odd digits to even digits   **a.** 5:4   **b.** 4:5   **c.** 4:8   **d.** 4:4

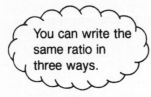

6. When you write a ratio as a fraction, which amount do you use

for the numerator? _____ *the first amount given*

93 **RETEACH** **Equal Ratios**

You can find equal ratios in the same way that you find equivalent fractions.

First, write the ratio as a fraction. Then, either multiply or divide the numerator and the denominator by the same number.

$\frac{4}{3} = \frac{}{15}$ $3 \times \blacksquare = 15$ $3 \times 5 = 15$

$\frac{8}{12} = \frac{}{3}$ $12 \div \blacksquare = 3$ $12 \div 4 = 3$

$\overset{\times 5}{\frac{4}{3}} = \underset{\times 5}{\frac{20}{15}}$

$\overset{\div 4}{\frac{8}{12}} = \underset{\div 4}{\frac{2}{3}}$

So, $\frac{4}{3} = \frac{20}{15}$.

So, $\frac{8}{12} = \frac{2}{3}$.

Write the missing number. Make sure each answer appears in the Answer Box.

1. $\frac{2}{5} = \frac{8}{\boxed{20}}$ $2 \times \blacksquare = 8$ $2 \times 4 = 8$

2. $\frac{20}{10} = \frac{\boxed{4}}{2}$ $10 \div \blacksquare = 2$ $10 \div 5 = 2$

3. $\frac{7}{8} = \frac{\boxed{14}}{16}$

4. $\frac{9}{3} = \frac{\boxed{3}}{1}$

5. $\frac{3}{5} = \frac{\boxed{15}}{25}$

6. $\frac{3}{4} = \frac{\boxed{36}}{48}$

7. $\frac{2}{12} = \frac{8}{\boxed{48}}$

8. $\frac{3}{4} = \frac{18}{\boxed{24}}$

9. $\frac{1}{2} = \frac{9}{\boxed{18}}$

10. $\frac{4}{5} = \frac{\boxed{28}}{35}$

11. $\frac{10}{4} = \frac{\boxed{5}}{2}$

12. $\frac{3}{8} = \frac{15}{\boxed{40}}$

13. $\frac{9}{7} = \frac{\boxed{27}}{21}$

14. $\frac{42}{18} = \frac{\boxed{7}}{3}$

15. $\frac{5}{20} = \frac{\boxed{1}}{4}$

16. $\frac{8}{25} = \frac{\boxed{16}}{50}$

17. $\frac{90}{20} = \frac{9}{\boxed{2}}$

Answer Box

28	14	1	40	15	48	2	7	20	36	24	3	18	4	16	5	27

94 RETEACH   **Writing Percents as Fractions**

You know that a percent represents a number of parts out of 100. All percents can be expressed as fractions with denominators of 100.

$35\% = \frac{35}{100}$ To write a percent as a fraction, first write the percent as a fraction with a denominator of 100.

$$\frac{35}{100} \overset{\div 5}{\underset{\div 5}{=}} \frac{7}{20}$$

Then you can write the fraction in simplest form. Remember: a fraction is in simplest form when neither the numerator nor the denominator can be divided by a whole number other than 1.

Write each percent as a fraction in simplest form. Make sure each answer appears in the Answer Box.

1. $6\% = \frac{6}{100} = \underset{\frac{3}{50}}{\underline{\hspace{2cm}}}$

2. $30\% = \frac{30}{100} = \underset{\frac{3}{10}}{\underline{\hspace{2cm}}}$

3. $80\% = \frac{80}{100} = \underset{\frac{4}{5}}{\underline{\hspace{2cm}}}$

4. $60\% \underset{\frac{3}{5}}{\underline{\hspace{2cm}}}$

5. $15\% \underset{\frac{3}{20}}{\underline{\hspace{2cm}}}$

6. $20\% \underset{\frac{1}{5}}{\underline{\hspace{2cm}}}$

7. $8\% \underset{\frac{2}{25}}{\underline{\hspace{2cm}}}$

8. $37\% \underset{\frac{37}{100}}{\underline{\hspace{2cm}}}$

9. $1\% \underset{\frac{1}{100}}{\underline{\hspace{2cm}}}$

10. $36\% \underset{\frac{9}{25}}{\underline{\hspace{2cm}}}$

11. $4\% \underset{\frac{1}{25}}{\underline{\hspace{2cm}}}$

12. $45\% \underset{\frac{9}{20}}{\underline{\hspace{2cm}}}$

13. $25\% \underset{\frac{1}{4}}{\underline{\hspace{2cm}}}$

14. $90\% \underset{\frac{9}{10}}{\underline{\hspace{2cm}}}$

15. $50\% \underset{\frac{1}{2}}{\underline{\hspace{2cm}}}$

16. $17\% \underset{\frac{17}{100}}{\underline{\hspace{2cm}}}$

17. $55\% \underset{\frac{11}{20}}{\underline{\hspace{2cm}}}$

18. $75\% \underset{\frac{3}{4}}{\underline{\hspace{2cm}}}$

Answer Box

$\frac{9}{20}$	$\frac{3}{50}$	$\frac{17}{100}$	$\frac{3}{5}$	$\frac{1}{100}$	$\frac{9}{10}$	$\frac{1}{25}$	$\frac{11}{20}$	$\frac{4}{5}$	$\frac{37}{100}$	$\frac{1}{2}$	$\frac{2}{25}$	$\frac{1}{5}$	$\frac{9}{25}$	$\frac{3}{4}$	$\frac{3}{20}$	$\frac{1}{4}$	$\frac{3}{10}$

95 ▸ RETEACH   Writing Percents as Decimals

Percents can be written as decimals.

Problem: | Write 20% as a decimal. |

Here is how to write a percent as a decimal:

Write it as a fraction with a denominator of 100.
Then write the decimal name for that fraction.

$$20\% = \frac{20}{100} = 0.20 = 0.2$$

Write each percent as a decimal. Make sure each answer appears in the Answer Box.

1. $80\% = \frac{80}{100} = 0.80$ or _____0.8_____

2. $4\% = \frac{4}{100} = $ _____0.04_____

3. $27\% = \frac{27}{100} = $ _____0.27_____

4. $10\% = \frac{10}{100} = $ _____0.10 or 0.1_____

5. $2\% = \frac{2}{100} = $ _____0.02_____

6. $16\% = \frac{16}{100} = $ _____0.16_____

7. 48% _____0.48_____

8. 90% _____0.90 or 0.9_____

9. 1% _____0.01_____

10. 55% _____0.55_____

11. 60% _____0.60 or 0.6_____

12. 40% _____0.40 or 0.4_____

13. 8% _____0.08_____

14. 12% _____0.12_____

15. 25% _____0.25_____

16. 96% _____0.96_____

17. 50% _____0.50 or 0.5_____

18. 7% _____0.07_____

19. 45% _____0.45_____

20. 75% _____0.75_____

Answer Box

0.4	0.16	0.04	0.27	0.48	0.8	0.08	0.02	0.1	0.9	0.55	0.12	0.6	0.01	0.25	0.07
0.96	0.45	0.5	0.75												

96 **RETEACH**   **Finding a Percent of a Number**

To find a percent of a whole number, you can write the percent as a fraction. Then multiply the fraction and the whole number.

Problem: | Find 20% of 25

$20\% = \frac{20}{100} = \frac{1}{5}$

$25 = \frac{25}{1}$

$\frac{1}{5} \times \frac{25}{1} = \frac{25}{5} = 5$

So, 20% of 25 is 5.

1. Write the percent as a fraction in simplest form.

2. Write the whole number as a fraction with a denominator of 1.

3. Multiply.

Find the percent of the number. Circle the letter of the correct answer.

1. 10% of 40 $10\% = \frac{10}{100} = \frac{1}{10}$
   (a.) 4
   b. 10
   c. 400

2. 25% of 96 $25\% = \frac{25}{100} = \frac{1}{4}$
   a. 25
   b. 384
   (c.) 24

3. 30% of 300
   (a.) 90
   b. 100
   c. $\frac{1}{10}$

4. 75% of 200
   a. 100
   (b.) 150
   c. 50

5. 45% of 80
   a. 28.8
   (b.) 36
   c. $\frac{9}{16}$

6. 60% of 85
   a. 65
   b. $\frac{12}{17}$
   (c.) 51

7. 20% of 125
   a. 20
   b. $2\frac{1}{2}$
   (c.) 25

8. 25% of 240
   a. 6
   (b.) 60
   c. 600

9. 12% of 50
   (a.) 6
   b. 38
   c. $\frac{6}{25}$

10. 26% of 500
   a. 1300
   b. 100
   (c.) 130

11. 5% of 40
   a. 20
   (b.) 2
   c. 8

Name _____ Date _____

You can find a percent of a whole number by first writing the percent as a decimal.

Problem: | Find 36% of 150

36% = 0.36	**1.** Write the percent as a decimal.
$\begin{array}{r} 1\,50 \\ \times\ \ 0.36 \\ \hline 9\,00 \\ 45\,00 \\ \hline 54.00 \end{array}$	**2.** Multiply. Be sure you place the decimal point in the product correctly.
So, 36% of 150 is 54.	

Write the percent of the number. Make sure each answer appears in the Answer Box.

1. 25% of 180

$\begin{array}{r} 1\,80 \\ \times 0.25 \\ \hline 45 \end{array}$

2. 5% of 320

$\begin{array}{r} 3\,20 \\ \times 0.05 \\ \hline 16 \end{array}$

3. 15% of 900

$\begin{array}{r} 9\,00 \\ \times 0.15 \\ \hline 135 \end{array}$

4. 50% of 628 = __314__

5. 72% of 400 = __288__

6. 8% of 150 = __12__

7. 12% of 700 = __84__

8. 22% of 200 = __44__

9. 60% of 120 = __72__

10. 65% of 220 = __143__

11. 99% of 800 = __792__

12. 85% of 60 = __51__

13. 38% of 500 = __190__

14. 45% of 80 = __36__

15. 75% of 244 = __183__

16. 64% of 125 = __80__

17. 55% of 920 = __506__

18. 82% of 450 = __369__

19. 18% of 300 = __54__

20. 16% of 725 = __116__

21. 95% of 320 = __304__

22. What is the first step you would take to find a percent of a number? __Write the percent as a fraction or as a decimal.__

_____

Answer Box

12	16	36	44	45	51	54	72	80	84	116	135	143	183	190	288	304	314
369	506	792															

12.12 ANOTHER LOOK

Exploring Probability

You can use what you have learned about ratios to help you predict the colors of cubes in a bag. In one of two bags, put 5 red, 5 green, and 5 blue cubes. Shake the bag and, without looking, pick 4 cubes and put them in the second bag. Put aside the first bag for now, and use the second bag containing the 4 cubes for steps 1–3:

1. Without looking, pick a cube. Look at the cube and record a tally mark under "Round 1" in the tally chart to show the color of the cube you picked. Put the cube back into the bag.

2. Continue picking cubes, recording their colors in the "Round 1" column of the tally chart. Replace each cube in the bag. Pick cubes 10 times.

3. Use the ratios in the chart to guess the colors of the 4 cubes in the bag. Make a prediction, and then look in the bag to check.

Predictions **Answers may vary.**

Round 1: _____

Round 2: _____

Round 3: _____

Put the four cubes back into the first bag. Shake the bag and pick 4 new cubes, and put them into the second bag. Repeat steps 1–3 two more times, recording your tally marks under "Round 2" and "Round 3."

What did you learn about making a prediction? **Answers may vary.**

_____

Color	Round 1	Round 2	Round 3
Red			
Green			
Blue			

Name_____ Date_____

12.13 ANOTHER LOOK

Probability and Ratio

Probability is a measure of chance.

Look at the number cube: each side has one number. The numbers are 1, 2, 3, 4, 5 and 6. If you roll the cube, each number has an equal chance of coming up.

The probability of any roll of the cube can be written as a ratio.

- There are 3 even numbers on the cube. So, the probability of rolling an even number is 3 out of 6 or $\frac{3}{6}$.

- There are no numbers greater than 6. So, the probability that the result of rolling the cube will be greater than 6 is 0 out of 6 or $\frac{0}{6}$, or just 0. The probability of any impossible event is 0.

- The probability that the result will be a number 6 or less is $\frac{6}{6}$ or 1. The probability of any event that is certain is 1.

Write each probability in the form of a ratio. Use a number cube to answer questions 1–4.

1. What is the probability of rolling an odd number? ___ $\frac{3}{6}$ or $\frac{1}{2}$ ___

2. What is the chance of rolling a number between 1 and 4? $\frac{2}{6}$ or $\frac{1}{3}$

3. What is the probability of rolling a 9? _____ $\frac{0}{6}$ or 0 _____

4. What is the chance of rolling a number less than 7? ___ $\frac{6}{6}$ or 1 ___

Use the spinner at the right.

5. What is the probability of spinning red? _____ $\frac{3}{8}$ _____

6. What is the chance of spinning green? _____ $\frac{4}{8}$ or $\frac{1}{2}$ _____

7. What is the probability of spinning blue? _____ $\frac{1}{8}$ _____

8. What is the chance of spinning yellow? _____ $\frac{0}{8}$ or 0 _____

9. Is there a greater chance of spinning red, blue, or green? <u>green</u>

R=red
G=green
B=blue

251

12.14 ANOTHER LOOK

Problem Solving: Using Strategies

The entire 5th grade voted for class president. Every two out of 6 boys voted for you. If 60 of the students in the class were boys, how many voted for you?

1. Understand

- You know that 2 out of 6 boys voted for you.

- You know that 60 students were boys.

- You need to find out how many boys voted for you.

2. Plan

- Write an equation about equal ratios to solve the problem.

3. Try it

- Write the equation using the information you have.

- Solve the equation.

$$\frac{2 \text{ boys voted for you}}{6 \text{ boys}} = \frac{\text{Total \# of boys voting for you}}{60 \text{ boys in class}}$$

So, $\dfrac{2}{6} = \dfrac{?}{60}$ ($\times 10$)

4. Look Back

- 20 boys from the 5th grade voted for you.

Use any strategy to solve.

1. Suppose you are at a bowling alley. For 2 games, you pay $5. If you want to bowl 10 games, how much will it cost you?

   $25

2. You are taking care of your neighbor's cats. There are 3 bags of cat food left for the week. The bags weigh 5.7 lb, 2.2 lb, and 8.1 lb. If the cats eat 3 lb of food each day, how long will your supply last?

   5 days

12.15 ANOTHER LOOK

Choose a Computation Method

At the regular price, a movie ticket is $7.25. You can save money if you buy a book of 6 tickets for $28.50. How much will you be saving on each ticket if you buy the book of 6?

1. Understand

- You know how much a regular movie ticket costs.

- You know how much a book of 6 movie tickets cost.

2. Plan

- Decide whether you will use a calculator or mental math. You will have to divide $28.50 by 6 to find the cost for one ticket.

- You will have to use subtraction to find the difference between the book price and the regular price.

- Because you need to do different operations, and the numbers are not easy to use with mental math, you should use a calculator to solve this problem.

3. Try It

- Divide $28.50 by 6: $28.50 ÷ 6 = $4.75. This is the price of each ticket in the book.

- Now, to find out how much you will save, subtract this price from the price of one regular ticket. One regular ticket is $7.25: $7.25 − 4.75 = $2.50.

4. Look Back

- You will save $2.50 on each ticket if you buy them in a book.

Decide whether to use a calculator or mental math. Then solve.

1. Johanna had 24 pencils. Over the year, she gave $\frac{1}{2}$ of the pencils away to her friends. She took $\frac{1}{2}$ of the remaining

   pencils home. How many pencils were left in her school box? _____ **6 pencils**

2. Suppose an amusement park train ride runs on a 415-foot loop. If the train travels at a speed of 25 feet each second, how long will

   it take to complete 1 loop? _____ **16.6 seconds**

Probability is a measure of the likelihood of an event occurring.

Suppose tiles for the word *carnation*
were mixed up and turned face down.
What is the probability of picking a *C*?

Since there are nine tiles, there are nine **possible outcomes.**
Each one has the same chance of being picked. There is only

one *C* tile, so the probability of picking a *C* is 1 out of 9, or $\frac{1}{9}$.

How many vowels are there? ___4___

What is the probability of picking a vowel? ___4 out of 9___

Since there are no *F* tiles, the probability of picking an *F* is

0 out of 6, or ___$\frac{0}{6}$___

**Suppose tiles for the word *begonia* are mixed up and turned
face down. Find the probability of picking each letter below.
Then circle the word that is below the correct probability.**

1. an N $\frac{1}{7}$ $\frac{7}{1}$

(all)   money

2. a T $\frac{0}{7}$ $\frac{7}{0}$

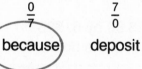

(because)   deposit

3. a vowel $\frac{7}{4}$ $\frac{4}{7}$

safe   (tellers)

4. an A or
an O $\frac{7}{2}$ $\frac{2}{7}$

if   (of)

5. a letter from the first
half of the alphabet, A − M $\frac{7}{5}$ $\frac{5}{7}$

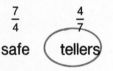

when   (the)

Unscramble the words you circled to solve the riddle.

Riddle: Why can't you keep secrets in a bank?

__because__   __of__   __all__   __the__   __tellers__

99 RETEACH

Suppose that you placed the number cards at the bottom of the page into a paper bag.

1. If you picked a card without looking, what is the probability that you would pick each of these?

a. 3 _____ 4 out of 10, or $\frac{4}{10}$ _____

b. 1 _____ 1 out of 10, or $\frac{1}{10}$ _____

c. 2 _____ 3 out of 10, or $\frac{3}{10}$ _____

d. 4 _____ 2 out of 10, or $\frac{2}{10}$ _____

Cut out the number cards. Fold them and place them into a box or a paper bag.

2. Suppose you make 20 picks and replace the card each time. Predict which number you would pick most often. Why?

_____ Answers may vary but may include: 3, because there are _____

_____ more 3's than any other number. _____

Now make 20 picks. Tally the results and replace the number card after each pick.

Number	\multicolumn{20}{c	}{Picks}
	1	2	3	4	5	6	7	8	9	10	11	12	13	14	15	16	17	18	19	20
1																				
2																				
3																				
4																				

3. Was your prediction correct? _____ Answers may vary. _____

4. Suppose you made 1000 picks. About how many times might you pick number 3? _____ Accept reasonable responses. _____

Name_____ Date_____

13.1 ANOTHER LOOK

Area of a Rectangle

The area of a figure is the number of units needed to cover the surface of the figure. Area is measured in square units such as square inches or square centimeters.

Each row of the rectangle at the right contains 4 small squares. Each small square is 1 square unit. There are 2 rows of small squares.

The area of the rectangle is 4 units × 2 units, or 8 square units.

You can use this rule to find the area of a rectangle:

Area of a rectangle = length × width

$A = l \times w$

$A = 4 \text{ units} \times 2 \text{ units}$

$A = 8 \text{ square units}$

Write the area of each rectangle. Check your answer by drawing the rectangle on the dot paper provided. Remember to use square units in your answer.

1. length = 5 units

width = 3 units

15 square units

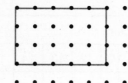

2. length = 6 units

width = 2 units

12 square units

3. length = 5 units

width = 4 units

20 square units

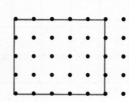

4. length = 6 units

width = 4 units

24 square units

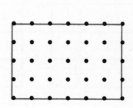

Write the area of each rectangle. Remember to use square units in your answer.

5. length = 15 ft

width = 9 ft

135 square ft

6. length = 50 cm

width = 30 cm

1500 square cm

7. length = 24 m

width = 20 m

480 square m

8. length = 6 cm

width = 3.4 cm

20.4 square cm

13.2 ANOTHER LOOK

Estimating Area

To estimate the area of a curved figure on a grid, first count the whole squares.

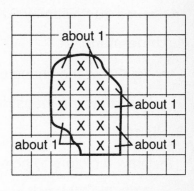

- In the figure shown at the right, whole squares are marked with an X. There are 10 whole squares.

- Next, find parts of squares that together make about 1 whole square unit. The partly-covered squares have a sum of about 4 whole squares.

- Then, add: area of whole squares + area of partial squares.

    10 square units + 4 square units = 14 square units

The total area of the figure is about 14 square units.

Estimate the area of each figure. Cross out parts of squares as you combine them to make a whole square. Write your answer in square units. Accept answers in range given.

1.

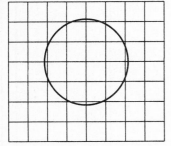

13–16 square units

2.

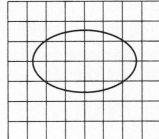

11–14 square units

3.

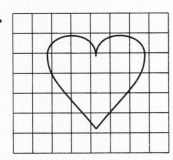

14–19 square units

4.

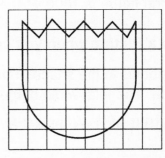

25–28 square units

13.3 ANOTHER LOOK

Problem Solving Strategy: Draw a Picture

A park has a flower garden in the shape of the letter *T*. The top of the *T* measures 20 ft wide by 40 ft long. The stem of the *T* measures 20 ft wide by 50 ft long. What is the garden's total area?

1. Understand

- You know the shape of the garden.

- You know the measurements of the top and stem of the *T*.

2. Plan

- Draw a picture to help you see what the garden looks like.

- Write the dimensions on the drawing.

- Look for rectangles. Then, find the area of each.

3. Try It

- The garden can be divided into two rectangles.

- One rectangle measures 20 ft × 40 ft. To find the area, multiply the length times the width: 20 ft × 40 ft = 800 ft².

- The other rectangle measures 20 ft × 50 ft: 20 ft × 50 ft = 1000 ft², so the area is 1000 ft².

- Add these areas together to find the total area of the figure: 800 ft² + 1000 ft² = 1800 ft².

4. Look Back

- The area of the figure is 1800 ft².

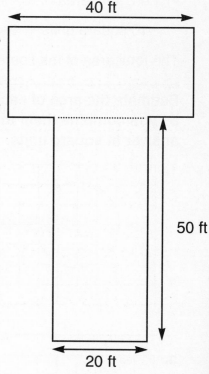

Solve. Use Draw a Picture when you can.

1. A swimming pool is in the shape of the letter *H*. It is 45 ft long on the left side. The total width of the pool is 45 ft. Each part of the *H* pool is 15 ft wide. What is the area of the pool? _____ 1575 ft²

2. You go to a square swimming pool that is 20 ft long on each side. Around the entire pool, there is a sidewalk that is 2 ft wide. The town wants to cover the sidewalk with a non-slip surface. How much of the non-slip surface will they need?

   176 ft²

_____

13.4 ANOTHER LOOK

Area of a Triangle

You can use the area of a rectangle to find the area of a right triangle.

- Figure WXYZ is a rectangle.

- Diagonal WY divides the rectangle into 2 congruent triangles: WZY and WXY.

- Triangle WZY and triangle WXY are right triangles. Each triangle contains a right angle.

The area of rectangle WXYZ is 12 square units.

The area of each triangle is 12 ÷ 2, or 6 square units.

Find the area of each rectangle. Then draw a diagonal and find the area of each triangle. The first one is done for you.

1.

Area of rectangle = 24 square units
Area of triangle = 12 square units

2.

Area of rectangle =
10 square units

Area of triangle =
5 square units

Draw a rectangle to find the area of each triangle.

3.

Area of rectangle =
20 square units

Area of triangle =
10 square units

4.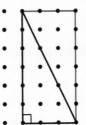

Area of rectangle =
18 square units

Area of triangle =
9 square units

Name _____ Date _____

13.5 ANOTHER LOOK

Problem Solving Decisions: One Answer or More

You and 3 friends search a park for cans to recycle. The park, shaped like a rectangle, is 11 ft long and 8 ft wide. How will the park be divided so that each of you covers the same amount?

1. Understand

- You know the dimensions of the area.

- You know the park must be divided equally among four people.

2. Plan

- Multiply the length by the width to find the area. Then use division to find the area each person covers.

- You can draw the rectangle using grid paper.

3. Try It

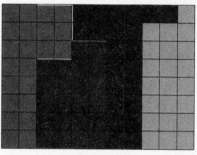

8 ft

- Multiply the length by the width to find the total area: $11 \times 8 = 88$.

- Divide the area by the number of people who will search the park: $88 \div 4 = 22$. Each person will search 22 sq ft.

- Shade your drawing to show where each person will search.

11 ft

4. Look Back

- There are many ways to divide the area.

- Check by counting squares to see that each person covers the same.

Decide whether the problem has more than one answer. Solve and explain.

1. A piece of carpet is 6 ft long by 8 ft wide. How can you cut it so it fits into a room 4 ft long by 5 ft wide? Show your work.

There is more than one answer. One possible answer: On the 6 ft side,

measure over 2 ft, cut down 5 ft and then over 4 ft.

260

100 **RETEACH**

Areas of Rectangles

How much tiling is needed to cover a floor area that is 3 feet wide and 5 feet long?

To find area, use square units. Think of these units as fitting together to cover a surface completely.

□
1 square unit

3 square units

10 square units

15 square units

If each □ represents one square foot, each side of the square has a measure of 1 foot. To find the area you can count the squares. Another way to find area is to multiply length by width.

width = 3 feet

length = 5 feet

Area = length × width

Area = 5 ft × 3 ft

Area = 15 square feet or 15 ft²

The area requires 15 square feet of tiling.

Write the area. Use square units in your answer. Make sure each answer appears in the Answer Box.

2 cm
4 cm

A = _____8_____ cm²

2.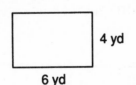
4 yd
6 yd

A = _____24_____ yd²

3.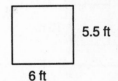
5.5 ft
6 ft

A = _____33_____ ft²

4.
5 m
7 m

A = _____35 m²_____

5.
6 yd
8 yd

A = _____48 yd²_____

6.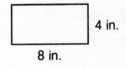
4 in.
8 in.

A = _____32 in.²_____

7. length 15.5 meters; width 7 meters

A = _____108.5 m²_____

8. length 15.4 cm; width 9 cm

A = _____138.6 cm²_____

Answer Box

| 24 | 48 yd² | 108.5 m² | 8 | 35 m² | 138.6 cm² | 32 in.² | 33 |

Name _____ Date _____

⎡ What is the area of a square that measures 6 meters on each side? ⎤

To find the area of a square, use square units.

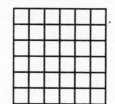

1 square unit   6 square units   _____36_____ square units

All 4 sides of a square have the same measure. To find the area of a square, multiply the measure of one side by itself.

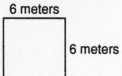

Area = side × side

Area = 6 m × 6 m

Area = 36 square meters or 36 m²

Write the area. Use square units in your answer. Make sure each answer appears in the Answer Box.

1.
10 m

$A =$ ___100___ m²

2.
20 mm

$A =$ ___400___ mm²

3.
2 m

$A =$ ___4___ m²

4.
5 yd

$A =$ ___25___ yd²

5.
9 km

$A =$ ___81___ km²

6.
7.5 cm

$A =$ ___56.25___ cm²

7.
8 in.

$A =$ ___64___ in.²

8.
6 ft

$A=$ ___36___ ft²

9. side = 3 yd
$A =$ ___9 yd²___

10. side = 5.4 m
$A =$ ___29.16 m²___

11. side = 8.4 cm
$A =$ ___70.56 cm²___

12. side = 9.6 km
$A =$ ___92.16 km²___

Answer Box

56.25	9 yd²	100	70.56 cm²	81	29.16 m²	25	4	92.16 km²	64	400	36

Name_____   Date_____

13.6 ANYTHER LOOK

Solids

Solids are made from plane figures or curved surfaces or both.
The base or bases of solids may be any plane figure. The bases in
the figures below are shaded.

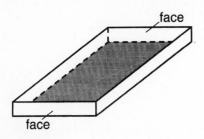

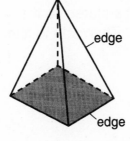

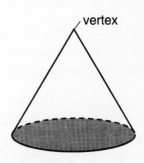

vertex

face

edge

edge

face

- Some solids have faces.
  A face is a flat surface of
  a solid.

- Some solids have edges.
  An edge is a line segment
  formed where two faces
  meet.

- Some solids have
  vertexes. A vertex is a
  corner of a solid.

Follow the directions to answer each question.

1.

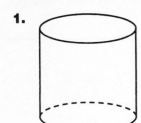

Color a face of the
cylinder red.
How many faces are
there on the cylinder?

2 faces

2.

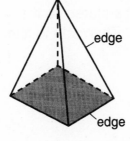

Color an edge of the
pyramid blue.
How many edges are
there on the pyramid?

6 edges

3.

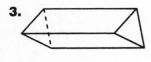

Mark a vertex of the
prism with a black dot.
How many vertices
are there on the
prism?

6 vertices

4.

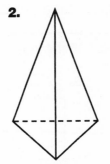

Color a face of the
pyramid green.
How many faces are
there on the pyramid?

5 faces

5.

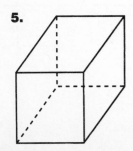

Color an edge of the
prism blue.
How many edges are
there on the prism?

12 edges

6.

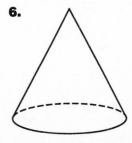

Color the face of the
cone yellow.
Could a cone have
more than one face?

No

13.7 ANOTHER LOOK

Surface Area and Solids

The surface area of a solid is the sum of the unit squares on all sides of the figure, including the top and bottom.

Use 4 centimeter cubes to make the solid at the right.

To find the surface area, count the unit squares on the top, bottom, and each side of the solid. Then add to find the total number of unit squares.

$$
\begin{aligned}
\text{top} &= 2 \text{ unit squares} \\
\text{side 1} &= 4 \text{ unit squares} \\
\text{side 2} &= 2 \text{ unit squares} \\
\text{side 3} &= 4 \text{ unit squares} \\
\text{side 4} &= 2 \text{ unit squares} \\
\text{bottom} &= 2 \text{ unit squares} \\
\text{surface area} &= 16 \text{ unit squares}
\end{aligned}
$$

Use 4 centimeter cubes to make the solid at the right.

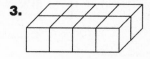

The surface area of this solid is 18 unit squares. This is the greatest surface area possible for a 4-cube solid.

Use cubes to make each solid. Write the surface area of each solid.

1.

22 unit squares

2.
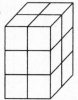

32 unit squares

3.
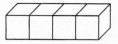

28 unit squares

Use the given number of cubes below to make the solid with the greatest surface area. Write the surface area of each solid.

4. three cubes

14 unit squares

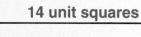

5. five cubes

22 unit squares

6. six cubes

26 unit squares

Name _____ Date _____

··

Volume of a Rectangular Prism

Volume is the amount of space taken up by a solid.

Fill the rectangle at the right with one layer of centimeter cubes. You will have 3 rows of 5 cubes each.

Build a second layer of cubes on top of the first layer. The solid you made is a rectangular prism.

You can find the volume of a rectangular prism by multiplying.

Volume = length × width × height
Volume = 3 cm × 5 cm × 2 cm

The volume of the rectangular prism is 30 cubic centimeters, or 30 cm³.

**Build each rectangular prism using centimeter cubes.
Then write the volume. Give your answer in cubic units.**

1. length = 3 cm
width = 3 cm
height = 3 cm

volume = ___27 cm³___

2. length = 5 cm
width = 4 cm
height = 3 cm

volume = ___60 cm³___

3. length = 6 cm
width = 2 cm
height = 3 cm

volume = ___36 cm³___

4. length = 6 cm
width = 6 cm
height = 10 cm

volume = ___360 cm³___

5. length = 5 cm
width = 5 cm
height = 5 cm

volume = ___125 cm³___

6. length = 8 cm
width = 3 cm
height = 2 cm

volume = ___48 cm³___

You can use a centimeter cube as a benchmark to estimate volume.

This prism is about 2 cubes high, 1 cube wide, and 2 cubes long. So, the volume is about 4 cubes, or 4 cm³.

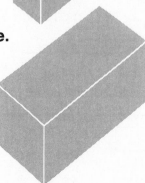

------ Benchmark ------

1 cubic cm, or cm³

Use the benchmark to estimate the volume.

7.

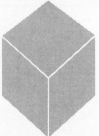

2 × 2 × 2 = 8 cm³

8.

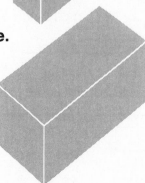

2 × 2 × 4 = 16 cm³

13.9 ANOTHER LOOK

Volume of Irregular Solids

You can make solids of different shapes by combining rectangular prisms.

Use centimeter cubes to make the two rectangular prisms below. Use red cubes for one prism and blue cubes for the other prism.

red

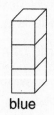

blue

The volume of the red prism is 4 cubic centimeters or 4 cm³.

The volume of the blue prism is 3 cubic centimeters or 3 cm³.

If you combine the two prisms to make one solid, the volume of the new solid will be 4cm³ + 3cm³ or 7 cm³.

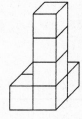

You can make other solids using the two prisms. Each solid will have a volume of 7 cm³.

Use centimeter cubes to make each prism shown below. Combine the prisms to form a new solid. Write the volume of the new solid.

1.

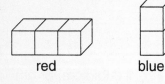

red   blue

_____ 5 cm³ _____

2.

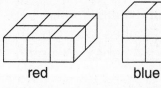

red   blue

_____ 10 cm³ _____

3.

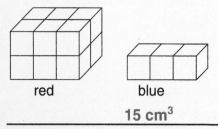

red   blue

_____ 15 cm³ _____

4.

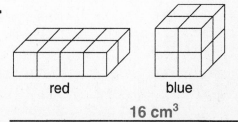

red   blue

_____ 16 cm³ _____

13.10 ANOTHER LOOK

Problem Solving: Using Strategies

Twenty-eight students will paint the gym wall. Covered with square tiles, it is 20 squares long and 15 squares high. The top 20 squares cannot be painted. How will you divide up the rest of the wall so that each paints the same amount?

1. Understand

- You know the dimensions of the area to be painted, and that the wall must be divided equally among 28 people.

2. Plan

- You can use the Draw a Picture strategy to help you.

- You can use multiplication to find the area of the wall. Subtraction will tell you the area that can be painted. Division will help you find the number of squares each person paints.

3. Try It

- Multiply 20 by 15 to find the area: $20 \times 15 = 300$.

- Subtract 20 from the total because the top 20 squares cannot be painted: $300 - 20 = 280$.

- Divide 280 by 28 to find the number to be painted by each student. Use mental math: $280 \div 28 = 10$. Draw a picture to show which tiles each person will paint.

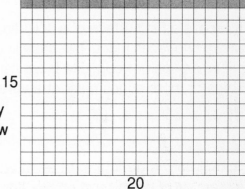

15

20

4. Look Back

- Each person will paint 10 tiles.

Use any strategy to solve.

1. It takes 400 cocoa beans to make one pound of chocolate. Suppose you ate one pound of chocolate every year for 25 years. How many cocoa beans would have been used to make the chocolate you ate?

    10,000 cocoa beans

    _____

2. Pablo, Jean, LaToya, and Rita play instruments. They play the flute, piano, guitar, and drums. Rita plays the flute. Pablo does not play the piano or guitar. If Jean does not play the guitar, what instrument does LaToya play?

    guitar

    _____

This figure is flat. It has two dimensions. The terms **width** and **length** are used to describe its dimensions.

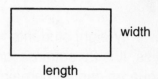

This picture represents a figure that is not flat. It is called a **solid** and it has three dimensions: **length, width,** and **height.**

Here are some other terms that are used to describe the features of solids.

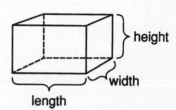

A **rectangular prism** has:
  8 vertices
  12 edges
  6 faces
  2 bases

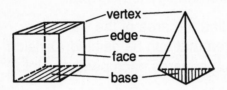

A **triangular pyramid** has:
  4 vertices
  6 edges
  4 faces
  1 base

A **face** is a flat surface of a solid figure. An **edge** is the segment where two faces meet. The **base** is a special face. On a rectangular prism, any pair of opposite faces can be considered the bases. Three or more edges meet at a **vertex.**

Complete the definition of each term. Then find lettered examples of each term on the figures at the right.

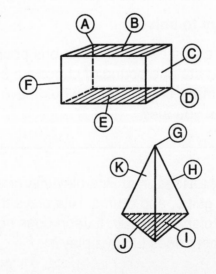

1. A ___vertex___ is a point where 3 or more edges meet. Examples are __A__, __G__, and __D__.

2. A ___face___ is a flat surface found on a solid. Examples are __B__, __C__, __E__, __K__, and __I__.

3. An ___edge___ is where two faces meet. Examples are __F__, __J__, and __H__.

Name _____   Date _____

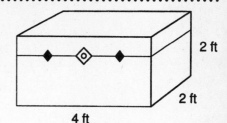
2 ft
2 ft
4 ft

Julio found a trunk in the attic. The trunk is 4 feet long, 2 feet high, and 2 feet wide. What is the volume of the trunk?

Volume is measured in cubic units. A **cube** has **length, width,** and **height.** When we measure the volume of a solid, we are finding the numbers of cubic units needed to fill it if it were hollow.

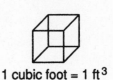
1 cubic foot = 1 ft³

Use this formula to find the volume of a rectangular prism:
Volume = length × width × height
So, for the problem above,
Volume = 4 ft × 2 ft × 2 ft
Volume = 16 cubic feet or 16 ft³

Look at the diagram at the right. What are the dimensions of the prism?

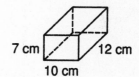
7 cm   12 cm
10 cm

width __10__ cm   height __7__ cm   length __12__ cm

What is the volume? __840__ cm³

Write the volume. Use cubic units in your answer. Make sure each answer appears in the Answer Box.

1.
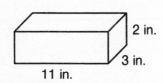
2 in.
3 in.
11 in.

2.
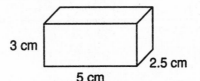
3 cm
2.5 cm
5 cm

3.

2 ft
3 ft
2 ft

Volume = __66__ in.³

Volume = __37.5__ cm³

Volume = __12__ ft³

4. length 9.4 cm
   width   7 cm
   height   4 cm

   Volume = __263.2 cm³__

5. length 12 ft
   width   8 ft
   height 12 ft

   Volume = __1152 ft³__

6. length 15 yd
   width 10 yd
   height 6 yd

   Volume = __900 yd³__

Answer Box

66	12	900 yd³	1152 ft³	263.2 cm³	37.5